SUPPORT FOR THE POOR
IN THE MISHNAIC LAW OF AGRICULTURE

Program in Judaic Studies
Brown University
BROWN JUDAIC STUDIES
Edited by
Jacob Neusner,
Wendell S. Dietrich, Ernest S. Frerichs,
Alan Zuckerman

Editorial Board

David Blumenthal, Emory University (Approaches to Medieval Judaism)
William Scott Green, University of Rochester (Approaches to Ancient Judaism)
Martin Hengel, University of Tübingen (Hellenistic Judaism)
David Hirsch, Brown University (Modern Jewish Literature)
Baruch A. Levine, New York University (Ancient Israel)
Alan Mintz, University of Maryland (Hebrew Literature)
Valentin Nikiprowetzky, University of Paris (Ancient Judaism)
Marc L. Raphael, Ohio State University (Approaches to Judaism in Modern Times)
Peter Schäfer, University of Cologne (Ancient Judaism)
Jonathan Z. Smith, University of Chicago (Studia Philonica)
Uriel Tal, Tel Aviv University (Modern Judaism)
David Vital, Tel Aviv University (Modern Judaism)
Geza Vermes, University of Oxford (Ancient Judaism)

Corresponding Editors

David Altshuler, George Washington University
Alan J. Avery-Peck, Tulane University
Baruch M. Bokser, Dropsie University
Joel Gereboff, Arizona State University
David Goldenberg, Dropsie University
Robert Goldenberg, State University of New York, Stony Brook
David Goodblatt, Haifa University
Peter Haas, Vanderbilt University
Martin Jaffee, University of Virginia
Shamai Kanter, Temple Beth El, Rochester, New York
Jack N. Lightstone, Concordia University
Irving Mandelbaum, University of Texas, Austin
Ivan Marcus, Jewish Theological Seminary of America
Louis Newman, Carleton College
Gary G. Porton, University of Illinois
Richard S. Sarason, Hebrew Union College–Jewish Institute of Religion, Cincinnati
Larry Schiffman, New York University
Tzvee Zahavy, University of Minnesota

Editorial Committee

Roger Brooks
Paul Flesher
Howard Schwartz
Judith Romney Wegner

Number 43

SUPPORT FOR THE POOR
IN THE MISHNAIC LAW OF AGRICULTURE:
TRACTATE PEAH

by
Roger Brooks

Support for the Poor in the Mishnaic Law of Agriculture: Tractate Peah

by

Roger Brooks

Scholars Press
Chico, California

SUPPORT FOR THE POOR
IN THE MISHNAIC LAW OF AGRICULTURE:
TRACTATE PEAH

by
Roger Brooks

© 1983
Brown University

The publication of this book was made possible by support from Friends of Judaic Studies at Brown University.

Library of Congress Cataloging in Publication Data
Brooks, Roger.
  Support for the poor in the Mishnaic law of agriculture, Tractate Peah.

  (Brown Judaic studies ; no. 43)
  Includes translation of: Peah.
  Includes index.
  1. Mishnah. Peah—Commentaries. 2. Agricultural laws and legislation (Jewish law). 3. Charity laws and legislation (Jewish law). I. Mishnah. Peah. English. 1983. II. Title. III. Series.
  BM506.P7B76 1983   296.1'2307   83-8719
  ISBN 0-89130-632-3

For Gayle

TABLE OF CONTENTS

Preface	1
Acknowledgements	3
Transliterations	5
Abbreviations and Bibliography	7
Introduction	17
Chapter One: Mishnah Peah Chapter One	41
Chapter Two: Mishnah Peah Chapter Two	53
Chapter Three: Mishnah Peah Chapter Three	61
Chapter Four: Mishnah Peah Chapter Four	71
Chapter Five: Mishnah Peah Chapter Five	87
Chapter Six: Mishnah Peah Chapter Six	101
Chapter Seven: Mishnah Peah Chapter Seven	121
Chapter Eight: Mishnah Peah Chapter Eight	137
Appendix: Mishnah Tractate Peah in Sifra and Sifre Deuteronomy	157
Notes	177
Index to Biblical Texts	203
Index to Classical Rabbinic Texts	204
General Index	207

PREFACE

Tractate Peah (The Corner-Offering for the Poor) prescribes how Israelite farmers must support poor people by giving them a portion of all crops that grow in the Land of Israel. It asserts that the poor constitute a special group, prevented by circumstances from owning a share of the Land. Like the priests, who are prevented by Scriptural legislation from owning a portion of the Land, poor people deserve some of the Land's yield. This is because God has promised that all Israelites will share equally in the bounty of the Land of Israel. As we shall see, the tractate's rules reflect Mishnah's authors' overall concerns in the period, around A.D. 200, in which Rome destroyed the Jews' Temple, defeated their armies, and finally prohibited them from inhabiting Jerusalem. Those authorities who formulated Mishnah responded to these events by creating, in their imaginations and in their writings, a world in which God, not Rome, ruled over the Land of Israel and demanded support for those under his special care, the poor. Far from being mere subjects of the Roman Empire, Mishnah's authors asserted, ordinary farmers must take responsibility for the welfare of others.

My study seeks to uncover Tractate Peah's meaning by explaining its laws as they were understood by their authors around A.D. 200. The methods I employ in the translation and commentary are designed to meet this end. The translation itself shows the formalized structure of Mishnaic Hebrew's literary patterns. These patterns, I argue, indicate the point of each passage, which I then fully explain in my commentary. My remarks also draw out from the discrete rules the larger implications for the framers' thought. I provide an introduction to each chapter of text so that the reader can easily understand how the diverse laws, when brought together and arranged by Mishnah's framers, systematically work through a principle or issue. Finally, my introduction to the study as a whole aims at grasping the central points of Tractate Peah when read as an essay produced in a particular historical context. Here I outline the tractate's structure, thereby explaining the message the authors wanted to convey by dealing with the topics in one particular order. Furthermore, the introduction places Tractate Peah in both diachronic and synchronic context. This enables us to see how Mishnah's framers related to ongoing Israelite culture as well as to their particular historical setting.

My study of Tractate Peah includes work on other documents of nascent Judaism--Tosefta, Sifra, and Sifre Deuteronomy--among which Tosefta Peah first deserves our attention. This tractate, redacted soon after Mishnah, sometime between the third and fifth centuries A.D., reflects the organizational structure and topical agendum of Mishnah. Furthermore, Tosefta Peah utilizes Mishnah's linguistic and literary style and attributes its rules to Mishnah's authorities. In all, Tosefta Peah constitutes an extremely important commentary, because of its conceptual and temporal closeness to

Mishnah. Accordingly, I have translated and commented upon the whole of Tosefta Peah, placing each pericope of Tosefta after the relevant unit of Mishnah. My analysis here focuses almost exclusively upon the relationship between Mishnah and Tosefta. That is, I wish to know only how each pericope of Mishnah is illuminated by understanding the related Toseftan material. I take up other issues only when they bear directly upon Tosefta's character as a commentary.

An appendix to this study contains the materials of two works of Scriptural exegesis--Sifra and Sifre Deuteronomy--that intersect with Mishnah Peah. These two documents, generally thought to have come to closure around the fourth century A.D., differ in an important respect from Mishnah in their treatment of poor-support. As these texts systematically work through Leviticus and Deuteronomy, they specify at each point how proper exegesis of Scripture, and that alone, allows one to derive Mishnah's principles and rules. This is an important claim, because, as we shall see, Tractate Peah scarcely cites the Mosaic Codes. In other words, Mishnah purports to be its own independent law, with authority equal to other revealed law. The framers of Sifra and Sifre claim, of course, that Mishnah is not at all independent of Scripture, but merely makes explicit what otherwise is implicit in the Hebrew Bible. By presenting these materials in translation, I hope to enable the reader more easily to perceive the claim basic to Mishnah's laws.

Tractate Peah is of interest to us because it takes up a problem persistent to our own day--poor-relief. This study places its emphasis on reconstructing Mishnah's authors' thoughts regarding this subject. It is hoped that the detailed translations and textual analyses below will enable us to perceive the framers' response to their age and the world view that underlay that response.

ACKNOWLEDGEMENTS

I extend my thanks to teachers and colleagues who supervised and otherwise contributed to my education and this study. Above all, I express my gratitude to Professor Jacob Neusner, whose careful critique shows throughout this study. The book was first presented in his graduate seminar and written under his guidance. I shall always appreciate how generously he gives of his instruction, time, and energy. The students in Professor Neusner's seminar over the past three years have improved my work through their comments and criticisms. I extend my thanks to Professors Alan Avery-Peck (Tulane University) and Louis Newman (Carleton College), as well as Mr. Howard Schwartz, Mrs. Judith Romney Wegner, and Mr. Paul Flesher. In addition, Mr. Arnold Sanders of Brown University's English Department read the entire manuscript and suggested numerous improvements in style and consistency. I gratefully acknowledge his help and friendship. I of course retain responsibility for any errors that may remain below.

Brown University has supported me throughout my graduate education with University and Teaching Fellowships, for which I am grateful. I wish to thank as well the Max Richter Foundation, for providing me with summer study grants that enabled me to continue work on this study. Finally, the Feder Fund for Judaic Studies at Brown University has enhanced my education, particularly by providing much needed travel grants.

The manuscript was prepared by Verbatim Word Processing. I extend special thanks to Ms. Catherine Hawkes, who typed most of the text.

This book is dedicated to my wife, Gayle Brooks, who supports me in more ways than I can enumerate.

September 7, 1983
Erev Rosh Hashanah, 5744
Providence, Rhode Island

Roger Brooks

TRANSLITERATIONS

א	=	ʾ	ל	=	l
ב	=	b	מ	=	m
ג	=	g	נ	=	n
ד	=	d	ס	=	s
ה	=	h	ע	=	ʿ
ו	=	w	פ	=	p
ז	=	z	צ	=	ṣ
ח	=	ḥ	ק	=	q
ט	=	ṭ	ר	=	r
י	=	y	שׁ	=	š
כ	=	k	שׂ	=	ś
ת	=	t			

My transliterations represent the consonantal structure of the Hebrew word, with no attempt made to vocalize. I do not distinguish between the spirantized and non-spirantized forms of b, g, d, k, p, and t. Proper names and commonly used words are reproduced in their most frequent usage, e.g. Eliezer, Mishnah, etc.

ABBREVIATIONS AND BIBLIOGRAPHY

Albeck	= Hanoch Albeck, The Six Orders of the Mishnah, 6 Vols., Jerusalem and Tel Aviv: Bialik/Dvir Press, 1957-1959.
Arak.	= Arakhin
ARN	= Abot de Rabbi Natan
[Avery]-Peck, Terumot	= Alan J. [Avery]-Peck, The Priestly Gift in Mishnah: A Study of Tractate Terumot, Chico: Scholars Press, 1981.
A.Z.	= Abodah Zarah
b.	= Babli, Babylonian Talmud, Vilna: The Widow and Romm Brothers Press, 1886, various reprints.
	= ben, "son of," as in Simeon b. Gamaliel.
B	= Mishnah Zeraim, MS. Berlin 93; see Sacks-Hutner, Vol. 1, pp. 43, 77-78.
Barr, "Typology of Literalism"	= James Barr, "The Typology of Literalism in Ancient Biblical Translations," in Mitteilungen Des Septuaginta-Unternehmens (MSU) XV, reprinted Göttingen: Vandenhoeck and Ruprecht, 1979.
Batey, The Poor	= Richard Batey, Jesus and the Poor, New York: Harper and Row, 1972.
Bauer	= Walter Bauer, Die Mischna. I. Seder Zeraim. Z. Traktat Pea (Vom Ackerwinkel). Text, Übersetzung und Erklärung, Giessen: Alfred Töpelmann, 1914.
B.B.	= Baba Batra
BDB	= F. Brown, S.R. Driver, and C.A. Briggs, eds., A Hebrew and English Lexicon of the Old Testament, Oxford: Oxford University Press, 1907, reprinted 1952.
Bek.	= Bekhorot
Ber.	= Berakhot
Bert	= Obadiah b. Abraham of Bertinoro, Commentary to Mishnah (fifteenth century), reprinted in Romm edition of Mishnah.
Beṣ.	= Beṣah
Bik.	= Bikkurim
Blackman	= Philip Blackman, Mishnayot, second edition, 6 Vols., New York: Jewish Publication Society, 1964.
B.M.	= Baba Meṣia
Brueggemann	= Walter Brueggemann, The Land: Place as Gift, Promise and Challenge in Biblical Faith, Philadelphia: Fortress Press, 1977.
B.Q.	= Baba Qamma

C	= Mishnah, early printed edition of unknown origin, probably Constantinople or Pisaro, c. 1516; see Sacks-Hutner, Vol. 1, pp. 64, 82-83.
Ca	= Mishnah, MS. Cambridge 470, 1, printed in W.H. Lowe, The Mishnah On Which the Palestinian Talmud Rests, Cambridge, 1883; reprinted Jerusalem, 1967; see Sacks-Hutner, Vol. 1, pp. 63, 67.
Carmichael	= Calum M. Carmichael, The Laws of Deuteronomy, Ithaca: Cornell University Press, 1974.
Constantelos	= Demetrios J. Constantelos, Byzantine Philanthropy and Social Welfare, New Brunswick: Rutgers University Press, 1968.
Countryman	= L.W. Countryman, The Rich Christian in the Church of the Early Empire: Contradictions and Accommodations, New York and Toronto: Edwin Mellen Press, 1980.
Danby	= Herbert Danby, trans., The Mishnah: Translated from the Hebrew with Introduction and Brief Explanatory Notes, London: Oxford University Press, 1933.
Davies	= W.D. Davies, The Territorial Dimension of Judaism, Berkeley: University of California Press, 1982.
Dem.	= Demai
Driver, Scrolls	= G.R. Driver, The Judean Scrolls: The Problem and a Solution, Oxford: Basil Blackwell, 1965.
Deut.	= Deuteronomy
E	= Tosefta, MS. Erfurt. See Lieberman, TZ, pp. 8-11.
EB	= Menahem Haran, "Poor-Offerings," in Encyclopaedia Biblica. Thesaurus Rerum Biblicarum Alphabetico Ordine Digestus (Heb.), Vol. 5, pp. 674-675, Jerusalem: Bialik Institute, 1968.
Ed.	= Eduyyot
ed. princ.	= Tosefta, editio princeps, Venice; Bomberg Press, 1521. See Lieberman, TZ, pp. 8-11.
EJ	= Encyclopedia Judaica, 16 Vols., Jerusalem: Keter Publishing House, 1972.
Elliger, Leviticus	= Karl Elliger, Leviticus, Tubingen: J.C.B. Mohr, 1966.
Epstein, Mabo	= Jacob Nahum Halevi Epstein, Introduction to the Text of the Mishnah (Heb.), 2 Vols., ed. by E.Z. Melamed, Jerusalem and Tel Aviv: Magnes Press, 1948; second edition, 1964.
Epstein, Mebo'ot	= Jacob Nahum Halevi Epstein, Introduction to the Tannaitic Literature (Heb.), 2 Vols., ed. by E.Z. Melamed, Jerusalem and Tel Aviv: Magnes Press, 1957.
Erub.	= Erubin
Ex.	= Exodus
Fish	= Stanley Fish, Is There a Text in This Class? The Authority of Interpretive Communities, Cambridge: Harvard University Press, 1980.

Abbreviations and Bibliography

Frisch	= Ephraim Frisch, <u>An Historical Survey of Jewish Philanthropy. From the Earliest Times to the Nineteenth Century</u>, New York: Macmillan, 1924.
G (+ raised number)	= Mishnah MSS. fragments from the Cairo Genizah, listed and numbered in Sacks-Hutner, Vol. 1, pp. 87-112.
Gen.	= Genesis
Gereboff, Tarfon	= Joel Gereboff, <u>Rabbi Tarfon: The Tradition, The Man, and Early Rabbinic Judaism</u>, Missoula: Scholars Press, 1979.
Git.	= Gittin
GRA	= Elijah b. Solomon Zalman ("HaGaon Rabbi Eliyahu" or "Vilna Gaon"), Lithuania, 1720-1797, Mishnah commentary, <u>Shonot Eliyahu</u>, reprinted in Romm edition of Mishnah.
Green, Approaches	= William S. Green, ed., <u>Approaches to Ancient Judaism</u>, Vol. 1, Missoula: Scholars Press, 1978; Vol. 2, Chico: Scholars Press, 1980; Vol. 3, Chico: Scholars Press, 1981.
Green, Joshua	= William S. Green, <u>The Traditions of Joshua ben Hananiah</u>, Part I: The Early Legal Traditions, Leiden: E.J. Brill, 1981.
Haas, Second Tithe	= Peter Haas, <u>A History of the Mishnaic Law of Agriculture: Tractate Maaser Sheni</u>, Chico: Scholars Press, 1980.
Ḥag.	= Ḥagigah
Ḥal.	= Ḥallah
Hands	= A.R. Hands, <u>Charities and Social Aid in Greece and Rome</u>, Ithaca and New York: Cornell University Press, 1968.
ḤD	= David Samuel b. Jacob Pardo, Italy, Austria and Palestine, 1718-1790, Tosefta commentary, <u>Sefer Ḥasdé David. I. Seder Zeraim</u>, Livorno, 1776; reprinted Jerusalem, 1970.
Hengel, Property	= Martin Hengel, <u>Property and Riches in the Early Church. Aspects of a Social History of Early Christianity</u>, Philadelphia: Fortress Press, 1974.
Hengel, Judaism	= Martin Hengel, <u>Judaism and Hellenism. Studies in Their Encounter in Palestine During the Early Hellenistic Period</u>, 2 Vols., Philadelphia: Fortress Press, 1974.
Hirsch, Validity	= E.D. Hirsch, <u>Validity in Interpretation</u>, New Haven and London: Yale University Press, 1967.
Ḥul.	= Ḥullin
ḤY	= Yehezqel Abramsky (1886-1976), <u>Ḥazon Yeḥezqel, Seder Zeraim</u>, Tosefta commentary, Vilna, 1925; second edition, Jerusalem, 1971.
IB	= Nathaniel Micklem, "Leviticus," in <u>The Interpreter's Bible</u>, Vol. 2, New York and Nashville: Abingdon Press, 1952.
IDB	= <u>The Interpreter's Dictionary of the Bible</u>, 4 Vols., New York and Nashville: Abingdon Press, 1962; Supplementary Volume, 1976.
Is.	= Isaiah

Jaffee, Lists	= Martin S. Jaffee, "Deciphering Mishnaic Lists: A Form-Analytical Approach," in Approaches to Ancient Judaism, Vol. 3, pp. 19-35.
Jaffee, Tithes	= Martin S. Jaffee, Mishnah's Theology of Tithing: A Study of Tractate Maaserot, Chico: Scholars Press, 1981.
Jastrow	= Marcus Jastrow, A Dictionary of the Targumim, the Talmud Babli and Yerushalmi, and the Midrashic Literature, 2 Vols., New York, 1895-1903; reprinted New York: Judaica Press, 1975.
JE	= The Jewish Encyclopedia, 12 Vols., New York and London, 1901-1906; reprinted New York: KTAV Press, 1975.
Jer.	= Jeremiah
Johnson	= Luke T. Johnson, Sharing Possessions: Mandate and Symbol of Faith, Philadelphia: Fortress Press, 1981.
K	= Mishnah, MS. Kaufman A 50; photocopy: Georg Beer, Faksimile-Ausgabe des Mischnacodex Kaufmann A 50, The Hague, 1929; reprinted Jerusalem, 1969. See Sacks-Hutner, Vol. 1, pp. 63, 65-66.
Kahana	= Abraham Kahana, ed., The Apocryphal Books (Heb.), 2 Vols., Jerusalem: Makor Publishing, 1978.
Kanter, Gamaliel	= Shamai Kanter, Rabban Gamaliel II: The Legal Traditions, Chico: Scholar's Press, 1980.
Kasovsky, Conc. Mish.	= C.Y. Kasovsky, Thesaurus Mishnae: Concordantiae Verborum Quae in Sex Mishnae Ordinibus Reperiunter, 4 Vols., Tel Aviv: Massada Press, 1957; reprinted 1967.
Kasovksy, Conc. Tos.	= C.Y. Kasovsky, Thesaurus Thosephthae: Concordantiae Verborum Quae in Sex Thosefthae Ordinibus Reperiunter, 6 Vols., Jerusalem: Massada Press, 1932-1961.
Kel.	= Kelim
Ket.	= Ketubot
Kid.	= Kiddushin
Kil.	= Kilayim
Klein	= Samuel Klein, Sepher Hayishub, (Settlements in the Land of Israel), Vol. I: From the Destruction of the Second Temple to the Arab Conquest of the Land, Jerusalem: Isaac Benzvi Press, 1977.
KM	= Joseph b. Ephraim Karo, 1488-1575, Kesef Mishnah, commentary to Maimonides' Mishneh Torah, in standard editions.
Kohut, Aruch	= Alexander Kohut, Aruch Ha-Shalem: Aruch Completum sive Lexicon Vocabula et res, quae in libris Targumicus, Talmudicus et Midraschicis, 6 Vols., Vienna, 1878-1892, reprinted Jerusalem.
L	= Palestinian Talmud, MS. Leiden; see Sacks-Hutner, Vol. 1, pp. 63, 72.
Lev.	= Leviticus

Abbreviations and Bibliography

Levy	= Jacob Levy, Neuhebräisches und Chaldäisches Wörterbuch uber die Talmudim und Midraschim, 4 Vols., Leipzig, 1876.
Lewis and Short	= C. Lewis and C. Short, A Latin Dictionary, Oxford: Oxford University Press, 1958.
Lieberman, TK	= Saul Lieberman, Tosefta Ki-fshutah: A Comprehensive Commentary on the Tosefta, Orders of Agriculture, Appointed Times, and Women, 8 Vols., New York: Jewish Theological Seminary of America, 1955-1977.
Lieberman, TR	= Saul Lieberman, Tosefeth Rishonim. A Commentary Based on Manuscripts of the Tosefta and Works of the Rishonim and Midrashim in Manuscripts and Rare Editions, 2 Vols., Jerusalem: Bamberger and Wahrmann, 1938.
Lieberman, TZ	= Saul Lieberman, ed., The Tosefta According to Codex Vienna, with Varients from Codex Erfart, Genizah Mss. and Editio Princeps, Orders of Agriculture, Appointed Times, and Women, 4 Vols., New York: Jewish Theological Seminary of America, 1955-1977.
Löw, Flora	= Immanuel Löw, Die Flora der Juden, 4 Vols., Vienna and Leipzig: R. Loewit Press, 1926.
M	= Babylonian Talmud, Codex Munich 95; photocopy: Hermann L. Strack, Talmud Babylonicum Codicis Hebraica Monacensis 95, Leiden, 1912; reprinted Jerusalem, 1971; see Sacks-Hutner, Vol. 1, pp. 63, 69-70.
M.	= Mishnah. All references are to M. Peah unless otherwise indicated.
Maas.	= Maaserot
MacMullen	= Ramsay MacMullen, Roman Social Relations. 50 B.C. to A.D. 284, New Haven: Yale University Press, 1974.
Maimonides, Commentary	= Maimonides, (Moses b. Maimon), 1135-1204, The Mishnah, With a Commentary by R. Moses b. Maimon, Translated from the Arabic on the Basis of the Original Manuscript. Introduction and notes by Joseph D. Kafaḥ, 3 Vols., Jerusalem: Rab Kook Foundation, 1964.
Maimonides, Gifts	= Maimonides, Mishnah Torah: Laws of Poor Offerings, in Israel Klein, The Book of Agriculture, New Haven: Yale University Press, 1979.
Mak.	= Makkot
Mandelbaum	= Irving Mandelbaum, A History of the Mishnaic Law of Agriculture: Kilayim, Chico: Scholars Press, 1982.
MB	= Samuel Avigdor b. Abraham Karlin, Minḥat Bikkurim, Tosefta commentary, 1842, in Romm edition of Babylonian Talmud.
Mekhilta, Horowitz-Rabin	= H.S. Horowitz and I.A. Rabin, eds., Mekhilta de-Rabbi Ishmael, original edition, 1930, reprinted Jerusalem: Wahrman Books, 1970.
Mekhilta, Lauterbach	= Jacob Lauterbach, Mekhilta de-Rabbi Ishmael, 3 Vols., Philadelphia: Jewish Publication Society, 1935, reprinted 1976.
Men.	= Menaḥot

Mid.	= Middot
M.Q.	= Moed Qatan
MR	= Ephraim Isaac of Premysla, Poland, <u>Mishnah Rishonah</u>, Mishnah commentary, 1882, reprinted in Romm edition of Mishnah.
MS	= Solomon b. Joshua Adeni, Yemen and Palestine, c. 1600, <u>Meleket Shelomoh</u>, Mishnah commentary, reprinted in Romm edition of Mishnah.
M.S.	= Maaser Sheni
ms.	= manuscript
N	= Mishnah, <u>ed. princ.</u>, Naples 1492; see Sacks-Hutner, Vol. 1, pp. 64, 81-82.
Naz.	= Nazir
Ned.	= Nedarim
Neusner, <u>Appointed Times</u>	= J. Neusner, <u>A History of the Mishnaic Law of Appointed Times</u>, 5 Vols., Leiden: E.J. Brill, 1981.
Neusner, <u>Cults</u>	= J. Neusner, ed., <u>Christianity, Judaism and Other Greco-Roman Cults: Studies for Morton Smith at Sixty</u>, 4 Vols., Leiden: E.J. Brill, 1975.
Neusner, <u>Damages</u>	= J. Neusner, <u>A History of the Mishnaic Law of Damages</u>, 5 Vols., Leiden: E.J. Brill, 1982.
Neusner, <u>Eliezer</u>	= J. Neusner, <u>Eliezer ben Hyrcanus: The Tradition and the Man</u>, 2 Vols., Leiden: E.J. Brill, 1973.
Neusner, <u>Holy Things</u>	= J. Neusner, <u>A History of the Mishnaic Law of HolyThings</u>, 6 Vols., Leiden: E.J. Brill, 1978-79.
Neusner, <u>Judaism</u>	= J. Neusner, <u>Judaism: The Evidence of the Mishnah</u>, Chicago, University of Chicago Press, 1981.
Neusner, <u>Method</u>	= J. Neusner, <u>Method and Meaning in Ancient Judaism</u>, Missoula: Scholars Press, 1979; Second series, Chico: Scholars Press, 1981; Third series, Chico: Scholars Press, 1981.
Neusner, <u>Modern Study</u>	= J. Neusner, ed., <u>The Modern Study of the Mishnah</u>, Leiden: E.J. Brill, 1973.
Neusner, <u>Pharisees</u>	= J. Neusner, <u>The Rabbinic Traditions about the Pharisees Before 70</u>, 3 Vols., Leiden: E.J. Brill, 1971.
Neusner, <u>Purities</u>	= J. Neusner, <u>A History of the Mishnaic Law of Purities</u>, 22 Vols., Leiden: E.J. Brill, 1974-77.
Neusner, "Redaction"	= J. Neusner, "Redaction, Formulation, and Form: The Case of Mishnah," <u>Jewish Quarterly Review</u> 70, 1980, pp. 1-22.
Neusner, <u>Talmud</u>	= Jacob Neusner, <u>The Talmud of the Land of Israel</u>, 35 Vols., Chicago: University of Chicago Press, 1982-.
Neusner, <u>Tosefta</u>	= J. Neusner, <u>The Tosefta Translated from the Hebrew</u>, 5 Vols., New York: KTAV Publishing House, 1977-81.

Neusner, Women	= J. Neusner, A History of the Mishnaic Law of Women, 5 Vols., Leiden: E.J. Brill, 1979-80.
Newman, Shebiit	= Louis Newman, The Sanctity of the Seventh Year: A Study of Mishnah Tractate Shebiit, Chico: Scholars Press, 1983.
Nickelsburg	= George W.E. Nickelsburg, Jewish Literature Between the Bible and the Mishnah, Philadelphia: Fortress Press, 1981.
Nid.	= Niddah
Noth	= Martin Noth, Leviticus, Philadelphia: SCM Press, 1963.
Num.	= Numbers
O^1	= MS. Oxford 366, Babylonian Talmud, Orders Zeraim and Moed; see Sacks-Hutner, Vol. 1, pp. 63, 68-69.
O^2	= MS. Oxford 393, Mishnah Zeraim, with Maimonides' commentary, autograph; see Sacks-Hutner, Vol. 1, pp. 63, 76-77.
Oh.	= Ohalot
Orl.	= Orlah
P	= Mishnah, MS. Parma DeRossi 138, photocopy: Jerusalem, 1970; see Sacks-Hutner, Vol. 1, pp. 63, 66-67.
Pa	= Mishnah, MS. Paris 328-329, photocopy: Jerusalem, 1970; see Sacks-Hutner, Vol. 1, pp. 64, 79.
Par.	= Parah
Pes.	= Pesaḥim
Porter	= J.R. Porter, Leviticus, Cambridge, Cambridge University Press, 1976.
Porton, "Dispute"	= Gary G. Porton, "The Artificial Dispute: Ishmael and Aqiba," in Neusner, Cults, Vol. IV, pp. 18-29.
Porton, Ishmael	= Gary G. Porton, The Traditions of Rabbi Ishmael, 4 Vols., Leiden: E.J. Brill, 1976-80.
Primus, Aqiba	= Charles Primus, Aqiva's Contribution to the Law of Zera^{c}im, Leiden: E.J. Brill, 1977.
Prov.	= Proverbs
Ps.	= Psalms
Qid.	= Qiddushin
R.	= Rabbi
Rabad	= Abraham b. David of Posquieres, ca. 1120-1198, glosses to Maimonides' Mishneh Torah, in standard editions.
Rashi	= Solomon b. Isaac of Troyes, France, 1040-1105, commentary to Babylonian Talmud, in standard editions.
RDBZ	= David ibn Zimra, 1479-1589, supercommentary to Maimonides' Mishneh Torah, in standard editions.

R.H.	= Rosh Hashanah
Romm Mishnah	= Standard printed version of Mishnah, Vilna: The Widow and Romm Brothers Press, 1908 (and reprints).
Rosh	= Asher b. Yeḥiel, Germany and Spain, 1250-1327, Mishnah commentary, in standard editions of Babylonian Talmud.
RSV	= H.G. May and B.M. Metzger, eds., The New Oxford Annotated Bible. Revised Standard Version Containing the Old and New Testaments, Oxford: Oxford University Press, 1971.
S	= MS. British Museum 403, Palestinian Talmud, Zeraim, with commentary of Solomon of Sirillo (see Sirillo); see Sacks-Hutner, Vol. 1, pp. 63, 73-75.
Sa	= Mishnah Zeraim, MS. Sassoon 531; see Sacks-Hutner, Vol. 1, pp. 63, 68.
Sacks-Hutner	= The Mishnah with Variant Readings, Order Zeraim, 2 Vols., Nissan Sacks, ed., Jerusalem: Institute for the Complete Israeli Talmud, 1972-75.
San.	= Sanhedrin
Sarason, Demai	= Richard S. Sarason, A History of the Mishnaic Law of Agriculture: A Study of Tractate Demai, Part One, Leiden: E.J. Brill, 1979.
Schäfer	= Peter Schäfer, Der Bar Kokhba-Aufstand. Studien zum zweiten judischen Krieg gegen Rom, Tübingen: J.C.B. Mohr, 1981.
Segal	= M.H. Segal, A Grammar of Mishnaic Hebrew, Oxford: Oxford University Press, 1958.
Shab.	= Shabbat
Sheb.	= Shebiit
Sheq.	= Sheqalim
Sens	= Samson b. Abraham of Sens, France, late twelfth - early thirteenth centuries, Mishnah commentary, reprinted in Romm edition of Babylonian Talmud.
Sifra	= I.H. Weiss, ed., Sifra debe Rab, hu Sefer Torat Kohanim, Vienna, 1862; reprinted New York: Om Press, 1946.
Sifre Deut.	= L. Finkelstein, with H.S. Horovitz, ed., Siphre ad Deuteronomium, Berlin, 1939; reprinted New York: Jewish Theological Seminary of America, 1959.
Sifre Bamidbar	= H.S. Horovitz, ed., Siphre de be Rab. Fasciculus primus: Siphre ad Numeros adjecto Siphre Zutta, Leipzig, 1917; reprinted Jerusalem: Wahrmann Books, 1966.
Sirillo	= Solomon b. Joseph Sirillo, d. 1558, commentary to Palestinian Talmud, Zeraim, Jerusalem: 1963.
Smallwood	= E. Mary Smallwood, The Jews Under Roman Rule: From Pompey to Diocletian. A Study in Political Relations, Leiden: E.J. Brill, 1981.

Smith, Map	=	Jonathan Z. Smith, Map Is Not Territory, Leiden: E.J. Brill, 1978.
Sot.	=	Sotah
Strack	=	Hermann Strack, Introduction to the Talmud and Midrash, Philadelphia: Jewish Publication Society, 1931; reprinted 1976.
Suk.	=	Sukkah
T.	=	Tosefta. All references are to T. Peah unless otherwise indicated.
T³	=	Mishnah Zeraim, MS. Temani, New York 30/31; see Sacks-Hutner, Vol. 2, p. 44.
Ta.	=	Taanit
Tanh.	=	Midrash Tanhuma, Jerusalem: Eshkol Press, 1975.
Tanh. Buber.	=	Solomon Buber, ed., Midrash Tanhuma, Attributed to Rabbi Tanhuma b. R. Abba, reprinted Jerusalem: Books Export Enterprises.
Tcherikover	=	Avigdor Tcherikover, Hellenistic Civilization and the Jews, Philadelphia: Jewish Publication Society, 1959.
Tem.	=	Temurah
Ter.	=	Terumot
Theophrastus, Enquiry	=	Theophrastus, Enquiry into Plants, trans. Sir Arthur Hart, 2 Vols., Loeb Classical Library, Cambridge: Harvard University Press, 1916.
Toh.	=	Tohorot
TYT	=	Yom Tob Lippmann Heller, Austria, Bohemia, Poland, 1579-1654, Tosefot Yom Tob, Mishnah commentary, in Romm edition.
TYY	=	Israel b. Gedaliah Lipschütz, Germany, 1782-1860, Tiferet Yisrael Yakin, Mishnah commentary, with supercommentary, Tiferet Yisrael Boaz, by his son, Baruch Isaac b. Israel Lipschutz, 1812-1877, both reprinted in Romm edition of Mishnah.
Uqs.	=	Uqsin
V	=	Tosefta, MS. Vienna Heb. 20; see Lieberman, TZ, pp. 11-12.
Vermes, DSSE	=	Geza Vermes, The Dead Sea Scrolls in English, second edition, Baltimore: Penguin Books, 1975.
Vermes, Perspective	=	Geza Vermes, The Dead Sea Scrolls: Qumram in Perspective, revised edition, Philadelphia: Fortress Press, 1977.
Von Rad, Deuteronomy	=	Gerhard Von Rad, Deuteronomy: A Commentary. Philadelphia: Westminster Press, 1966.
Von Rad, Studies	=	Gerhard Von Rad, Studies in Deuteronomy, Chicago: Henry Regnery Co., 1953.
Weinfeld	=	Moshe Weinfeld, Deuteronomy and the Deuteronomic School, Oxford: Oxford University Press, 1972.

Welch, Origins	= Adam C. Welch, <u>The Code of Deuteronomy: A New Theory of Its Origins</u>, London: James Clark and Co., 1924.
White	= K.D. White, <u>Roman Farming</u>, Ithaca: Cornell University Press, 1970.
Y.	= <u>Yerushalmi</u>, Palestinian Talmud, <u>ed. princ.</u>, Venice, 1520-23, reprinted Jerusalem. All references are to Y. Peah unless otherwise indicated.
Yad.	= Yadayim
Yalon	= Hanoch Yalon, <u>Introduction to the Vocalization of the Mishna</u> (Heb.), Jerusalem: Bialik Institute, 1964.
Yeb.	= Yebamot
Z	= Mishnah, MS. Paris 362, with commentary of Sens; see Sacks-Hutner, Vol. 1, pp. 64, 79-80.
Zeb.	= Zebahim
Zuckermandel	= Moses Samuel Zuckermandel, <u>Tosefta, based on the Erfurt and Vienna Codices, with Parallels and Variants</u>; revised edition with supplement by Saul Lieberman, Jerusalem: Wahrmann Books, 1970.
Zahavy, Eleazar	= Tzvee Zahavy, <u>The Traditions of Eleazar ben Azariah</u>, Missoula: Scholars Press, 1977.

INTRODUCTION

I. Poor and Priests: The Message of Tractate Peah

Tractate Peah asserts that needy Israelites are entitled to a portion of each crop that grows on the Land of Israel. The householder must designate some of his produce to meet this entitlement, while other gifts become the property of the poor entirely through processes of accident.[1] What these various types of food have in common is the fact that they are reserved for the poor alone--no one else may eat them. So the fundamental claim of this tractate is that the poor should receive some bit of the Land's yield for their exclusive use. This notion of poor-relief emerges through Mishnah's discussion of the procedures for designating and distributing the several poor-offerings mentioned in Scripture. Tractate Peah deals with each offering specified in the Mosaic Codes in the order in which they are separated during the harvesting process: that which grows in the rear corner of the field (peah; Lev. 19:9; 23:22), gleanings (Lev. 19:9; 23:22), forgotten sheaves (Deut. 24:19), separated grapes (Lev. 19:10), defective clusters (Lev. 19:10; Deut. 24:21), and poorman's tithe (Deut. 26:12). In sum, the tractate takes as its topic the entire repertoire of Scriptural references to poor-offerings.

In their discussion of these offerings, Mishnah's framers appear to be concerned with a single question: Within the holy life of Israel, how do we account for poor people's exclusive right to produce set aside as poor-offerings? To anticipate at the outset what answer we shall find, we shall examine the somewhat analogous case of the priests and the rations they receive, an analogy suggested to begin with by the tractate's setting within Mishnah's Division of Agriculture. That division deals primarily with the priestly caste and with the types of food set aside for its members.[2] Its tractates outline the various priestly rations--for example, tithes, heave offering, and first fruits--all of which are reserved for consumption by the priests and their families.[3] But the poor, too, are entitled to certain food that no other Israelite may eat. So by placing the tractate in this context, Mishnah's redactors indicate that in their view the poor, and the poor-offerings due them, are in some way analogous to the priests, and the priestly rations given them. In fact, Mishnah's framers make this analogy explicit when they compare the poor with the priests (see M. 1:6, 4:6-8) and assert that just as the priestly caste receives tithes from each householder, so the poor should receive a part of each crop. God grants both an exclusive right to a portion of crops grown on the Land of Israel. The poor, no less than the priests, seem to be counted as a distinctive caste of Israelite society.

What conception stands behind this analogy between the poor and the priests? It is their common claim on God for protective support. Because neither group possesses a portion of the Land of Israel, neither can produce the food it needs. The priests, for their part, are forbidden by Scriptural law to own land (see Deut. 18:1-5). Instead, they act as

- 17 -

God's servants in the Temple and are accorded food on that account. Similarly, the poor have lost whatever portion of the Land they may have possessed, and so are entitled to receive some of its yield. God supports both the priests and the poor because they neither own land nor attain the economic prosperity promised to all Israelites who live in the Land (see Deut. 8:7-10).[4]

These claims on God are satisfied through the action of the ordinary Israelite householder. As a tenant farmer, he works God's Land and enjoys its yield, with the result that a portion of all that he produces belongs to God. In order to pay this obligation, Israelites render to the priests grain as heave offering, tithes, and other priestly rations.[5] Similarly, a specific portion of the Land's yield is set aside, by chance alone,[6] for the poor. So underlying the designation of both priestly rations and poor-offerings is a single theory: God owns the entire Land of Israel and, because of this ownership, a portion of each crop must be paid to him as a sort of sacred tax (see Lev. 27:30-33). According to Mishnah's framers, God claims that which is owed him and then gives it to those under his special care, the poor and the priests.

The tractate reinforces its implicit comparison of the poor and the priests in its discussion of the manner in which poor-offerings are set aside. Only when accident separates grain from a normal crop is the food deemed to have been set aside by God for the poor. We therefore speak of produce that is set aside without any identifiable cause. Since neither the householder, his workers, nor anyone else has acted to identify which produce within a crop is to be designated, we know that God alone has reserved this particular food for the poor. Whether it is the grain that happens to grow in the rear corner of a field (and that the farmer himself will later designate as peah), or the stalks that by chance fall aside from the edge of the farmer's sickle (gleanings), all this food apportioned seemingly by accident must be left for the poor. So the framers of Mishnah believe that God alone determines what produce falls into the category of poor-offerings. In fact, the deepest expression of God's wishes for the produce of his Land is carried in the random separation of a small amount of food.[7] This random character is reflected likewise in the designation of produce for the priests. For example, when a farmer designates heave offering from the produce he has collected at his threshing floor, he declares that the heave offering is isolated in one part of the pile. When he lifts out this produce, whatever he grabs immediately takes on the status of heave offering. He may not measure this produce or attempt to designate any specific grain.[8] Rather, it is through chance alone that God detemines which particular grain in which quantity will fall into the category of priestly rations. So in this important regard, poor-offerings are like priestly rations. In both cases, God claims a portion of his Land's yield through chance designation.[9]

Throughout the tractate, the basic similarity between poor-offerings and priestly rations is clear.[10] Each time the householder asserts his ownership of the Land's yield, God demands a portion for those under his protective care, the poor and the priests. Thus in the course of reaping and processing grain, God's interest in the crop is aroused at two distinct points, once in behalf of the poor, once in behalf of the priests. First, as the householder harvests the grain in his field, thereby claiming it for himself, God causes a portion to be set aside. This bit of food, separated seemingly at random, then is available for the poor alone. (In the case of peah, of course, the poor must wait for the householder to explicitly designate what God has set aside.) Second, when the farmer later collects the food at his threshing floor, God again asserts his ultimate ownership of the Land's yield by removing some for the priests.[11]

Although, as we have now seen, poor-offerings and priestly rations are analogous, they also differ in an important respect. The farmer plays no active role in identifying the produce to be set aside as poor-offerings, while he acts as God's agent in designating priestly rations. The steps a householder must take in supporting the poor and the priests all maintain this distinction. When setting aside poor-offerings, a farmer merely leaves some of his grain unharvested as peah,[12] accidentally drops a few stalks as gleanings, or forgets to collect some of his sheaves. In the process through which this food is set aside for the poor, the farmer does nothing purposive. Rather, God alone determines which particular grain must be given to the poor and separates this food from the remainder of the crop. Furthermore, as we shall see, the farmer is forbidden to dispense the offerings, lest he put them to his own purposes, not God's. So the householder has no part at all in separating poor-offerings. In identifying the portion of a crop to be offered as priestly rations, by contrast, the farmer does take an active role. Here the householder is the one who reaches into a pile of grain to set aside produce for the priests. That which he grasps, a random handful, must be given directly to a priest. The farmer thus functions as God's agent by lifting out this random portion of the crop and delivering it to its proper recipients.[13]

What theory accounts for the differing roles assigned to the farmer in the process through which poor-offerings and priestly rations are separated? The answer lies in the householder's relationship to the poor and to the priests. The poor have no immediate claim for support on the householder. The priests, by contrast, deserve his direct aid, because they serve in the Temple as the Israelite's respresentatives before God. They alone can offer animals in the Temple, thus performing an indispensable service for ordinary farmers. In return for the priests' services, the householder must maintain them by acting as God's partner in designating their food. The poor are another matter. Unlike the priests, the poor perform no service in behalf of the householder, and so have no direct claim upon him. As owner of the Land of Israel, God alone owes them sustenance to keep the promise he made to all Israelites who live in the Land. So God alone determines what grain should be given to the poor and separates this from those crops that the householder is about to reap and take as his own. The householder is entirely excluded from this process; he must not interfere in God's allotment. So the two types of offerings are analogous in all respects but the manner in which they are designated. In that regard, the contrast stems directly from the different sorts of claims these two groups assert for a portion of the Land's yield.

II.   The Logical Unfolding of the Harvesting Process: The Structure of Tractate Peah

When we turn to the structure of Tractate Peah, we find that it presents a systematic review of the farmer's acts in harvesting his crops. The tractate details his reaping grain and fruit, binding this produce into sheaves, and transporting it to the threshing floor. Through these varied agricultural activities, taken up in sequential order, the farmer asserts his claim upon produce of the Land of Israel. When he begins to harvest a field, he expresses his desire to take the yield of the Land for his own use. Later, when the householder actually cuts a few stalks with his sickle, he establishes a direct claim upon those particular stalks. Then, when he binds the grain into sheaves for easy transportation to his own threshing floor, he reasserts his claim on the produce. At precisely these points, God affirms his ultimate ownership of the Land and all of its produce. This he does by taking away from the householder some grain, which then must be given over to the poor.

The logical unfolding of the harvest process thus serves to organize the entire tractate. The framers first discuss peah, the offering set aside as the farmer begins to reap his crop. Second, they treat gleanings, an offering that falls to the ground as the householder cuts the individual stalks, and, third, forgotten sheaves, food accidently left behind during the binding process. Having finished discussing those offerings that the poor take in the field itself, the sages move on to describe a type of support given to the poor after the food has been removed for processing. They briefly treat poorman's tithe, one of the several tithes designated at the threshing floor. Having worked their way through the entire harvest process, the framers now take up issues entirely outside the framework of the agricultural calendar. They briefly discuss those types of community charity given out during the entire year, and define the category of "poor." As the complement of the discussion of poor-offerings set aside during the reaping and processing of the Land's yield, these brief definitions could have been placed at either the beginning or end of the tractate's essay. Yet Mishnah's philosophers chose to dwell on these issues only after their main point has emerged: there exists a perfect correspondence between the farmer's reaping his field and God's setting aside produce for the poor. Each time the farmer claims some of the produce for his own use, God too demands a portion for the poor, who are under his special care.

Within each of the tractate's major units, the framers also follow a logical program of inquiry. They typically begin at the foundation of the matter by defining each poor-offering under discussion. Next, the sages address the distribution of this food, over and over again making the point that God alone determines what particular produce falls to each poor person. Householders must not in any way interfere as God apportions the grain. Finally, each of the units concludes with a transition that follows a set pattern. This involves shifting the topic of discussion from one particular poor-offering to rules governing poor-offerings in general; the framers thereby indicate their intention to close discussion of one particular poor-offering and move on to the next.

Introduction

I. **PEAH**: The poor-offering set aside when the farmer begins to harvest his entire field (M. 1:1-4:9):

   A. Basic Definition: Amount, Location, Types of Produce Subject (M. 1:1-6):

   1. Amount:

      M. 1:1 — Homiletical introduction: Five things that have no limit, including the amount of produce designated as peah. Four things the benefits of which a person enjoys both in this world and in the world to come.

      M. 1:2 — The amount of produce designated as peah must be at least one-sixtieth of the crop. The amount of peah must correspond to the size of the field, the number of poor people, and the size of the yield.

   2. Location:

      M. 1:3 — Produce may be designated as peah in any part of the field. Simeon: in the rear of the field. Judah: peah must be differentiated from the remainder of the crop.

   3. Types of Produce Subject to the Law:

      M. 1:4-5 — All produce that is (1) edible, (2) tended, (3) grown on the Land of Israel, (4) harvested as a crop and (5) can be stored is subject to the laws of peah.

      M. 1:6 — Produce designated as peah is exempt from the separation of tithes; so too ownerless produce, grain used as animal feed, or seed all are exempt from the separation of tithes.

   B. Definition: The area of land defined as a field from which a single portion of peah must be designated (M. 2:1-3:8):

   1. Grain fields:

      M. 2:1-2 — The boundaries of grain fields are established by physical barriers such as rivers, ponds and roads.

   2. Orchards:

      M. 2:3-4 — The boundaries of orchards are established by fences. Gamaliel and Eliezer: each species of tree constitutes an orchard.

   3. Ambiguous cases in which one field is treated as two, or in which two fields are treated as one:

      M. 2:5-6 — A single field planted with two species of a single genus: if harvested separately, the two types define distinct field from each of which peah must be set aside; if harvested at one time, the entire tract of land constitutes a single field from which only one portion of peah is separated.

      M. 2:7-8 — A single field, half of which is destroyed, harvested by thieves, or sold, and the remaining half of which the Israelite farmer reaps: whoever harvests the rear corner must designate peah for the entire field, for the obligation to set aside peah inheres only in the grain that grows in the rear corner.

	M. 3:1-4	Houses-disputes in which a single field is harvested in more than one part because of spatial, temporal, or purposive considerations. Shammaites: a separate portion of produce must be set aside from each individually harvested patch. Hillelites: a single portion of produce should be separated as peah on behalf of the entire field.
	M. 3:5	A single field jointly owned: the owners together set aside a single portion of produce as peah. A single field owned in two distinct parts: each owner separates a portion of peah on behalf of his own part of the field.

    4.   The Minimum Size of a Field:

	M. 3:6	Eliezer, Joshua, Tarfon, Judah b. Beterah: small tracts of land are inconsequential, so peah need not be designated on their behalf. Aqiba: all tracts of land, however minuscule, constitute real estate, and so are subject to the laws of peah.
	M. 3:7-8	Cases in support of Aqiba's view: a miniscule area of land indicates a householder's intentions for his entire estate.

C.   Distributing Peah to the Poor (M. 4:1-5):

	M. 4:1-2	The poor themselves are allowed to gather and divide the produce set aside as peah; the householder is permitted to interfere only to prevent damage to his property.
	M. 4:3-4	Each poor person is entitled only to the amount of produce that he can gather by hand and carry.
	M. 4:5	Poor people must be allowed to gather the peah three times each day; Gamaliel: to allow them easy access. Aqiba: to assure that the poor need not waste time waiting for the farmer to allow them to gather the produce.

   D.   Transition: A general discussion of when produce becomes subject to the laws of gleanings, forgotten sheaves, and peah (M. 4:6-9):

	M. 4:6-7	These laws apply at the time when the field is reaped. Judah: the law of the forgotten sheaf takes effect only after the produce is bound into sheaves.
	M. 4:8	Comparison: Produce becomes subject to the separation of tithes when the grain pile at the threshing floor is smoothed-over.
	M. 4:9	Poor-offerings designated from a field belonging to a gentile are subject to the separation of tithes.

In the opening unit, A, the framers take up three central issues: (1) the amount of food to be set aside as peah, (2) where within each field the farmer must leave this grain, and (3) the types of produce subject to the laws of peah. This arrangement of topics seems to bear no particular meaning, yet the framers' discussion in fact constitutes a suitable introduction because it serves to define the category of peah. The quite lengthy unit B takes up a logically consequent topic, the definition of a field. The householder must know what area of his land constitutes a field in order to properly designate the produce that grows in the rear corner of each field. Sections B1 and B2 propose definitions for two main types of agricultural tracts, grain fields and orchards. From this information, the framers move on to typical ambiguities (B3) concerning a single field delimited by the above criteria, yet harvested in more than one part or owned by more than one farmer. The discussion of a field's definition concludes by addressing at B4 a secondary point, a field's minimum size.

In section C the framers turn to the distribution of peah to the poor, the next logical topic after discussing (at A and B) how this produce is set aside. The discussion here is shaped entirely by the tractate's notion that all poor people own the produce left as peah. It follows that all must have fair access to the food separated as peah.

A short transition at D signals the conclusion of the tractate's treatment of peah and prepares the way for a new topic. This is accomplished throughout the tractate by shifting the subject from peah in particular to poor-offerings in general. The sages here identify the moment when each law takes effect and they discuss the status of poor-offerings deriving from fields owned by gentiles.

In the second act of harvesting to be considered, the farmer reaps individual stalks of grain. As he or his workers claim these stalks, some of the grain falls entirely by accident and is designated by God for the poor alone.

II. GLEANINGS: The poor-offering separated when the householder cuts individual stalks (M. 4:10-5:6):

    A. Definition (M. 4:10-5:2):

        1. Gleanings:

            M. 4:10   During the harvest, that which falls entirely at random enters the category of gleanings.

        2. Ambiguous cases:

            M. 4:11   Grains of wheat found in ant-holes: if at the bottoms of the ant holes, we assume that ants stole the grains and that they are not in the status of gleanings; if at the tops, we assume the grains fell during the harvest and are in the status of gleanings. Meir: all such produce must be given to the poor, for produce in a doubtful status is deemed to be in the category of gleanings.

            M. 5:1-2   Cases of doubt caused when produce in the status of gleanings becomes mixed together with ordinary produce. The poor receive all of the grain in a doubtful status for this is deemed to be in the category of gleanings. Simeon b. Gamaliel, Eliezer: the poor receive only the amount of food they actually lost in the mixture.

    B. Distribution (M. 5:3)

        M. 5:3   Householders may not irrigate a field until the poor have gathered the gleanings because it might make the collection difficult.

    C. Transition: the collection of poor-offerings in general (M. 5:4-6):

        1. Poor-offerings gathered by rich people:

            M. 5:4   A travelling rich person may collect gleanings, forgotten sheaves, and peah. Eliezer: he must repay when he returns home. Sages: he need not repay because in effect he was poor.

2. Poor-offerings gathered by poor field-owners:

M. 5:5   Sharecroppers or hired laborers who are paid part ownership in the crop may not gather poor-offerings from that field.

M. 5:6   Former owners of a field are entitled to gather the poor-offerings designated from it. Field owners and their families who collect poor-offerings from their own fields steal from the poor.

Mishnah's authors open this discussion by defining gleanings as produce that falls for no apparent reason during the harvest (A1). Having delimited this category, they turn to ambiguous cases (A2) in which there is a doubt whether or not a particular stalk should be deemed a gleaning. Their focus on such liminal cases generates a series of disputes that add precision to the preceding definition of the category of gleanings.

At B, Mishnah's authors characteristically shift their focus from the process by which gleanings are separated to God's dividing the food among the poor. As with all other poor-offerings, only God may dispense this food. To allow this, householders must guarantee the poor unimpeded access to their produce.

The transitional section, C, once again takes up a topic relevant to poor-offerings in general (cf. the parallel section at I.D). Through this by now familiar redactional technique, the framers prepare to move from their discussion of gleanings. The main point is that people may not collect the poor-offerings designated from their own fields even if these individuals otherwise qualify as poor. Since these people have direct access to the fruits of the Land, they have no right to collect an additional allotment as poor-offerings.

After the farmer has reaped a field, he binds the grain into sheaves and carries these bundles to the threshing floor for processing. Proceeding through its step by step review of the harvesting process the tractate next considers the law governing sheaves that a householder forgets in the field. Once again, Mishnah's redactors begin by defining the category of forgotten sheaves and then move on to ambiguous cases. The main point of the entire discussion is that only sheaves left in the field entirely by accident must be given to the poor. God has caused this produce to be set aside, with the result that the sheaves become the property of the poor. That which the farmer purposely leaves behind, by contrast, does not fall into the category of forgotten sheaves, because it never was forgotten at all.

III. <u>FORGOTTEN SHEAVES</u>: The offering separated after the farmer has completed reaping the field when he binds the grain into sheaves (M. 5:7-6:11):

A. Definition (M. 5:7-6:3):

1. What falls into the category of "Forgotten..."

M. 5:7   Only sheaves that have been forgotten by all involved in processing enter the status of the forgotten sheaf. Those that are hidden by the poor or remembered by even one worker need not be left for the poor.

2. What falls into the category of "...Sheaf"

    M. 5:8 Only produce bound into a sheaf for transportation to the threshing floor is subject to the law. Both prior to this binding and after the produce reaches the threshing floor, the law cannot apply.

3. Ambiguous cases: Houses-disputes regarding the definition of "forgotten sheaf" and, by extension, "ownerless property":

    M. 6:1a Hillelites: produce declared ownerless belongs to all, even if the farmer declares it reserved for poor-people. Shammaites: the farmer validly may declare produce ownerless, yet reserved for the poor alone.

    M. 6:1b-6:2 Hillelites: All sheaves that the householder leaves behind are subject to the restrictions of the forgotten sheaf, even if he clearly intends to gather them later. Shammaites: sheaves that the householder intends to gather at a later time are not subject to the law, even if the householder has left them behind.

    M. 6:3 Sheaves laid out for later collection, sheaves that the householder has picked up in order to take them to the city for sale--both Houses agree that they are not subject to the restrictions of the forgotten sheaf.

B. Scriptural basis: Deut. 24:19's injunction that one should not return to gather sheaves forgotten during the binding process (M. 6:4):

   M. 6:4 Once the workers have had a chance to collect a sheaf, but nonetheless have passed by it, the sheaf falls into the category of the forgotten sheaf. But sheaves that they have not yet passed cannot enter this status because the workers need not "return" in order to collect them.

C. Ambiguous cases: Sheaves that the householder leaves behind, yet does not forget, with the result that they are exempt from the law of the forgotten sheaf (M. 6:5-7:2):

   1. Quantity:

       a. Number: more than two sheaves are exempt from the law:

           M. 6:5 Hillelites: Two bundles left together in a field are subject to the law of the forgotten sheaf; three such bundles are exempt, for they are deemed to be in temporary storage. Shammaites: Three bundles are subject to the law, four are exempt.

       b. Volume: more than two seahs are exempt from the law:

           M. 6:6a Sheaves that contain more than two seahs, but are left in a field apparently forgotten, are not subject to the law's restrictions.

           M. 6:6b Two sheaves that together contain two seahs. Gamaliel: exempt from the restrictions of the law. Sages: subject.

           M. 6:7 A standing crop that contains two seahs cannot fall subject to the restrictions regarding forgotten produce, even if apparently forgotten.

	M. 6:8	If a householder remembers that a standing crop remains in the field, we know he will return; hence nearby sheaves do not enter the status of forgotten sheaves; this applies even if the standing crop consists of only one stalk.
	M. 6:9	Two one-<u>seah</u> parcels of a single species of grain join together to form two <u>seahs</u> of produce not subject to the law of the forgotten sheaf. Two separate species do not join together. Yosé: separate lots of produce join together only if not physically separated by food that belongs to the poor.
2.	Types of produce intentionally left in the field:
	M. 6:10a	Produce set aside for use in the field as fodder or for binding other sheaves is not subject to the law, since the householder wishes to keep it in the field.
	M. 6:10b	Tubers left in a field: Judah: exempt from the law, because the farmer left them in storage. Sages: subject to the law, because they have been left behind, forgotten.
	M. 6:11a	One who harvests while blind or unable to see--the produce he binds is subject to the law of the forgotten sheaf, because his actions show that he accepts his handicap, and intends to gather all of the sheaves.
	M. 6:11b	One who intends to leave the small sheaves in the field--those sheaves that he leaves are exempt from the law, because he did not forget them.
	M. 6:11c	One who claims that he later will gather all of the sheaves that he now forgets--the produce is subject to the law, because his intention does not have the power to abrogate the law.
3.	Olive trees with distinctive features and the laws of forgotten produce:
	M. 7:1a	Produce on olive trees that have distinctive features, such as location, reputation, or production, is not subject to the law, because we may assume that the farmer will remember to return and harvest the tree.
	M. 7:1b	All other trees--two left unharvested are subject to the law, three left unharvested are exempt, because the amount of produce left behind is too great for the farmer to have forgotten.
	M. 7:2a	A tree distinguished by its location--exempt.
	M. 7:2b	A tree that contains more than two <u>seahs</u> of produce is exempt, because we may assume that the farmer remembers the large amount of produce.

The section begins by clarifying the conceptions of "forgotten" and "sheaf," thus delimiting the type of produce that falls into the category of forgotten sheaves. From this main definition, it turns to ambiguous cases (A3) concerning whether or not the law applies to a sheaf that the farmer leaves behind yet fully intends to gather at some later time. The opening unit is supplemented at B by a reference to the Scriptural basis for the law of the forgotten sheaf, Deut. 24:19.[14] Taken together, these first two units, A-B,

Introduction   27

comprise Mishnah's entire theory of forgotten sheaves. That is to say, by comparing sheaves accidentally left behind with those purposely left in the field, they make the single point that only what God set aside through random circumstance must be given to the poor. Given this theory, the two sections that follow in fact introduce nothing new. C merely works out in greater detail the ambiguous cases presented at A3. Similarly, D applies thoroughly familiar rules to the case of produce left unharvested on olive trees, as indicated by Deut. 24:20.

After the topic of reaping fields of grain or olive groves, the next step in reviewing the harvesting process is to consider poor-offerings set aside while reaping other sorts of crops, namely grape vineyards. In this regard, Scripture specifies two offerings that accident alone sets aside and that the householder must leave for the poor to gather: separated grapes and defective clusters.

IV. SEPARATED GRAPES AND DEFECTIVE CLUSTERS: Offerings set aside while the householder harvests his vineyard:

   A. Separated Grapes (M. 7:3):

      1. Definition:

         M. 7:3a   Single grapes that fall due to no identifiable cause during the harvest.

      2. Free access to the separated grapes:

         M. 7:3b   Workers who attempt to catch the separated grapes before they fall to the ground are deemed thieves.

   B. Defective Clusters (M. 7:4-8):

      1. Definition:

         M. 7:4a   Clusters without shoulders or pendants are deemed defective, and must be given to the poor.

      2. Ambiguous cases:

         M. 7:4b   Well-formed clusters that appear to be defective; if they are harvested along with the well-formed clusters, then they are deemed well formed. But if they are not harvested with the normal clusters, they are deemed defective, and must be left for the poor.

         M. 7:4c   Grapes that grow singly on the vine, without any cluster at all; Judah: In the status of well-formed clusters, for the produce's lack of a shoulder and pendant is not a defect. Sages: In the status of a defective cluster, for the grape lacks a shoulder and pendant.

      3. When does the law of the defective cluster begin to apply?

         M. 7:5   One who thins a vineyard; Judah: he may thin both the well-formed and the defective clusters, because the poor have no claim on the defective clusters until the entire vineyard is harvested. Meir: he may not thin the defective clusters, because these belong to the poor from the moment they appear on the vine.

4. Interruption: Defective clusters, separated grapes, and four-year-old vines.

> M. 7:6   Hillelites: produce of a four-year-old vine is entirely analogous to produce in the status of second tithe, and so is exempt from the laws of defective clusters and separated grapes. Shammaites: these types of produce are subject to opposite rules, with the result that the produce of a four-year-old vine is subject to the laws of defective clusters and separated grapes.

5. Ambiguous case regarding the definition of defective clusters:

> M. 7:7   A vineyard that contains only defective clusters; Eliezer: since this is the norm within the vineyard, the clusters are not deemed defective. Aqiba: since the clusters lack shoulders and pendants, they fall into the the category of the defective cluster.

6. Reprise: When does the law of the defective cluster begin to apply?

> M. 7:8   Before the defective clusters appear, one may dedicate his entire vineyard to the Temple. Once these clusters appear, however, they belong to the poor and the farmer cannot dedicate them. Yosé: if the farmer dedicates his vineyard after the defective clusters appear but before the harvest, he should give to the poor the defective clusters, and to the Temple the amount of produce that grew in the interim.

C. Transition: Poor-offerings in general: their status after the harvest has been completed, yet before the processing at the threshing floor (M. 8:1):

> M. 8:1   All people, rich and poor alike, may take gleanings separated grapes, defective clusters, and forgotten olives after the poor have had an adequate opportunity to gather the offerings.

In a single terse rule concerning the law of the separated grape, the framers provide a basic definition, A1, and discuss how the householder and his workers must take pains not to deprive the poor of God's gift.

The law of the defective cluster also commences with matters of definition, B1: any cluster that has neither a shoulder nor a pendant the framers classify as malformed. This definition is followed by cases of ambiguity in which bunches of grapes appear to be defective, even though in fact they are well formed. As usual, the framers supplement their definition by taking up a problem related to God's apportioning the produce to the poor. Here they dispute at what point in the growth of a year's crop the defective clusters become the property of the poor.

The orderliness of the treatment of the law of the defective cluster is interrrupted at M. 7:6. This tangentially related rule has been included here because it mentions defective clusters, but there is no apparent reason why it has been inserted in the midst of an on-going discussion.

In C, essentially separate from the foregoing, we move from poor-offerings set aside during reaping to those separated during processing at the threshing floor. This unit thus comprises a transition focusing on the span of time after the householder has finished his work in the field, but before he begins to thresh the grain. By concentrating on this

Introduction   29

intermediate period of time, the sages conclude one discussion and set the stage for the unit to come.

The following section carries forward the systematic review by taking up the next stage in the harvest, during processing, when food is set aside for the poor. While processing his crops at the threshing floor, the householder must designate all of the required tithes and priestly rations. In the third and sixth years of the sabbatical cycle, these tithes include poorman's tithe, the subject of the following discussion:

V. POORMAN'S TITHE: The offering separated at the threshing floor:

    A. Introduction: The poor's claims regarding poor-offerings and poorman's tithe (M. 8:2-4):

        1. Under what circumstances are poor people who wish to sell produce believed if they claim that the food derives from poor-offerings or poorman's tithe and so is exempt from further separation of tithes?

            M. 8:2   They are believed so long as it is the proper time of year for them to possess poor-offerings (i.e., around the harvest season).

            M. 8:3-4   If they claim that the food derives from poorman's tithe, they are believed with regard to the types of of food that householders usually give them--namely, uncooked, unprocessed food.

    B. Definition: The proper amount of food to give to each poor person as poorman's tithe (M. 8:5-6):

        1. Proper measures:

            M. 8:5   Various measures for wheat, barley, spelt, beans, figs, wine, and olive oil. Abba Saul: the poor should be given enough of each type of food for two meals.

        2. Equitable distribution of poorman's tithe:

            M. 8:6a   The measures of M. 8:5 apply when giving to all poor people, whether Israelites, Levites, or priests.

            M. 8:6b   If the householder has too little produce to give each poor person a proper measure, he allows them to divide the food, lest he favor one or another individual.

    C. Types of charity given throughout the year, from one harvest season to the next (M. 8:7):

        1. The transient poor:

            M. 8:7a   The amount of food given to the transient poor: a loaf of bread for a day trip; two meals if one stays overnight; three meals if one spends the Sabbath.

        2. The community institutions of charity:

            M. 8:7b   Who is eligible to gather food from these institutions? Soup kitchen: anyone in immediate need, without enough food for two meals. The community fund: anyone without enough food for the near future, i.e., with less than a week's food supply.

The framers introduce their treatment of poorman's tithe with a common redactional technique: they inquire first about poor-offerings in general and then about poorman's tithe in particular (A; cf. I.D and II.C). This shift in topic sets the stage for a discussion that follows that established pattern. We move from definitions specifying what quantity of food each poor person should receive as poorman's tithe to the problem of distribution, namely, how to ensure that all poor people have equal access to the produce.

Having completed their systematic review of the harvest process, the framers at C describe two institutions for giving charity throughout the year, the soup-kitchen and the community fund. This discussion clearly is unrelated to the harvesting process and so stands outside the framework that organizes the tractate as a whole. Still, it has been placed at the end of the essay so as not to detract from the main point: each time the householder reaps and claims some the Land's yield for himself, God takes a portion of the produce and sets it aside for the poor.

The tractate as a whole concludes by identifying who falls into the category of a poor person and so is eligible to collect the poor-offerings discussed above. Apparently, the sages have relegated discussion of this central matter to the end of their essay in order not to interrupt the systematic review of the farmer's agricultural activities.

VI. CONCLUDING DEFINITION: Who falls into the category of "Poor"? (M. 8:8-9):

    A. Definition (M. 8:8-9):

        M. 8:8   Anyone with less than two hundred zuz in liquid assets is deemed poor.

        M. 8:9a   Anyone with as little as fifty zuz utilized as captial is not deemed poor, and may not gather poor-offerings, because he can live off the income from his money.

        M. 8:9b   Those who pretend to be in need eventually will be forced to gather poor-offerings; those who refuse to collect poor-offerings, even though entitled, eventually will be able to support others from their own fortunes.

The simple definition is accompanied by a concluding homily that marks the end of the entire tractate by taking up exegesis of several verses of Scripture.

The foregoing outline as a whole shows the care with which the framers created their essay. The logical arrangement of each thematic unit points out the message Tractate Peah expresses when read as an essay: each time the farmer reaps or processes produce, he claims some of the Land's yield for himself. Then some of the food also must be set aside for the poor. This ensures that God's share of the Land's yield goes to its intended recipients, the poor.

III.   Mishnah in Its Larger Cultural Setting: The Context of Tractate Peah

We now shift our attention to the broader context in which Mishnah's system took shape and ask what Tractate Peah's framers inherited from the Israelite culture that preceded them and what they themselves contributed. In order to establish this diachronic context, we must turn to Mishnah's literary antecedent, Scripture. This is the logical starting point, because Mishnah's authors ignore all else. So far as Tractate Peah is concerned, the Hebrew Bible provides the sole framework upon which to build a system of poor-relief. Scripture's basic sense in this regard--that farmers must aid the needy by setting aside various offerings from their crops--provides the fundamental principles of Tractate Peah. It follows that by understanding the Biblical rules governing poor-support, we may better understand Mishnah's system. As we shall see, the framers of Mishnah follow with only minor variation the precedent set by the Hebrew Bible. They place Scripture's rules in a fresh order, and only briefly consider some issues outside the concerns of Scripture.

In order to clarify these generalizations, let me begin by explaining Scripture's rules on poor-relief. The Hebrew Bible contains two main treatments of poor-support, one in the Holiness Code (Lev. 19:9-10; 23:22), the other in the Deuteronomic Code (Deut. 24:19-22; 26:12). Since these rules derive from different writers and settings, I shall examine each system separately. The relevant passage from Leviticus is as follows:

> When you reap the harvest of your land, you shall not reap your field to its very border, neither shall you gather the gleanings after your harvest. And you shall not strip your vineyard bare [of defective clusters], neither shall you gather the fallen grapes of your vineyard. You shall leave them for the poor and for the sojourner: I am the Lord your God (Lev. 19:9-10).

The Holiness Code directs that a portion of the yield of grain fields and vineyards be rendered to the poor. Setting aside these offerings, according to the Priestly Writer, constitutes one element in Israel's life of holiness.[15] By supporting the poor, therefore, the farmer acts in a holy manner as he works God's holy Land.

The poor-offerings, Leviticus commands, must be given to "the poor and to the sojourners." Within the priestly conception of the world here envisaged, why should underprivileged people receive such special rights? The answer emerges when we consider that, according to the Priestly Writer, all of God's Holy people are entitled to receive a portion of the Land's yield, whether ordinary Israelites, priests, sojourners, or the poor (see Lev. 27:30; Num. 18:8-19, 21-23). The poor and sojourners, like the priests, possess no share of the Land of Israel (see Num 18:20,24).[16] Nonetheless, these groups have the right to be sustained by God with a portion of the Land's produce. That is to say, the Priestly Writer directs that they receive what they would be able to produce for themselves if they owned a piece of the Land.

The Holiness Code contains one further reference to poor-relief:

> And when you reap the harvest of your land, you shall not reap your field to its very border, nor shall you gather the gleanings after your harvest. You shall leave them for the poor and for the sojourner: I am the Lord your God (Lev. 23:22).

This verse, which repeats Lev. 19:9 nearly verbatim,[17] has been included here to complete the Priestly Writer's presentation of the agricultural calendar. These rules pertain to the reaping and processing of a householder's crops, so they are placed in the logical point in the calendar to correspond to the fall harvest season.

Scripture's second system of poor-support is contained in the Deuteronomic Code:

> When you reap your harvest in your field, and have forgotten a sheaf in the field, you shall not go back to get it. It shall be for the sojourner, the

fatherless, and the widow, that the Lord your God may bless you in all the work of your hands. When you beat your olive trees, you shall not go over the boughs again. It shall be for the sojourner, the fatherless, and the widow. When you gather the grapes of your vineyard, you shall not glean it afterward [of the defective clusters]. It shall be for the sojourner, the fatherless, and the widow. You shall remember that you were a slave in the land of Egypt, therefore I command you to do this (Deut. 24:19-22).

The main point is made explicitly in Deut. 24:22. According to the Deuteronomist, Israelites once were members of an unprotected class of slaves in Egypt and now must protect the rights of under-privileged classes within their midst. Israel's oppression in Egypt thus serves to justify the fact that farmers must give to sojourners, orphans, and widows a portion of the produce of grain fields, vineyards, and olive orchards.[18]

Deuteronomy knows one other offering given to the poor, poorman's tithe:

When you have finished paying all the tithe of your produce in the third year, which is the year of tithing, giving it to the Levite, the sojourner, the fatherless, and the widow, that they may eat within your towns and be filled, then you shall say before the Lord your God, "I have removed the sacred portion out of my house, and moreover I have given it to the Levite, the sojourner, the fatherless, and the widow, according to all your commandment which you have commanded me. I have not transgressed any of the commandments, neither have I forgotten them (Deut. 26:12-13).

This rule takes its place in the unfolding of Scripture's system of tithes (Deut. Ch. 26). The main point is to assure that underprivileged groups have enough food to support themselves, and so every third year farmers must set aside a portion of their tithes for Levites, sojourners, orphans, and widows.

Having reviewed these two Scriptural systems of poor-relief, let us now consider their relationship to Mishnah's system. With regard to details and theories, Mishnah merely repeats what Scripture has already told us. So, to begin with the obvious, Mishnah's framers treat Scripture as a homogeneous book, without parts or divisions. Each offering mentioned in either of Scripture's two codes thus receives the full attention of Mishnah's authors.[19] Furthermore, the overall conceptions that characterize Mishnah's system of poor-relief--that the poor, like the priests, deserve a portion of the produce of a Land they cannot own--are derived directly from the Priestly Writer.

Mishnah's distinctive contribution to the laws of poor-relief, however, emerges only when we consider its arrangement of the various offerings described in the Hebrew Bible. The two Biblical codes loosely organize their discussion by species, considering first fields of grain (Lev. 19:9; Deut. 24:19-20), then vineyards (Lev. 19:10; Deut. 24:21), and olive groves (Deut. 24:20). Mishnah's authors, as we saw in the outline presented above, took a different tack. They placed in chronological order of the harvesting process all of the offerings due from each farmer. The following chart shows clearly how the framers improve upon Scripture's arrangement of the poor-offerings:[20]

Introduction

The Relationship Between Mishnah and Scripture

Mishnah		Issue	Scripture
1:1-4:9	I.	Peah: given at the beginning of the harvest.	Lev. 19:9a
4:10-5:6	II.	Gleanings: given as each stalk is reaped.	Lev. 19:9b
5:7-7:2	III.	Forgotten Produce: set aside while binding grain.	Deut. 24:19-20
7:3	IV.A.	Separated Grapes: given while harvesting a vineyard.	Lev. 19:10b
7:4-8:1	IV.B.	Defective Clusters: given after harvesting a vineyard.	Lev. 19:10a; Deut. 24:21
8:2-6	V.A-B.	Poorman's Tithe: given at the threshing floor.	Deut. 26:12-13
8:7	V.C.	Community Charity: given throughout the year.	--
8:8-9	VI.	Who Is Poor?	Lev. 19:10c; Deut. 24:19,21

The framers' contribution, as the chart indicates, is to present a systematic review of the harvesting process from the point when the householder reaps the first stalk (I) to the point when he processes the produce (V.A-B), and then beyond into the year (V.C). At each point, they fit into this scheme the relevant information from Scripture's two codes. Only at the end, in a brief unit (VI) do they pause to take up an issue not directly related to Scripture or the harvesting process.

But to say that Tractate Peah merely repeats, in its own words and order, the facts presented by Scripture does not constitute an adequate evaluation of the text. This very repetition constituted an enormous choice. In order to understand the possibilities before Mishnah's sages and the importance of the choice they made, we must now briefly consider the far different options taken by other Israelite groups in treating the topic of poor-support. We shall review three literary sources, The Wisdom of Ben Sira, The Dead Sea Scrolls, and the writings of earliest Christianity, because these are the only other Israelite groups that take an active interest in the subject.[21] As we shall see, the discussion of poor-support contained in each reflects the larger system of thought of that particular document as a whole.

The Wisdom of Ben Sira, written ca. B.C. 175, emerges out of the Israelite wisdom tradition, a fact indicated by the book's opening and concluding poems about Wisdom (Chs. 1-2; 51:13-22).[22] The wisdom genre of the book as a whole shapes the entire treatment of poor-relief. Aid for the poor is the subject of quite general aphorisms, such as, "Do not withhold a gift from the miserable, nor ignore the pleas of the downtrodden" (Ben Sira 4:4). Furthermore, advice about the proper dispensation of one's possessions (see Ben Sira 11:10-14:19) merely allows the author to make his main point: by supporting the needy, one indicates that he has attained true wisdom. Since the author of Ben Sira never concretely discusses the offerings of Leviticus and Deuteronomy, we may conclude that his interest in the topic of poor-support scarcely intersects with program of Mishnah's authors.

The Dead Sea Scrolls, generally thought to have been produced by Essenes living at Qumran (ca. 150 B.C. to 70 A.D.),[23] are concerned primarily with maintaining the holiness and purity of a monastic community.[24] The Scrolls' discussions of topics related to poor-relief reflect this emphasis on community holiness. For example, the Covenanters of the Damascus Rule were required to give to the guardians and judges two days' earnings in each month from which to support widows, orphans, the sick, and the aged.[25] By maintaining the community's less fortunate member, the Covenanters believed that the community as a whole would purify itself for the eschaton.

The Community Rule presents a different view. The authors of this scroll claimed that one who renounced all possessions and voluntarily submitted to poverty would lead a life of personal holiness.[26] According to this view, all personal property would have been turned over to a bursar who would administer it for the community's benefit.[27] The community members thus would hold all possessions in common. No individual needed to give poor-relief because all shared equally in the communal property.

From either point of view, the contrast to Mishnah should be clear. Mishnah's framers clearly assume a world in which individuals possess personal property. The responsibility of one Israelite for another almost never is surrendered to the community at large.[28] The sages further assert that proper support of the poor constitutes part of the expression of God's ownership of the Land of Israel and acknowledges his right to determine how its yield is distributed. The householder thus must abandon his claim upon some of his produce, namely, that which God sets aside for the poor. In short, Mishnah's authors simply do not focus upon the eschaton, and, in their view, neither poor-relief nor communality of property comprise a proper mode of attaining personal holiness.

Finally, we turn to views of poor-support held by the earliest Christians, as represented in Jesus' sayings in the Gospels and in Paul's letters. Here again, each system as a whole dictates what the authors say regarding poor-relief. Jesus' sayings in general speak of the drawing near of the Kingdom of God. His view of poor-support likewise looks ahead directly to the eschaton. Jesus urged all the wealthy to sell their possessions and give the receipts as alms[29] because, in the eschatological order he imagined, the poor would have precedence over the rich (see, for example, Luke 16:19-31).[30] Similarly, Jesus claimed "It is easier for a camel to go through the eye of a needle than for a rich man to enter the Kingdom of God" (Mark 10:25). The new economic order proclaimed by Jesus, as I said, reflects the apocalyptic emphasis of his sayings in general.[31]

Paul's description of poor-relief also takes its place in his overall scheme of reconciling Jewish and gentile Christians for the coming kingdom.[32] Thus in his letters to the churches in Corinth and Galatia, Paul urged that the Christian brethren "remember the poor" (Gal. 2:10) by collecting money for those in Jerusalem. By gathering money for the predominantly Jewish Jerusalem church, Paul hoped to improve relations between the Jewish and gentile Christian communities.[33] So the writers of the Gospels and Paul treat the topic of poor-relief quite differently from Mishnah's framers. Mishnah, as we recall, developed its points about poor-support in detailed laws that carry forward the authoritative codes of Leviticus and Deuteronomy. Now in the early Christian sources, discussion of aid for the poor does in fact take place in the context of homilies focused upon Lev. 19:11-18. Yet poor-relief here serves primarily to emphasize points about the drawing near of the eschaton. Mishnah, by contrast, focuses not upon the end of time, but upon the present moment. For the sages, the Land of Israel is God's possession, deemed holy here and now. Their treatment of poor-offerings therefore arises out of the holiness inherent in God's Land, its produce and inhabitants. So Mishnah and the early Christian sources represent far different choices, which primarily reflect the points of insistence of the two systems viewed whole.

This discussion of the variety of ways in which earlier and contemporary Israelite groups had treated the topic of poor-support shows us that the sages could have done many things with the issue, but chose only to parrot Scripture.[34] If we view Mishnah's system as a whole, we can understand why the framers find Scripture's rules on poor-relief compelling.

Within Mishnah as a whole, the Israelite householder, through his actions and intentions, is deemed the center of the world. What he thinks and does determines in many cases how the law applies. Tractate Peah, like the rest of the Division of Agriculture, adheres closely to this principle. The framers therefore arrange their discussion of the various offerings around the householder's acts in reaping the Land. At each point when the farmer takes some of the Land's yield for himself, God demands a portion of the crop. As landlord and owner of the Land of Israel, God determines what shall be done with the Land's yield and that the poor and priests should be supported.

It remains only to ask why these points, taken directly out of the Mosaic Codes, should have proven so important to Mishnah's framers. The answer emerges only when we consider Mishnah's context in the first two centuries in Palestine. We recall that the framers brought Mishnah to closure around A.D. 200, at the end of two centuries that had been disastrous for the Israelites. One hundred years after instituting provincial rule over the Land of Israel in 64 B.C., Roman soldiers had destroyed the Israelites' Temple (A.D. 70), crushed their messianic revolt (A.D. 132-135), and forbade them to occupy Jerusalem (from A.D. 135 onward). The deep impact of these events on the material life of the Israelite population is concisely summarized by Mary Smallwood:

> Inevitably Palestine was in low economic water after Bar Cochba's revolt. The cessation or curtailment of the agricultural operations on which the national economy was based and the devastation of the country, especially in Judea during the later stages of the war, the breakdown of normal trade and industry, the confiscation of much Jewish Land by Rome, and the serious reduction in Jewish numbers resulted in widespread hardship and poverty for some time... (Smallwood, p. 426).

After A.D. 135, Israel was a defeated people, both politically and economically. In the face of this defeat, the framers turned to Scripture because it provided a convincing solution to the problem posed by the Roman conquest of Palestine. The message of Scripture, now reaffirmed in Tractate Peah and in the entire Division of Agriculture, is that God, not Rome, rules sovereign over the Land of Israel. God alone tells the farmer how to dispense his crops. God has a special concern for poor and indigent Israelites who suffer because of recent events. These people must be supported by the remainder of the

Israelite community because this is God's will. Given what must have seemed an insurmountable defeat, Mishnah's repetition of Scripture transmits a powerful message: The welfare of each Israelite is important to God, who remains the sole ruler of the Land of Israel.

IV. Original Meaning: The Goal of Analyzing Tractate Peah

The foregoing conclusions about the meaning and structure of Mishnah's system of poor-relief stem from my analysis of Tractate Peah. My goal in this study is to discover the meaning of Mishnah Peah for those who redacted the tractate in the second century A.D. What message did the authors wish to convey by creating this particular tractate? By asking what the framers themselves intended,[35] we can distinguish between what I call the original meaning of the law and various other interpretations that Mishnah's rules might support. By original meaning, I refer to the message the authors wished to communicate, so far as we are able to reconstruct their intention. This original meaning of the law enables us to make judgments about the authors' own world view, and so allows us to see the shape and texture of the Judaism represented by Tractate Peah in particular and Mishnah in general.

I delineate the framers' original meaning by paying careful attention to the way these authors use Mishnaic Hebrew. The framers' logic, and so the intended meaning of the Mishnaic law, emerges through syntactic analysis of the authors' sentences and through literary study of their essay as a whole.[36] How does knowledge of the language itself make the original meaning accessible to us? The framers cast virtually all of their rules within a small repertoire of syntactic forms. These range from simple declarative sentences--"One who does X, lo, he is exempt"--to complex structures called "apocopation"--"One who does X to object Y--lo, the object is clean."[37] These syntactic forms provide us with the first clue toward determining how the framers think, because they mark the beginning and end of each complete thought in Mishnaic discourse. Moreover, within their discussion of a given topic, Mishnah's authors typically utilize a single form over and over again, organizing their thematic units into a limited number of larger patterns: for example, "A householder who does X, lo, he is exempt; but one who does Y, lo, he is liable."[38] Again, these formulary patterns point toward the relationship of one rule to another, and so help to indicate the meaning of each thematic unit.

We now turn to four specific syntactic constructions and patterns that characterize Tractate Peah. In each case, I shall explain how formal analysis enables us to reconstruct the original meaning of the law.

The most distinctive literary form in this tractate is the list.[39] This form consists of a superscription followed by a number of items that fall under its general rubric, for example:

M. 2:1

A. These landmarks establish the boundaries of a field for purposes of designating peah:

B. (1) a river, (2) pond, (3) private road, (4) public road, (5) public path, (6) private path that is in regular use both in the dry and in the rainy season, (7) uncultivated land, (8) newly-broken land, and (9) an area sown with a different type of seed.

The superscription at A indicates that, for the framers, a single principle unites all of the items in the list. Accordingly, the exegete must find the common thread among the various entries and show how all items relate to the superscription. That is to say, we can understand why the authors put this information together in just this manner only by paying attention to the relationships among the members of the list and between these members and their superscription. The form used by Mishnah's framers thus is the key to our understanding the original meaning of a list.

A second common literary form utilized in Tractate Peah is the dispute.[40] This form begins with a superscription followed by at least two contrasting ruling, for example:

M. 3:1

A. As regards rectangular plots of grain sown among olive trees--

B. the House of Shammai say, "Peah is designated separately from each and every one of the plots."

C. The House of Hillel say, "Peah is designated from one plot on behalf of all the plots together".

The legal point at issue is indicated by the superscription, A, and the alternative rulings, B and C, show the range of solutions possible. As before, however, the formal aspects of the dispute shape the intended meaning of the rule at hand. By framing matters in just this way, Mishnah's editors tell us that the main point is found not in one or the other response to the superscription; rather, the meaning of such a dispute emerges when we understand how each disputing position constitutes a fitting answer to the dilemma posed by the superscription. The dispute form not only carries two possible solutions to an issue, but also manifests the larger principle that represents the point of the construction as a whole.

We now turn to a third case, in which the law's meaning emerges out of the repetition of a single form such as the simple declarative sentence.[41] For example, we might find several such rulings, all sharing a common apodosis:

M. 1:6

A. One may do X, until the grain-pile has been smoothed over.
B. One may do Y, until the grain-pile has been smoothed over.
C. One may do Z, until the grain-pile has been smoothed over.

The parallel structure of these rules indicates that the framers have constructed them to convey a single principle. The exegete's task is to identify that principle by understanding why the single apodosis governs the various cases brought together in this repetition. The reader must pay attention to the formal similarities of these rules in order to grasp the point of the entire construction.

Finally, let us consider a special type of repetition very common in Tractate Peah, the triplet. In this pattern, the framers typically begin with two straightforward and unambiguous rules. The point of the whole, however, emerges only when we take account of the climactic third case:[42]

M. 2:5

I. A. One who plants a field with wheat must designate a single portion of produce as peah, even if he reaps the grain in two separate stages and processes it at two separate threshing floors.

II. B. One who plants a field with wheat and barley, two entirely different species of grain, must designate a separate portion of produce as peah from each of the two fields that the different species delimit.

III. C. But if he sowed a field with two distinct types of wheat--

D. if he reaps and processes the grain in a single lot, he designates a single portion of produce as peah on behalf of the entire field.

E. But if he reaps and processes the grain in two separate lots, he must designate two separate portions of produce as peah, one from each type of wheat.

The triplet in fact makes a single point. We discern the message of the whole by noting that the first two cases, A and B, limn the area of unambiguous law. This sets the stage for the third case which addresses an ambiguity inherent in the law and resolves it. The point of the entire construction does not lie in the details of the three cases read in isolation. Only by paying attention to the larger pattern can we discover the main point of ambiguity and the solution presented by the final case.

V. Translation and Commentary: The Exegesis of Tractate Peah

Let me now explain in detail the chapter by chapter literary analysis found below. I begin my comments upon each chapter of Mishnah by presenting a brief introduction.[43] These overviews alert the reader to important formal patterns in the chapter as a whole, and to underlying principles that unite the diverse rules. By presenting a context of legal issues for each chapter, I provide the reader with a framework within which to understand the tractate's laws.

As I turn to individual rules, I begin with a fresh translation of each pericope. Here I strive to reveal the underlying structure of Mishnah's language by imitating, as far as English permits, the word order of Mishnaic Hebrew.[44] I identify each component of the framers' thought with a letter of the English alphabet. When Tractate Peah's authors arrange formally parallel rules to form an ongoing discussion of a particular topic, I indicate the constituents of their construction with Roman numerals. In all, the translation is designed to allow the reader to recognize a given pericope's literary forms and patterns. This information, as I stated above, guides my attempt to reconstruct the framers' original meaning.[45]

Several aspects of the textual apparatus used in the translations now need to be explained. First, I expand the translations by adding in square brackets [ ] the legal principles that underlie Mishnah's rules. This first step in interpreting the law allows the reader to make sense of Mishnah's own terse phrasing. Second, I indicate, also in brackets, words implied by the Hebrew but not present in the text (e.g., [olive]-oil). Third, parentheses ( ) are used to indicate transliterations of idiomatic Hebrew phrases, which I translate, whenever possible, into equally idiomatic English. By supplying transliterations, I allow the reader access to the original text of terms and phrases that elude precise translation. Finally, I have dealt, primarily in footnotes, with textual variants, as listed in the critical edition of Sacks-Hutner.[46] This allows the reader to read a translation relatively unencumbered by critical apparatus, yet provides access to important textual traditions behind Tractate Peah. In preparing the translation, I followed the text provided by Albeck, and made reference to earlier translations of Danby, Blackman, and Bauer. I also have reproduced following each pericope the list of parallel passages found in the apparatus of Sacks-Hutner.

My commentary on each unit of law is found after the translation. In each case, my remarks follow a set pattern. I first state the main point of the pericope--that is, the original meaning for the framers--as well as the overall world view, if any, implied by this message. Then I show how I derive these conclusions by pointing out the literary forms and patterns present in the rule and by explaining how these determine my interpretation. Next, when necessary I explain principles or rules, usually stated only in other Mishnaic contexts, that form the legal matrix into which the pericope falls. These unstated assumptions on the part of Mishnah's framers often are central to discovery of Tractate Peah's meaning. Finally, should there exist several equally likely interpretations of a rule, I argue for my explanation by outlining the exegetical possibilities and stating why I think one alternative is preferable.

In addition to analysis of Mishnah Peah, I present in its entirety Tractate Peah in Tosefta, Mishnah's companion document, redacted around A.D. 350 in the Land of Israel. Because of its temporal and conceptual closeness to Mishnah,[47] Tosefta provides important data for our reconstruction of the meaning of the Mishnah's rules. Accordingly, I present each unit of Tosefta after the pericope of Mishnah it serves. This mode of presentation best displays Tosefta as a commentary to Mishnah, even if at times it disrupts the redacted order of Tosefta. The translation here utilizes the same strategy as my translations of Mishnah, except that Mishnah-passages are underscored to show when Tosefta cites Tractate Peah's rules. My remarks focus exclusively on how each Toseftan passage relates to the corresponding pericope of Mishnah.[48] At the end of the study, in an appendix, I provide the relevant materials from Sifra and Sifre, two works of Scriptural exegesis from the fourth century A.D.[49] These documents carry on an extended polemic, arguing that Mishnah has no standing as independent law, but that its principles can and must be derived solely from proper exegesis of the Mosaic Codes. Sifra and Sifre show an alternative way of dealing with Scripture's topic of poor-support, and so emphasize the choices made by Mishnah's framers in formulating their rules. The translations here follow the aims and format of those provided for Tosefta.

The centuries of traditional rabbinic commentaries have added greatly to my analysis of the tractate. Their comments often supply the legal matrix critical to any understanding of the laws before us. Similarly, they often lay out the full range of possible interpretations of words, phrases, and pericopae. Their work provides the interpretive tradition that enables me to take up the task of determining Mishnah Tractate Peah's original meaning. But my study also represents a break with the interpretive tradition of rabbinic commentators. The traditional commentators' goal was not the delineation of the original meaning of Mishnah's rules, as I have explained that concept, but rather, to explain Mishnah as part of an ongoing system of law, the halakhah. For their purposes, the meaning imputed to a Mishnaic rule by the Talmuds or by a medieval law code is authoritative. This is the case even if such interpetations do not seem to reflect the rhetoric or concerns of Mishnah's own rules. In other words, these commentaries are concerned with determining the proper legal stand on various issues as matters stood at the time they were written. With notable exceptions (Maimonides, MR), most of these exegetes are unconcerned with the meaning of Mishnah's rules in their own right, apart from the interests and concerns of the later, developed Rabbinic law--concerns often unknown within Mishnah itself. The result is that the structure of the tractate is overlooked, as is the point of the essay as a whole.[50]

It remains now to place this work in the context of modern scholarship on Tractate Peah and Mishnah. The overall approach, with its careful attention to the interplay of form and meaning in Mishnah, carries forward the pioneering work of Jacob Neusner in A History of the Mishnaic Law of Purities (22 Vols., Leiden: E.J. Brill, 1974-1977). My claim that the formal characteristics of Tractate Peah indicate the original meaning of its rules rests directly upon Neusner's work. He has shown that the present formulation of Mishnah's rules is the product of those who redacted the document around 200 A.D. Within the bounds of this assumption, we may claim that these syntactic and literary patterns attest to the framers' choices for Tractate Peah, and not to those of earlier generations who might have contributed particular rules or later authorities who interpreted the tractate. Neusner's case for our access to the meaning intended by the framers themselves is so strong that I can move beyond much of current scholarship. Modern work on Tractate Peah has focused, first, on providing the English reader with new translations and, second, on presenting new Hebrew editions. Each of these improved upon the last, contributing philological insights and creating English technical terms to match the Hebrew. Of particular importance are the works of Danby, Blackman, Albeck, and Sacks. The only extended treatment of Tractate Peah is Bauer's German translation and commentary. He provides philological comments as well as brief explanations of the law. His focus, however, rests upon each rule read individually, not upon the tractate as the framers' essay. The methods employed here are important because they reveal Tractate Peah as a source that allows us to understand the religious imagination and world view of those who framed the document in the late second century A.D.

CHAPTER ONE
PEAH CHAPTER ONE

The tractate begins by addressing three fundamental issues regarding the law of peah. First, we wish to know how much produce must be designated as peah (M. 1:2, 1:3C-E). A second unit (M. 1:3A-B) asks which produce within each field, whether that in the front, middle, or rear, validly may be designated. Finally, Mishnah delimits the types of edibles that are subject to the law (M. 1:4-5+6). These three issues are introduced by a homiletical statement regarding Torah-piety (M. 1:1) that serves the entire Division of Agriculture. By defining these basic notions, Chapter One clarifies the complex issues to be addressed in the remainder of the tractate. With this overview of the chapter in hand, let us now turn to the specifics of the rules before us.

Peah is presented as a progressive tax (M. 1:2). Each householder must designate an amount of food proportionate to his own wealth. But the farmer's responsiblity is further determined by the needs of the poor, who have the right to be adequately supported by those who are more prosperous. The effect of this tax, then, is to narrow the gap between the richest and the poorest Israelites. Householders must give up some of what they own, while the poor are entitled to receive what they need.

Tractate Peah next turns to an issue of definition (M. 1:3). Does the word "peah" mean the "rear corner of the field" or does it merely refer to a "portion" of the crop, that is, any bit of food that the householder designates? The latter position, that peah may be designated from any portion of a crop, would mean that all of a field's produce in essence is the same. Grain growing in any part of the field could validly be designated as peah. The contrary view, expressed in Simeon's gloss (M. 1:3B), claims that peah is specific to the rear corner of the field. By definition, only grain growing in that part of the field may qualify as peah.[1]

Finally, Mishnah describes the types of produce that are subject to designation as peah (M. 1:4-5). The law governs only those plants that a householder cultivates for himself on God's Land. That is to say, only produce upon which both God and Israelite have a claim is subject to designation. The underlying theory seems to be that the Israelite is a tenant farmer who must render a portion of all that he grows to his landlord, God. An important secondary issue is addressed at M. 1:6. The poor need not separate tithes from the peah they receive, for God has given them this produce as tax-exempt charity. The remaining produce kept by the Israelite farmer, however, is subject to further taxation in the form of tithes.

1:1

A. These are things that are not [subject to a specific] measure:

B. (1) [the quantity of produce designated as] peah,[2]

(2) [the quantity of produce designated as] first fruits, [and brought to the Temple on Pentecost] (see Deut. 26:1-11),

(3) [the value of] the appearance-offering, [brought to Jerusalem on each of the three pilgrimage festivals] (see Deut. 16:16-17),[3]

(4) [the quantity of] righteous deeds [performed],[4]

(5) and [time spent in] study of Torah.

C. These are things the benefit of which (prwtyhn) a person enjoys in this world, while the principal (hqrn)[5] remains for him in the world-to-come:

D. (1) [deeds done in] honor of father and mother,

(2) [performance of] righteous deeds,

(3) and [acts that] bring peace between one person and another (byn 'dm lḥbrw).

(4) But the study of Torah is equivalent to all of them [together].

M. 1:1 (M. Bik. 2:4; T. Qid. 5:16; B. Shab. 127a; B. Ḥag. 6b; B. Yeb. 109a; B. Ned. 6b; B. Qid 39b-40a, 82a; ARN 40; B. Men. 77b; B. Ḥul. 137b; Tanḥ. Yitro 14; Sifra Ṣav 7:2 [Weiss, p. 35a]; Sifre Deut. #336 [Finkelstein-Horowitz, p. 386])

The pericope as a whole asserts that study of Torah is the most meritorious of all actions (D4). The two lists that comprise the unit, however, clearly are separate from each other, for their elements repeat (B4 and D2) and contradict (B5 and D4) one another. Let us therefore turn separately to the details of each section.

The first list (A+B1-5) is relevant to Tractate Peah only at B1, which accounts for the pericope's inclusion here. In order to understand this list's point, we must examine its core, the three offerings at B1-3.[6] Each of these offerings is presented in thanks to God for bounty and prosperity (see Deut. 26:19; 26:1-11; 16:16-17), and so is subject to no specific limits. Although any act of thanks to God, however small, is deemed sufficient, no gift possibly could be large enough. The last two of the list's elements (B4-5) are not offerings, and so seem entirely separate from the foregoing.[7] Nonetheless, they do fall under the rubric of A, for any number of these acts is deemed valuable.[8]

Turning now to the second list (C+D1-4), we again find a core of three rules (D1-3), each dealing with the proper treatment of others. Those who follow these rules earn rewards of two kinds. They benefit in this world, for others treat them properly in return, and they are rewarded in the world to come, for God repays those who perform his commandments (Maimonides, Commentary). The point of this list, and of the entire pericope as well, becomes clear at D4. Although treating others properly earns double rewards, study of Torah, the source of all proper actions, is deemed even more praiseworthy.

T. 1:2-4

A. For these things they punish a person in this world, while the principal [i.e., eternal punishment] remains for the world-to-come:

B. (1) for [acts of] idolatrous worship,
(2) for incest,
(3) for murder,
(4) and for gossip, [which is] worse than all of them together.

C. Doing good (zkwt) creates a principal [for the world-to-come] and bears interest (pyrwt) [in this world].[9]

D. As it is stated [in Scripture], "Tell the righteous that it shall be well with them, for they shall enjoy the benefits (pry) [of their deeds"] (Is. 3:10).

T. 1:2

E. A transgression creates a principal [i.e., eternal punishment, in the world-to-come] but bears no interest (pyrwt) [in this world].

F. As it is stated [in Scripture], "Woe to the wicked! It shall be ill with him, [for what his hands have done shall be done to him]" (Is. 3:11). [Note that the term pyrwt, this worldly interest, does not occur in the verse.]

G. If so, how shall I interpret [the following verse]: "[Because they hated knowledge and did not choose the way of the Lord, would have none of my counsel and despised all my reproof], therefore they shall suffer the consequences (pry) of their way" (Prov. 1:29-31)?

H. [The verse should be interpreted to mean:] A transgression that bears fruit (pyrwt) [i.e., causes other transgressions] brings a penalty (pyrwt) [in this world].

I. [But] one that does not bear fruit (pyrwt) [i.e., does not cause other transgressions] brings no penalty (pyrwt) [in this world].

T. 1:3

J. [As regards] a good intention--the Omnipresent, blessed be He, refines[10] [it, so that it produces] a corresponding deed.[11]

K. [As for] an evil intention--the Omnipresent does not refine [it, so that it does not produce] a corresponding deed.[12]

L. As it is stated [in Scripture], "If I had cherished iniquity in my heart, the Lord would not have listened" (Ps. 66:18).

M. But how shall I interpret [the following verse]: "Hear O earth! Behold I am bringing evil upon this people, the fruit (pry) of their intentions" (Jer. 6:19)?

N. [The verse should be interpreted to mean: As regards] an evil intention that bears fruit (pyrwt) [i.e., causes other transgressions]--the Omnipresent refines [it, so that it produces] a corresponding deed, [for the performance of which the person will be punished].[13]

O. [But as for] an intention that bears no fruit (pyrwt) [i.e, does not cause other transgressions]--the Omnipresent does not refine [it into] a corresponding deed, [and so one is not punished for his evil intention].

T. 1:4

Two units (A-B, C-O) take up issues completely outside the concerns of Tractate Peah, yet they respond to the form of Mishnah. The list of transgressions at A-B mirrors the list of M. 1:1D-F. Mishnah's list deals with those actions that bear rewards, while Tosefta's treats those that bring punishment. The two lists have similar superscriptions, the same number of elements, and identical formal endings (M. 1:1D4; T. 1:2B4).

The second unit, C-O, takes up the this-worldly consequences of: (1) M. 1:1D-E's list of good actions, C-D; (2) A-B's list of transgressions, E-I; (3) good intentions, J; and (4) evil intentions, K-O. The analysis shows that good deeds earn rewards both in this world and in the world-to-come, while punishment for transgressions is limited to the world-to-come. This entire section is tied together by a continued focus on the word pyrwt, lit. fruit, which is taken to mean the this-wordly consequences of one's actions and intentions.

1:2

A. They may designate as peah no less than one-sixtieth [of a field's produce].
B. And even though they said, "Peah has no [specified] measure" (see M. 1:1B),[14]
C. [the quantity designated] should always accord with:
  (1) the size of the field,
  (2) the number of poor people [in the vicinity],
  (3) and the extent of the yield (^{c}nwh).[15]

M. 1:2 (Y. Peah 3:1 [15a]; Y. Bik. 3:5 [65c]; B. Ḥul. 137b)

At issue is the proper amount of produce to be designated as peah. The first rule, A, openly contradicts M. 1:1B1, and fixes an absolute minimum amount of food.[16] This has the effect of assuring some degree of support for the poor. I cannot, however, account for the specific measure, one-sixtieth of a field's yield.[17]

The quite separate material that follows,[18] B+C1-3, explicitly clarifies M. 1:1B1's claim that no specific measure governs the designation of peah. The amount of food designated must accord with two criteria: the wealth of the householders who give, and the needs of the poor people who receive (Maimonides, Commentary, and Sens).[19] Householders who own large fields (C1) or abundant crops (C3) thus have a responsibility to leave additional produce unharvested for the poor. This will not place an undue burden upon the householders and will greatly benefit the poor. Similarly, if there are many poor people in the locale, farmers must designate an amount of food large enough to sustain all of them (C2).

T. 1:1

A. [These are] things that have no [specified] measure:
   (1) [the quantity of produce designated as] peah,
   (2) [the quantity of produce designated as] first fruits,
   (3) [the value of] the appearance-offering,
   (4) [the quantity of] righteous deeds [performed],
   (5) and [time spent in] study of Torah (M. 1:1A-B).
B. Peah has a minimum measure [specified], but it has no maximum measure [specified].
C. [As regards] one who declares all of [the produce in] his field to be peah--
D. [the produce he has designated] is not [deemed] peah.

Tosefta harmonizes the contradiction between M. 1:1's statement that peah has no specified measure and M. 1:2's claim that peah must constitute at least one-sixtieth of the field's produce. B claims that both rules are correct, for peah has a minimum measure but no maximum. M. 1:1 thus refers to the maximum measure for peah (there is none), while M. 1:2 refers to the minimum measure (one-sixtieth of a field's yield).

Next C-D take up a problem left open by the foregoing discussion. If peah has no upper limit, a farmer might wish to designate his entire field's produce for the poor (see M. 1:3C-D). Such an offering, however, would not be differentiated from the remainder of the field's produce. Since this differentiation is a necessary feature of all agricultural offerings, the crop designated does not qualify as peah.

While the pericope is applicable to M. 1:2, Tosefta's redactor has chosen it to begin Tosefta Tractate Peah. The material that corresponds to M. 1:1, it seems, has been subordinated because it does not deal with the central issues of the tractate. Tosefta thus begins with the first sustantive concern of the tractate, How much produce must be designated as peah? Only then does it go on to take up the unrelated topic of rewards and punishments for one's actions (cf. T. 1:2-4).

1:3

A. They may designate [produce as] peah [while harvesting] the front of the field and [while harvesting] the middle [of the field].[20]
B. R. Simeon says, "[This is true] providing that [the farmer] designates [as peah] the [required] measure [of produce while harvesting] the rear [of the field]."[21]
C. R. Judah says, "If [the farmer] retained (šyyr)[22] one stalk [of grain for himself, he may declare the] adjoining [field] (swmk lw) as peah [for the poor].
D. "But if [he did] not [retain at least one stalk for his own use, but rather designated the entire field's produce as peah], he has not [actually] designated [the produce in the field as peah].
E. "Rather, [he has designated it] as ownerless property."

M. 1:3 (B. Shab. 23a; Sifra Qid. 1:9 [Weiss, pp. 87a-b])

Two separate rules (A-B, C-D+E)[23] have been drawn together because both address a single topic, the meaning of the word "peah" in Lev. 19:9, "You shall not harvest the corner (peah) of your field." At issue is whether the farmer must designate produce from the rear corner of his field, in accord with the word's literal meaning. The alternative is that any portion of the yield may qualify as peah, so that the householder may designate produce from all parts of his field. Let us unpack this subtle issue by turning to the cases before us.

A-B dispute this very issue, whether or not peah is specific to the rear corner of the field. One theory, expressed at A, is that all of a field's produce essentially is the same. Any of the grain in any part of the field can become peah upon the householder's designation. "Peah" thus refers to any "portion" of the crop. Simeon (B) interprets "peah" more literally. The farmer must designate the proper amount of grain while harvesting the rear corner of his field, even if he already has designated produce at the front or middle. In Simeon's view, "peah" refers first and foremost to the produce in the rear corner of the field.

Judah's lemma, C-E, is totally separate from the foregoing. He loosely interprets "peah" as any "portion" of the yield. It follows, he claims, that the farmer cannot designate his entire crop, but must retain at least a minuscule amount for his own use (C). This ensures that that householder's produce is differentiated from that which he gives to the poor, as required for all agricultural offerings.[24] If the farmer does not retain some grain for himself, however, by definition he cannot designate a portion as peah. Since he forgoes this right, the produce immediately is deemed ownerless and available for all to take, rich and poor alike (E).

T. 1:5a

A. A farmer may designate [produce as] peah [while harvesting] the front, the middle, or the rear [of his field] (cf. M. 1:3A).

B. And if he has designated [this produce as peah], whether [while harvesting] the front, the middle, or the rear [of his field], he has fulfilled [his obligation regarding peah].

C. R. Simeon says, "If he has designated [produce as peah], whether [while harvesting] the front, the middle, or the rear [of his field]--lo, [that which he has designated] is deemed peah.

D. "But he must designate [as peah] the [required] measure [of produce while harvesting] the rear [of the field]" (M. 1:3B).

E. R. Judah says, "If [the farmer] retained one stalk of grain [for himself, he may declare the] adjoining [field] as peah [for the poor]. But if [he did] not [retain at least one stalk for his own use, but rather designated the entire field's produce as peah], he has not [actually] designated [the produce in the field as peah]. Rather, [he has designated it] as ownerless property" (M. 1:3C-E).

F. Said R. Judah, "Under what circumstances does this [namely, A-D] apply?

G. "[It applies] when [the farmer] has designated [the required amount of produce in the rear corner of his field], and wishes to add [to it]."

Tosefta sharpens the dispute between M. 1:3A and Simeon, M. 1:3B, by clearly stating at A-D the contrary opinions of the two authorities. The material that follows, E+F-G, appears to cite and explain M. 1:3C-D. The setting provided by E, however, is inappropriate to Judah's explanation, F-G. Instead, it seems that Judah harmonizes A-B and C-D (Lieberman, TZ, p. 42). He claims that A-B apply only after the farmer has given the required amount of produce in the rear corner of his field. This being the case, A-B and C-D make precisely the same point: peah may validly be designated in any part of the field, so long as the proper amount of produce is designated while harvesting the rear corner of the field. It therefore appears that E was added after the pericope was redacted, probably due to the mention of Judah at F.

T. 1:6

A. R. Simeon said, "For [the following] four reasons, a person must designate [produce as] peah only [while harvesting] the rear [of his field]:

B. "On account of:
   (1) robbery from the poor,
   (2) the idleness of the poor,
   (3) appearance's sake,
   (4) and deceivers.

C. "Robbery from the poor--how so?

D. "This assures that the time will never come when there is no [poor] person there [in the field to collect peah], such that [the farmer] may say to a poor relative (^{c}ny md^{c}tw),[25] 'Come and collect [all of] this peah for yourself.' [If the farmer was allowed to designate all of the peah for his own family, the other poor people in the town would not have fair access to the produce, thus robbing them of what rightfully is theirs (cf. M. 8:6).]

E. "The idleness of the poor--how so?

F. "This assures that poor people will not be sitting around and watching [the farmer] all day, saying, 'Now he is designating peah, now he is designating peah!' Rather, since [the farmer] designates [produce as] peah [while harvesting] the rear [of his field, the poor person] may go about his business, and may return to collect [the peah] at the end [of the harvest].

G. "Appearance's sake--how so?

H. "This assures that passers-by will not say, 'Behold how so-and-so harvested his field and did not designate [any produce as] peah!' For so it is written in Torah, "You shall not harvest the corner of your field" (Lev. 19:9). [That is, since the produce actually designated as peah will have been collected before the farmer finishes harvesting his field, when he does finish it will appear that he never designated any produce.]

I. "Deceivers--how so?

J. "This assures that [the deceivers] cannot say, 'We have already designated [produce as peah while harvesting the other parts of our fields.]'

K. "Another explanation [of the case of deceivers]:
L. "This assures that [the deceiver] does not retain the highest quality [produce for himself], and designate [peah] from the lowest quality. [Instead he must designate produce while harvesting the rear of his field, regardless of its quality, high or low.]"

Tosefta clearly presents Simeon's reasons for insisting that the householder designate peah while completing the harvest of his field (M. 1:3B).

T. 2:6

A. [As regards] a householder who designated peah for the poor,
B. [and] they said to him, "Designate [produce] for us on that side [of the field]"--
C. [if] he designates for them both [the produce on] this [side] and [the produce on] that [side],
D. lo, this [produce he designates, on both sides of the field] is in the status of peah.

Tosefta reiterates the point of M. 1:3A. The farmer may designate peah in any part of the field, whether at his own initiative, or at the request of the poor.

1:4-5

A. They stated a general principle governing [the designation of produce as] peah:
B. Whatever is
   (1) edible,
   (2) cultivated [as private-property] (nšmr),[26]
   (3) grown from the Land [of Israel],
   (4) harvested as a crop,
   (5) and can be preserved in storage,
   is subject to [designation as] peah.
C. Grain and legumes are included in this general principle.

M. 1:4

D. And among [types of] trees,
E. [the fruit of] (1) a sumac tree, (2) carob trees, (3) walnut trees, (4) almond trees, (5) grape vines, (6) pomegranate trees, (7) olive trees, (8) and date palms,[27] is subject to [designation as] peah.

M. 1:5 (M. Maas. 1:1; T. Pes. 2:20 [3:20]; Y. Peah 3:2-3 [17c]; Y. Shab. 7:1 [9a]; Y. Pes. 4:9 [31b]; B. Shab. 68a; B. Pes. 56b; B. Ḥul. 131a; B. Nid. 50a; Sifra Qid. 1:7-8 [Weiss, p. 87a])

The main point of the five part list at B is that the law governs only agricultural produce of the Land of Israel (B1-3). This is because Mishnah's framers regard the Land as the exclusive property of God. When Israelite farmers claim it as their own (B2) and grow food on it (B1, 3) they must pay for using God's earth. Householders thus must leave a portion of the yield unharvested as peah, and give this food over to God's chosen representatives, the poor. The underlying theory is that householders are tenant farmers who pay taxes to their landlord, God.

In addition to conditions applicable to all agricultural offerings (B1-3),[28] we are presented with two constraints particular to peah (B4-5). The first arises because, as we shall see (M. 1:6), peah must be designated during the harvest. But a farmer who picks a single piece of fruit cannot possibly leave behind a portion as peah. What follows is that edibles picked individually are exempt from the law, while those reaped as a crop are subject. Finally, since produce set aside as peah remains in the field until the poor come to collect it (M. 4:1), food that easily spoils is not subject to the law (B5).

The secondary material that follows (C, D-E) focuses on the claim that only produce harvested as a crop is subject to the law (B4). The two species at C present a gray area, for they neither are harvested as a crop nor picked individually. In the cases of both grain and legumes, the householder reaps small patches of produce, as they ripen. Since it is possible for him to leave standing as peah some of the yield each time he harvests a small area, the entire crop is deemed subject to the law (C).[29] Trees present a further ambiguity (D-E), for their fruit usually ripens and is picked one piece at a time.[30] The specific trees listed, however, bear fruit that is harvested as a crop. Hence a portion may be left for the poor as peah, and the law applies.

T. 1:7

A. [As regards] vegetables--even though they are harvested as a crop (cf. M. 1:4B4), they cannot be stored (cf. M. 1:4B5). [Hence they are not subject to designation as peah.]

B. [As for] figs, even though they can be stored, (cf. M. 1:4B5), they are not harvested as a crop (cf. M. 1:4B4). [Hence they are not subject to designation as peah.]

C. R. Yosé in the name of R. Judah says, "Figs [that are picked immediately after they ripen, while they still are] moist [and full], are exempt from [designation as] peah, since the first and the last do not ripen at the same time [lit., the first do not wait for the last]." [This being the case, they are not harvested as a crop (cf. M. 1:4B4).][31]

D. R. Eleazar in the name of R. Sadoq says "Jujubes[32] are subject to [designation as] peah."

E. Others say, "So too the fruit of white fig-trees[33] and peas[34] [are subject to designation as peah]."

50   Support for the Poor

Tosefta continues to adjudicate ambiguous cases. The species listed at A-B exhibit some, but not all, of the criteria for liability, and so are exempt from the law of peah. Yosé (C), Eleazar (D), and others (E) focus on the manner in which produce is harvested (cf. M. 1:4B4-5). Moist figs (C) are harvested individually, as each ripens, and so they are not subject to the law of peah. Jujubes (D), the fruit of white fig-trees (E), and peas (E), by contrast, are harvested in small patches, as areas of the field ripen. They therefore fall into the same operative category as grain and legumes (M. 1:4C), and are subject to designation as peah.

1:6

I. A. "At any time [after the harvest, the farmer] may designate [produce] as peah, [with the result that the produce he designates] is exempt from [the separation of] tithes,

   B. "until [the grain-pile] is smoothed-over.[35] [At this point the entire heap of grain becomes subject to the separation of tithes (see M. Maas. 1:6). The farmer therefore must tithe the produce, and then designate peah.]

II. C. "And [the farmer] may give away [produce] as ownerless property, [with the result that the produce he gives away] is exempt from [the separation of] tithes,

   D. "until [the grain-pile] is smoothed-over. [At this point the produce become subject to the separation of tithes and remains so even if he later declares it to be ownerless.]

III. E. "And [the farmer] may feed cattle, wild animals, and fowl [from the produce that he harvests, with the result that the produce he feeds them] is exempt from [the separation of] tithes,

   F. "until [the grain-pile] is smoothed-over. [At this point, the produce becomes subject to the separation of tithes.]

IV. G. "And [the farmer] may collect [grain] from the threshing floor, and sow [it, with the result that the grain he sows] is exempt from [the separation of] tithes,

   H. "until [the grain-pile] is smoothed-over. [At this point the produce becomes subject to the separation of tithes]," the opinion of R. Aqiba.

V. I. [As regards] a priest and a Levite who bought [grain at] the threshing floor[36] --the tithes [that otherwise would be separated from the produce that they have purchased] belong to them,

   J. unless [the grain-pile] is smoothed-over. [If this is the case, the farmer must separate tithes before he sells the produce, and may give them to the priest of his choice.]

VI. K. [As regards] one who dedicates [produce to the Temple], and then redeems [it--the produce he redeems] is subject to [the separation of] tithes,

   L. unless [the Temple]-treasurer smoothed-over [the grain-pile]. [If this is the case, the farmer incurs no liability to separate tithes when he redeems the produce, for the Temple owned the produce when it normally would have become subject to the separation of tithes.]

> M. 1:6 (T. Dem. 7:6; Y. Peah 1:1 [16c], 2:4 [17b], 4:1 [18a]; Y. Maas. 5:1 [51c-d]; B. Ber. 31a; B. B.Q. 94a; B. San. 88a; B. Mak. 16b; B. Tem. 6a)

Six formally parallel rules present a single principle regarding the separation of tithes. The repeated apodosis (B, D, F, H, J, L) makes the point that produce becomes subject to tithing as soon as the farmer processes it, the critical moment when he takes possession of the food.[37] Before smoothing over the grain-pile he may dispose of the food freely; he has not yet claimed full ownership of it, and so need not separate tithes (cf. M. Maas. 1:1). Once he has processed the grain, by contrast, the farmer has claimed exclusive ownership of it. This arouses the intense interest of God, the farmer's agricultural partner. The householder must pay to God, so to speak, a part of the profits. With the main point in hand, let us turn to the specific rules.

The first four cases (A-H), attributed to Aqiba, provide straightfoward illustrations of this principle and require no further discussion. Two rules concerning ownership complete the unit (I-J, K-L). Produce that priests, Levites, or the Temple own at the moment of processing is not subject to the separation of tithes. The priests and Levites themselves may eat the tithes that otherwise would be separated from food they possess (I-J). Grain owned by the Temple is exempt because God's appointees already own it (K-L). If at a later point the farmer redeems the produce, he still need not separate tithes. At the crucial moment of processing, when the law might have taken effect, the Temple owned the food. Apparently, Mishnah's redactors have included the entire unit here because peah is mentioned at A-B.

T. 1:5b

A. [If the farmer] did not designate some of the standing [crop as peah], he should designate some of the [grain bound into] sheaves.
B. [If he] did not designate some of the [grain bound into] sheaves [as peah], he should designate some of the [grain in the] stack.
C. [If he] did not designate some of the [grain in the] stack [as peah], he should designate some of the [produce in the] grain-pile.
D. [This rule applies] so long as he has not smoothed-over [the grain-pile].
E. But once he has smoothed-over [the grain-pile, the farmer] must [first] designate tithes [from the produce], and [then] designate [peah as well].

Tosefta explains how the situation described at M. 1:6 A-B could come about. A farmer should designate peah during the harvest (A). If he does not, however, he may designate the produce at any stage in processing. Once he finishes processing the food, however, he first must separate tithes, and then designate peah (E). This is because processing renders produce subject to the separation of tithes, as at M. 1:6.

CHAPTER TWO
PEAH CHAPTER TWO

The definition of a field, the basic unit of land in which peah must be set aside, occupies this entire chapter of Tractate Peah. This matter is crucial because M. 1:3, we recall, has informed us that the farmer must leave unharvested a separate portion of peah from each field he owns.[1] In order properly to comply wih the law, he must know what constitutes this area of land.[2] This main principle of the chapter's first unit (M. 2:1-4) is that whatever the farmer harvests as a single entity is deemed a field. For each patch of grain the householder reaps separately a distinct portion must be left standing as peah. This single principle generates two rules governing the apportionment of peah from grain fields (M. 2:1-2) and from orchards (M. 2:3-4). In the former case natural barriers such as rivers or hills mark off a field's boundaries. Each of these areas, defined by the land's physical characteristics, constitutes a separate unit for purposes of peah. Orchards present a different problem, for a single grove of trees may cover such a vast area of land that the farmer, while harvesting the trees, will ignore the land's physical features. As a result, natural landmarks do not suffice to establish an orchard's boundaries. Instead, a grove of trees is delimited by a fence that the householder erects to indicate his intention to harvest the enclosed trees as a single unit.

Only Eliezer (M. 2:4F+H) rejects the notion that physical barriers, whether natural or man-made, determine which trees a farmer will reap at one time. Rather, he claims, householders harvest all trees of a single species together, irrespective of landmarks or fences. Since all trees of one species ripen at the same time and are harvested in the same manner, they comprise a single orchard. In Eliezer's view the distinctions between natural categories of produce determine what constitutes an orchard or field.[3]

After introducing these two principles the chapter turns to ambiguous cases (M. 2:5-8). A farmer might harvest a single field delimited by physical barriers in two separate lots, or he might harvest two fields in one lot. In both cases the same questions arise: Are the land's physical features decisive, as sages hold above? Or do the farmer's actions determine the field's boundaries? The chapter takes the position that a single portion of produce must be designated on behalf of an entire field even if the grain is harvested at several different times (M. 2:5A-D, 2:7-8). Because the householder has ignored the boundaries clearly established by the field's physical characteristics, his actions have no effect. In the final ambiguous case (M. 2:6E-L), the chapter considers a tract of land planted with two different species of a single genus. Since it is unclear whether this tract constitutes one field or two, the farmer's actions are decisive. Whatever he harvests as a single unit is regarded as a field from which he must designate a separate portion of peah. As we might expect, the terrain of the fields and the

2:1

A. And these [landmarks] establish [the boundaries of a field] for [purposes of designating] peah:

B. (1) a river, (2) pond, (3) private road, (4) public road, (5) public path, (6) private path that is in regular use (hqbw^C) both in the dry season and in the rainy season, (7) uncultivated land, (8) newly-broken land, (9) and [an area sown with] a different [type of] seed.

C. "And [as regards] one who harvests unripe grain[4] [for use as fodder]--[the area he harvests] establishes [the boundaries of a field, since it now may be deemed uncultivated land; see B7]," the opinion of R. Meir.

D. But sages say, "[The area he harvests] does not establish [the boundaries of a field], unless he also has ploughed [the stubble] under, [thereby creating newly-broken land; see B8]."[5]

M. 2:1 (Y. Peah 3:1 [17c]; B. B.Q. 61a; B. B.B. 55a; B. Men. 71b; Sifra Qid. 2:1 [Weiss, pp. 87c-d])

The definition of a field is an issue of central importance because the farmer must know what constitutes this unit of land in order properly to set aside peah from each field.[6] The basic rule is contained in A-B: landmarks that prevent a householder from harvesting a large tract of land in a continuous action establish a field's boundaries. When physical barriers (B1-8) or a change in the type of crop (B9) force the farmer to stop harvesting, he has reached the edge of his field. The decisive criterion is the farmer's ability to continue reaping. With this definition in hand, the framers of Mishnah turn to a characteristic dilemma (C-D). Does a small tract of land that the farmer already has harvested serve to mark off separate fields on both of its sides? The ambiguity arises because such an area, while recently tilled by the householder, no longer is cultivated (see B7).[7] Meir (C) claims that the harvested area does establish a boundary between two adjacent fields, for it no longer is the subject of the farmer's agricultural work. Sages (D), by contrast, hold that the farmer indeed has cultivated the area, even if he already has harvested it. Accordingly, this harvested area establishes a boundary only if the farmer ploughs it, thus creating newly-broken soil (see B8).

T. 1:8a

A. These [landmarks] establish [the boundaries of a field] for [purposes of designating] peah:

(1) a river, (2) pond, (3) private road, (4) public road, (5) private path, (6) public path that is in regular use in the dry season and in the rainy season,[8] (7) uncultivated land, (8) newly-broken land, (9) [an area sown with] a different [type of] seed (M. 2:1A-B),

B. (10) one who harvests [unripe grain] for use as fodder (M. 2:1C),
C. (11) and three [unplanted] rows of a furrowed field.

Tosefta adds another element to M. 2:1's list (C). Three unplanted rows establish a field's boundary, since they constitute newly-broken land (see M. 2:1B8).

T. 1:9b

A. [As regards] embankments that are higher than ten-handbreadths--
B. [the farmer] designates [a separate portion of produce as peah from each [of the fields that they demarcate].
C. But if the ends of the rows touch one another [because the embankments have broken down] (r'šy šwrwt m^{c}wrbyn)--
D. [the farmer] designates peah from one [of the areas that the embankments demarcate] for all [of the areas together].

We now append one further landmark to the list at M. 2:1. Embankments that are ten handbreadths high interrupt the harvest, and so establish a field's boundaries. If these embankments break down so that they do not stop the farmer while he harvests, all of the areas together are deemed a single field (C-D).

2:2

A. [As regards] an irrigation ditch that [divides a tract of land so that the tract] cannot be harvested as one--
B. R. Judah says, "[It] establishes [the boundaries of a field]."
C. "And any hills that are hoed with a mattock" [i.e., hills that divide a tract of land and that are hoed manually] (Is. 7:25)--
D. even though an ox cannot cross over [them] with its plough,
E. [the farmer] designates peah for the entire [tract of land, as one field].

M. 2:2 (M. Sheb. 1:5; Sifra Qid. 2:2 [Weiss, p. 87d])

The pericope presents two extensions of M. 2:1's principle. First, Judah rules that an irrigation ditch, like a river (see M. 2:1B1), constitutes a barrier that prevents the farmer from continuing to harvest (A-B).[9] Such a ditch therefore establishes a field's boundary. Second, hills over which an ox cannot pass with its plough are deemed uncultivated land (C-D; see M. 2:1B7 and Maimonides, Commentary), and such hills mark off a boundary. Nevertheless, if the farmer hoes them by hand (E) and plants them, the hills no longer delimit separate fields because they do not constitute a barrier that prevents the farmer from continuing to harvest (see Sens).

T. 1:8b

A. And <u>an irrigation ditch that [divides a tract of land so that the tract] cannot be harvested as one</u> (M. 2:2A)--
B. R. Judah says, "If [the ditch is so wide that the farmer must] stand in the middle [of the irrigation ditch, in order to] harvest [the produce] on either side, [the ditch] establishes [the boundaries of a field (cf. M. 2:2B)].[10]
C. "But if [the ditch is sufficiently narrow that the farmer does] not [need to stand in the middle, but can harvest the produce on both sides while standing on one side of the ditch, the irrigation ditch] does not establish [the boundary between two fields]."

Tosefta has Judah (B-C) qualify his position of M. 2:2A, cited at A. An irrigation ditch establishes a boundary only if it stops the farmer from continuing to harvest (B). If the ditch presents no barrier, of course, it does not establish a boundary (C).

2:3-4

A. All [of the landmarks listed at M. 2:1] establish [the boundaries of a field planted with] seeds,
B. but as for establishing [the boundaries of an orchard of] trees, only a fence [does so].
C. But if the branches [of several trees] are intertwined with each other (ś'r kwtš),[11] [even a fence] does not establish [a boundary between them].
D. Rather, [the farmer] designates [a single portion of produce as] <u>peah</u> on behalf of all [of the trees whose branches are intertwined].

M. 2:3

E. And as regards carob trees, [which have extensive root systems that intertwine, as do the branches at D], all that are within sight of each other[12] [constitute a single orchard, and a single portion of fruit is designated as <u>peah</u> on behalf of all of them together].[13]
F. Said Rabban Gamaliel, "In my father's household they used to designate one [portion of produce as] <u>peah</u> on behalf of all of the olive trees that they owned in every direction [i.e., all that they owned together].
G. "But as regards carob trees, all that are within sight of each other [constitute a single orchard, and a single portion of produce is designated as <u>peah</u> for all of them together]" (cf. E).
H. R. Eliezer bar Ṣadoq says in [Gamaliel's] name, "So too: [They designated one portion of produce as <u>peah</u> for all] of the carob trees that they owned in the locale, [whether or not they were in sight of each other]."

M. 2:4 (Y. Peah 2:1 [16d]; Sifra Qid. 2:3-4 [Weiss, p. 87d])

The boundaries of an orchard present a special problem because trees are planted at great distances from each other. A single orchard thus may encompass several landmarks such as rivers or roads. These barriers, listed at M. 2:1, cannot serve to delimit groups of trees into distinct orchards. The pericope offers a simple solution to this problem. An orchard consists of those trees that a farmer harvests as a single unit. For example, a fence (A-B) marks off several trees that are in close proximity to each other, and these the farmer will harvest at one time. The farmer thus designates a single portion of fruit as peah on their behalf. C-D and E present parallel exceptions to this rule. Trees that are planted close to each other may intertwine, either in their branches (C-D) or in their extensive roots (E). Because these trees physically touch one another they form a single unit even if a fence divides them. The householder must designate a single portion of produce as peah for all of the trees together.

Gamaliel's lemma, loosely attached to the foregoing, repeats E verbatim at G. This ruling, however, presents us with two problems. First, while it is included here to serve as a precedent for E,[14] it clearly is not original to this context.[15] This is shown by the reference to olive trees (F), which is completely unrelated to the preceding material.[16] A second problem is more substantive, however, because Gamaliel's rule also espouses two contradictory theories. As we already have seen at G, Gamaliel endorses the notion that trees in close physical proximity to one another form an orchard and must have a single portion of fruit left behind as peah (cf. E). At F, though, Gamaliel has claimed that each species of trees belonging to a single farmer constitutes a separate orchard, and a distinct portion of produce must be designated as peah on behalf of each species even if the trees are planted at great distances from each other.[17] According to this theory, then, taxonomic groups determine what falls into the category of a field, for purposes of designating peah. Eliezer (H) presents a different version of Gamaliel's lemma, and so eliminates this contradiction.[18] He claims that for carobs, like olives, all of a farmer's trees of one species form an orchard. The practice of Gamaliel's father's household, in Eliezer's view, rejects E, and supports the theory that only natural categories, not physical proximity, determines what is a single unit for purposes of designating peah.

2:5-6

I. A. One who sows his field with [only] one type [of seed], even if he brings the crop to the threshing floor in two lots (^{c}wshw šty grnwt),[19]
    B. designates one [portion of produce as] peah [from the entire crop].
II. C. [But if he] sowed [his field] with two types [of seeds], even if he brings [both crops] to the threshing floor in only one lot,
    D. [he] designates two [separate portions of produce as] peah, [one from each type of produce].
III. E. He who sows his field with two [distinct] types of wheat--
    F. [if] he brings all of [the wheat] to the threshing floor in only one lot, [he] designates one [portion of produce as] peah.
    G. [But if he brings the wheat] to the threshing floor in two lots, [he] designates two [portions of produce as] peah.

M. 2:5

H. Once R. Simeon of Mişpah sowed [his field with two types of wheat].

I. [The matter came] before Rabban Gamaliel. So they went up to the Chamber of Hewn Stone, and asked [about the law regarding sowing two types of wheat in one field].

J. Said Nahum the Scribe,[20] "I have received [the following ruling] from R. Miasha, who received it from his father, who received it from the Pairs,[21] who received if from the Prophets, [who received] the law [given] to Moses on Sinai, regarding one who sows his field with two types of wheat:

K. "If he brings [the wheat] to the threshing floor in only one lot, [he] designates one [portion of produce as] peah.

L. "If he brings [the wheat] to the threshing floor in two lots, he designates two [portions of produce as] peah."

M. 2:6 (Y. Hag. 1:8 [76d]; B. Shab. 28b; B. Naz 65b; Tanh. Bamidbar 22 [Buber, Bamidbar 27])

The triplet before us supplements M. 2:1B9's claim that adjacent plots of land sown with two different types of produce constitute separate fields. In the case at hand a farmer has ignored the boundary between two such areas in order to harvest them as a single unit. Or the farmer might have harvested a single field in two separate lots. As the rules at A-B and C-D state, the farmer's actions in so reaping the field have no effect. The physically distinct plots of grain require separate designations of peah. These cases set up the conclusion of the triplet, E-G, in which a householder plants his land with two distinct species of a single genus. This creates an ambiguous situation. Does the crop constitute two fields, each planted with a different species, or only one field sown with a single genus? In this case the farmer's actions are decisive. Whatever he harvests as a single entity is regarded as one field from which a single portion must be set aside as peah.[22] The precedent at H-L lends authority to this rule by claiming that it derives from revelation at Sinai.

2:7-8

A. [As regards] a field that:
  (1) gentiles harvested [without the permission of the Israelite owner],[23]
  (2) robbers harvested,
  (3) ants destroyed,[24]
  (4) or that wind or cattle devastated--

B. [the produce of such a field] is exempt [from designation as peah].

C. [If a farmer] had harvested half [of his field], and robbers [then] harvested [the remaining] half--

D. [the produce that the farmer harvested] is exempt [from designation as peah], since the obligation [to designate] peah pertains to the [produce that] stands [in the rear corner of the field, and that robbers later harvested].[25]

M. 2:7

E. If robbers had harvested half [of a field], and [then the farmer] harvested [the remaining] half--
F. [the farmer] must designate peah, from that which he harvested, [on behalf of the entire field].
G. [If the farmer] had harvested half [of his field], and [then] sold [the remaining] half--
H. the buyer must designate peah on behalf of the entire [field].
I. [If the farmer] had harvested half [of his field], and [then] dedicated [the remaining] half [to the Temple]--
J. he who redeems the produce from the [Temple]-Treasurer is the one who designates peah on behalf of the entire [field].

M. 2:8 (Y. Peah 2:1 [16d], 3:5 [17c]; Sifra Qid. 1:6 [Weiss, p. 87b]; Sif. Deut. #282 [Finkelstien-Horowitz, p. 298])

Whoever completes the harvest of a field must designate peah on behalf of the whole, because he alone controls the grain that grows in the rear corner. As we recall (see M. 1:3A-B),[26] only this produce can take on the status of peah when left unharvested and then designated by the householder. The five cases before us (A-B, C-D, E-F, G-H, I-J) apply this principle in exhaustive detail. The farmer at A-B, for example, never harvests any part of his field, and so does not incur the responsibility to designate peah. This obvious case sets up a contrasting pair (C-D and E-F) in which thieves harvest half of the field. As D explicitly states, the farmer need not designate peah unless he himself reaps the field's rear corner. The final two cases (G-H and I-J) restate the obvious. The buyer or the person who redeems the produce will harvest the grain in the rear of the field, and so becomes responsible for designating peah on behalf of the entire field.

T. 1:8c-1:9a

A. [As regards an area within a field that]
(1) grasshoppers ate,
(2) edible locusts ate,
(3) ants destroyed,
(4) or which wind or cattle destroyed (see M. 2:7A3-4)--
B. all agree that if [the farmer] ploughed [the stubble] under, [the newly broken ground that he creates] establishes [a boundary] (cf. M. 2:1D).
C. If [the farmer] did not [plough the stubble under, the area that was destroyed] does not establish [a boundary].

T. 1:8c

D. [If the farmer] harvested half [of his field], and then sold this harvested produce (cf. M. 2:8G),

E. [of if he] harvested half [of his field], and then dedicated [to the Temple] this harvested produce (cf. M. 2:8I)--

F. [the farmer] designates peah from the one [remaining half] for the entire [field].

T. 1:9a

Tosefta (A-C) applies the principle of M. 2:1C-D to M. 2:7A. Only if the farmer ploughs the area destroyed by pests does that area establish a boundary between the unharvested areas on either side. D-F merely rephrases the ruling of M. 2:8G-J. The farmer harvests half of his field and then sells or dedicates the produce that he has harvested. Following Mishnah's reasoning, the farmer must designate peah for the entire field because he is the one who will complete the harvest.

CHAPTER THREE
PEAH CHAPTER THREE

This chapter further pursues the complex problem of defining fields. One theory holds that the householder's actions in harvesting comprise the decisive criteria. He establishes the boundaries of his fields by reaping an area of land separately from others, regardless of the land's topographical features: each discrete parcel that he reaps constitutes a distinct field. The second theory, already introduced in Chapter Two, claims that the land's topographical characteristics delimit fields. Rivers, hills, and other physical barriers set off one agricultural unit from another, regardless of the householder's actions while reaping the produce.

These two possibilities form the core of a series of disputes (M. 3:1-4), each concerning crops planted within a single topographical area yet harvested in more than one part. The Hillelites and sages hold that the land's features are determinative. Thus, the entire crop would constitute a single field and the farmer should designate one portion of produce as peah on behalf of the whole. However, according to the Shammaites, Aqiba, and Yosé, the farmer's actions establish boundaries and this same hypothetical crop might comprise several fields. This second view requires the householder to designate a separate portion of produce as peah for each small plot he harvests. The series of disputes culminates at M. 3:5, an anonymous ruling that supports the latter theory. The farmer's actions during the harvest might be determined solely on the basis of ownership, without reference to the land's physical features. Since each Israelite harvests only what he owns, he determines the boundaries of his fields.

An appendix (M. 3:6-8) completes the chapter by providing one further criterion for defining a field. Here Mishnah's framers seek to identify the minimum area of land that can constitute this unit. One opinion, held by Eliezer, Tarfon, Joshua, and Judah b. Beterah (M. 3:6A-D+E), is that small amounts of land are insignificant and do not comprise fields at all. Produce growing within such areas therefore is exempt from the law. Aqiba (M. 3:6F) presents the opposite opinion. In his view any area of land, however small, has infinite value. For this reason, even minuscule areas are deemed real estate and subject to the laws of peah. This position carries forward Aqiba's earlier ruling (M. 3:2F) that the Israelite's actions determine what is important. That is to say, human intention decides which areas of land are subject to the rules governing real estate, just as it determines what is a field. The anonymous pericopae that conclude the chapter (M. 3:7-8) support Aqiba's view by asserting that the transfer of a minuscule area of land is of consequence, and serves to indicate the householder's intention for his entire estate.

3:1-4

I. A. [As regards] rectangular [plots] (mlbnwt) of grain [sown] among olive trees--
    B. the House of Shammai say, "Peah [is designated separately] from each and every one [of the plots]."
    C. The House of Hillel say, "[Peah is designated] from one [plot] on behalf of all [of the plots together]."
    D. And [the Shammaites] concede [to the Hillelites] that if the ends of rows [at the edge of each plot] touch [one another] (r'šy šwrwt mᶜwrbyn), [the farmer] designates peah from one [plot] for all [of the plots together].

    M. 3:1

II. E. [As regards] one who reaps [the ripe portions] of his field (hmnmr 't śdhw),[1] having left the unripe stalks [unharvested]--
    F. R. Aqiba says, "He designates [a separate portion of produce] as peah from each and every [area, as he harvests it]."
    G. But sages say, "[He designates peah] from one [area] on behalf of all [of the areas together]."
    H. And sages concede to R. Aqiba that one who sows dill or mustard in three [distinct] places designates [a separate portion of produce as] peah from each and every [plot].

    M. 3:2

    I. One who picks fresh onions [in order to sell them] in the market, and who allows dried [onions to remain in the ground in order later to bring them] to the threshing floor (wmqyym ybšym lgwrn),
    J. designates peah from the former [i.e., the fresh onions] by themselves and from the latter [i.e., the dried onions] by themselves.
    K. And [this ruling applies] to beans and to [the produce of] a vineyard.
    L. He who thins [his vines] designates [peah] from the remaining [produce] (mn hmš'r) on behalf of that which he has left (ᶜl mh ššyr).
    M. But if he clears [part of his field, intending to use both that which he clears and that which he leaves] for a single purpose (m'ḥt yd),[2] he designates [peah] from the remaining [produce] on behalf of all [of the produce, i.e., on behalf of both the produce he clears and the produce that remains in the field].
    N. Parent-onions (h'mhwt šlbṣlym) are subject to [designation as] peah.
    O. But R. Yosé declares them exempt.

    M. 3:3

III. P. [As regards] rectangular [plots] of onions [sown] among [plots of] vegetables--
     Q. R. Yosé says, "[The farmer designates] peah from each and every one [of the plots of onions]."

R.   But sages say, "[He designates peah] from one [plot] for all [of the plots together]."

M. 3:4 (Y. Peah 2:1 [16d], 2:4 [17a], 3:1 [17c]; Y. Ḥag. 1:89 [76d]; B. Naz. 56b; B. Men. 71b; B. Nid. 50a, 51a)

The discussion focuses upon the status of a single crop divided into two or more parts. This issue occupies the three parallel disputes (A-B vs. C, E-F vs. G, P-Q vs. R) that form the core of the unit before us. In each of these cases we wish to know if each part comprises a distinct field and so, when it is harvested, requires its own designation of peah. The alternative is that the entire crop planted within a single area constitutes one field for purposes of the law. In this instance the fact that the farmer might reap the crop in several parts would be irrelevant. He must designate peah only once on behalf of the entire field.

In these disputes, the Shammaites (B), Aqiba (F), and Yosé (Q) all take the former view. Consider the householder who would have to harvest the crop in several parts because trees (A-C) or plots of vegetables (P-R) divide it into distinct sections or because small patches of the produce ripen at different times (E-G). Although these physical characteristics by themselves would not establish the boundaries of a field (see M. 2:1-2), the farmer treats the field as several distinct entities and so must designate a separate portion as peah from each small area.

The Hillelites (C) and sages (G-R), by contrast, claim that the farmer designates only one portion of peah on behalf of the entire field. In their view the fact that the produce grows within a single topographical area takes precedence over the householder's actions. Even if he stops harvesting when he reaches a tree, the larger tract of land remains a single field. This view, of course, carries forward Chapter Two's notion that the boundaries of a field are determined only by landmarks that interrupt the harvest.

Having explained the core of this unit, I now turn to secondary materials: the glosses at D and H, the anonymous rules at I-M, and a short section regarding parent-onions, N-O.

Two formally parallel stichs (D, H) gloss the foregoing disputes. First, the Shammaites (D) concede to the Hillelites that small plots of grain that are contiguous comprise a single field. The farmer therefore designates one portion of peah from all of the patches together. This hardly represents a concession, however, for the Shammaites' overall theory claims that each individually harvested area of land forms a distinct field. Since the plots under discussion are contiguous, the farmer will harvest all of them at one time as a single unit. At H, sages agree with Aqiba that physically distinct plots constitute separate fields. In this case a farmer has planted spices in small patches wherever he has unused land. Since these plots are not sown within a single area, the farmer must designate peah separately on behalf of each patch. Once again, this constitutes no concession. Consistent with their basic theory, sages merely agree that the spices never were planted as a single field and so must be treated as individual fields of produce.

The rules at I-M, while not formally parallel to the surrounding disputes,[3] in fact take up the same issue. Here the farmer harvests a single crop in two lots and intends to use each batch of produce for a different purpose. At I-J he wishes to sell some of the onions and to keep the rest for his own use. Similarly at M-N he cuts off some portions of his vines so that the remaining grapes will have adequate room to grow. The point of both rules, made explicit at M, is that whatever the farmer reaps for a single purpose, that is, as a single unit, must have its own portion of peah. In line with the Shammaites, Aqiba, and Yosé, Mishnah's framers rule that human actions and intentions are decisive.

The dispute regarding parent-onions (N-O) is unrelated to the issue of this entire contruction.[4] These onions have an ambiguous status, however, for although they are edible, they are left in the ground to sprout, and so never are eaten. Are they subject to designation as peah? The answer turns on our understanding of the word n'kl in M. 1:4, a pericope that defines the range of produce to which the law applies. This word may refer to all produce that is "edible," or only to that which is "eaten."[5] The anonymous rule at N takes into account only that parent-onions are edible. For this reason, they are subject to the law. Yosé (O), on the other hand, rules that parent-onions are exempt from this designation. In his view, the decisive fact is that the onions never are eaten.

T. 1:9b

A. One who selects [the ripe onions from his field and leaves the others to dry]--
B. is obligated [to designate peah from] the former, [ripe onions], and is obligated [to designate peah from] the latter, [dry onions] (cf. M. 3:3A-B).

Tosefta paraphrases M. 3:3A-B, without which it would be incomprehensible.

T. 1:10-11

A. [If a farmer] had four or five vines,[6]
B. he may harvest the grapes and bring them into his house,
C. [with the result that they] are exempt from the laws of the separated [grape], forgotten sheaf, and peah.
D. But the grapes are subject to the law of gleanings.
E. If he left [some of the grapes on the vines], he designates [peah] from the remaining [produce] on behalf of [this same] remaining produce (M. 3:3D).
F. He who thins [his field] designates [peah] from the remaining [produce] on behalf of [this same] remaining [produce] (M. 3:3D).
G. Said R. Judah, "Under what circumstances [does this apply]?
H. "[It applies if the farmer] thins [his field in order to sell the produce he thins] in the market.
J. "But if he thins [his field in order to bring the produce] into his home, he designates [peah] from the remaining [produce] on behalf of all [of the field's produce]."

T. 1:10

K. He who plucks [produce] and brings it into his house,
L. even if he plucks the entire field,
M. is exempt from the law of gleanings, the forgotten sheaf, and from peah.
N. But he is responsible [for separating] tithes.

T. 1:11

Three units expand the rules provided at M. 3:3. The first (A-E) applies the law of M. 3:3C to a vineyard. A farmer may harvest grapes for use as a random snack without incurring liability for the offerings listed at C because he has not harvested a crop (Lieberman, TK, p. 138). Such grapes are subject to the law of gleanings, however, since this law applies to all produce whether or not it is harvested as a crop. While A-D are unrelated to Mishnah, they allow Tosefta to make its point at E. Grapes left on the vine after some have been picked for a random snack are like produce left in a field after it has been thinned (M. 3:3D). The farmer need designate peah only for what remains, since the grapes that were eaten as a random snack were not subject to designation as peah.

In the second section (F-J) Judah qualifies M. 3:3D. In order to understand his ruling we must make two assumptions. First, the onions that the farmer brings to the market are exempt from designation as peah.[7] Second, the onions that remain in the field will be used for food in the farmer's house. Now if the farmer brings the onions to the market, only those that remain in the field are subject to designation as peah (H). If the farmer brings the thinned onions into his house, by contrast, all of the onions will be used for the same purpose. This being the case, the farmer designates peah for the entire crop.

The third unit (K-N) is parallel to A-D. The food is not harvested as a crop, and so is not subject to the offerings (cf. M. 1:4-5). Such produce, however, is subject to the separation of tithes (see M. Maas. 1:1).

3:5

A. [Two] brothers who divided [ownership of a field that they had inherited],
B. give two [separate portions of produce] as peah [i.e., each designates peah on behalf of the producing growing in his half of the field].
C. [If they] once again jointly owned [the field],
D. [together] they designate one [portion of produce] as peah [on behalf of the entire field].
E. Two [householders] who [jointly] purchased a tree,
F. [together] designate one [portion of produce] as peah [on behalf of the entire tree].
G. But if one purchased the northern [part of the tree], and the other purchased the southern [part of the tree],
H. the former designates peah by himself, and the latter designates peah by himself.
I. [As regards] one who sells [only] the trees in his field, [but not the earth in which they are planted] (qlby 'yln)[8]--

66   Support for the Poor

   J.   [the buyer] designates peah from each and every [tree]. [The trees do not
        comprise an orchard, because the buyer does not own the land in which they
        grow.]
   K.   Said R. Judah, "Under what circumstances [does this apply]?
   L.   "[It applies] if the owner of the field does not retain [any of the trees for
        himself].
   M.   "But if the owner of the field had retained [some of the trees for himself],
   N.   "[the owner] designates peah for all [of the trees, i.e., both those that he sells
        and those that he retains]."
                                       M. 3:5

Ownership has a direct bearing on the status of a field, for it determines which tracts of land the farmer will reap as a single unit. This point is made in the pair at A-D and E-H, cases in which two farmers own separate halves of a tree or of a tract of land (A-B, G-H). As a result, each must designate peah separately while harvesting his own portion of the yield. Two individuals who maintain joint ownership of a field (C-D, E-F), by contrast, each have an equal claim on the whole. The entire field is regarded as a single entity, and both owners together must designate a single portion of produce. The basic notion here is that in defining fields ownership takes precedence over the physical boundaries listed at M. 2:1-2. This notion surely is remarkable, because it undermines all of the foregoing discussion.

The secondary material at I-N concerns a slightly different issue, prepared for by the preceding discussion of joint ownership. Now one householder owns a grove of trees, while another owns the land in which they are planted (I-J). Since each tree is a separate entity, unconnected to the others, the buyer must designate peah separately from each one. Judah (K-N) qualifies this ruling. If the seller retains some of the trees, he still owns an orchard. Since he has not affected the status of the orchard, the owner must designate peah on behalf of the entire crop from the produce that remains.[9] That is to say, he designates peah both for the trees he sells and for those he keeps.

                                       3:6
   A.   R. Eliezer says, "[An area] of land [within which is planted] a quarter-[qab of
        seed] is subject to [the laws of] peah."
   B.   R. Joshua says, "[An area of land that] produces two seahs [of grain is subject
        to the laws of peah]."
   C.   R. Tarfon says, "[An area of land measuring] six-by-six handbreadths [is
        subject to the laws of peah]."
   D.   R. Judah b. Beterah says, "[An area of land that produces] sufficient [grain
        that the farmer must] cut twice (kdy lqṣwr wlšnwt) [i.e., with two strokes of a
        sickle,[10] is subject to the laws of peah]."
   E.   And the law accords with his opinion.

F. R. Aqiba says, "Land of any size at all,
- (1) "is subject [to the laws of] peah and [to the laws of] first fruits (cf. Deut. 26:1),
- (2) "[and is sufficient] for writing against it a prozbul. [This is a document that prevents the Sabbatical year from cancelling the obligation to repay a loan. It may be written only if the borrower owns real estate.][11]
- (3) "[Finally, even a minuscule area of land may be used] thereby to acquire ownership of movable property, along with [an exchange of] money, a deed, or [an act of] usucaption."

M. 3:6 (M. Sheb. 10:6; Y. Qid. 1:1 [60d]; Y. B.B. 9:7 [17a]; B. Qid. 26a; B. Git. 37a; B. B.B. 27a, 150a)

From the discussion of a field's boundaries the tractate now turns to a separate issue regarding its definition. The sages dispute whether or not a field must contain some minimum amount of land, or yield a minimum amount of grain, in order to be subject to the law. Two opposing theories are presented in the dispute at A-D+E vs. F. The four authorities at A-D all rule that minuscule tracts of land are inconsequential, and that peah need not be designated from produce that grows in them. As I shall explain below, these rulings differ only in their specific minimum measure of a field subject to peah. An opposing theory is presented by Aqiba (F).[12] He reasons that any piece of land, however small, has lasting value. All tracts of land therefore have the status of real estate, and are subject to the rules spelled out at F1-3.

Each authority at A-D defines the minimum amount of land that may be regarded as a field.[13] Eliezer (A) refers to an area within which is planted a quarter-qab of seed, the amount of land that must separate two fields of grain lest they be deemed a mixture of diverse kinds (M. Kil. 2:10). He claims that since this area is large enough to separate two tracts of land, it also may be deemed a field. Joshua (B) claims that an area has the status of a field only if it produces more than two seahs of grain. This is because, as we shall see, so small an amount of grain automatically must be left for the poor, in accordance with the law of the forgotten sheaf (see M. 6:7). In an area that yields less than this measure of grain, the householder will harvest nothing and cannot designate a portion as peah. At C Tarfon reminds us that six square handbreadths of land must separate two fields of vegetables (M. Kil. 2:10). He thus deems such an area to be a field. Finally, Beterah's rule (D) is based on a practical consideration that arises from designating peah during the harvest. After the farmer swings his sickle once, there must remain some standing produce (i.e., that which a second sickle stroke would cut) for the farmer to designate as peah. Therefore, a field must produce enough to require at least two sickle strokes during the harvest. E adjudicates the dispute between these four authorities in favor of Beterah.

3:7-8

I. A. [As regards] one who had consigned his property [to others] while he lay on his death bed (škyb mr^c), [but then recovered]--

B. [if in his consignment] he had retained [for himself] any land at all, his gift is deemed valid (mtntw mtnh).

C. [If] he had retained no land at all, his gift is deemed invalid, [and the others must return what they had received].

II. D. One who consigns his property to his sons--

E. [if] he had consigned any land at all to his wife, she forfeits [the settlement guaranteed by] her marriage-contract.[14]

F. R. Yosé says, "If she accepted [some land from the husband, as a gift] even though he had not consigned it to her [in writing], she forfeits [the settlement guaranteed by] her marriage-contract.

M. 3:7

III. G. One who consigns [all of] his property to his slave--

H. [the slave] becomes a free person, [because the slave, as part of the estate, now owns himself].

I. [If in his consignment the property owner had retained any land at all--the slave does not become a free person, [for we assume that the property retained includes the slave].

J. R. Simeon says, "Under any circumstances (l^{c}wlm) [i.e., whether o ot the property owner retains some land for himself], the slave is free,

K. "unless the [property owner] says, 'Lo, all of my possessions are given to so-and-so, my slave, except for one ten-thousandth part of them.'"

M. 3:8 (T. B.B. 9:11; Y. Ket. 12:5 [35c]; Y. Git. 1:1 [43a], 5:1 [46d]; B. Ket. 55a, B. Git. 8b, 42a; B. B.B. 132a-b, 146b, 149b, 150a-b; Tanḥ. Lekh Lekha 8)

The entire pericope carries forward Aqiba's notion that even tiny pieces of land have inestimable value (cf. M. 3:6F). This point is made in three formally parallel cases (A-C, D-F, G-K), which address the following situation. A householder consigns his property to others, either while on his deathbed or simply while making up his will. In each case, his transfer or retension of a minuscule amount of land serves to indicate his intentions for the transaction. With this basic principle in mind, let us now turn to the specifics of the three cases.

The deathly-ill property owner at A-B has made provision for his own well-being should he recover, for he has retained some land. What follows from this is that his consignment of property was not conditional upon his death. If he had not retained any land for himself, by contrast, we might infer that he gave away his property under the false assumption that he would die (C). When he recovers, the property he consigned must be returned to him. Similarly, at G-H a landowner consigns all of his property to his slave who thereupon owns himself and is a freeman. If the property owner retains even a tiny bit of land, however, we assume that he wishes to retain control of his entire estate. The slave therefore would remain the householder's property (I). The middle case (D-E+F) illustrates the same point--a minuscule area of land has inestimable value.[15] Here the husband signs over to his wife a small piece of land. The real estate, in the view of Mishnah's framers, has huge value and so is worth more than the two hundred zuz that the husband has guaranteed his wife in her marriage contract (see M. Ket. 1:2). By consigning this land to her, therefore, the husband has paid her marriage-settlement and debarred her from collecting any further amount from his estate. Yosé (F) applies this principle to a slightly different case in which the wife agrees to accept a gift of land. Once again, she forfeits her marriage settlement. Because the woman already has agreed to forgo her right to any additional claim on the estate it makes no difference whether or not her husband consigns the property to her in writing.

We must now explain Simeon's gloss (J-K). He holds that all types of property, not just land, may serve to indicate a householder's larger intentions.[16] Thus if a property owner retains a small amount of his property, even one part in ten thousand, he retains control of his entire estate.

T. 1:12

A. <u>One who consigns his property to his sons--if he had consigned any land at all to his wife, she forfeits [the settlement guaranteed by] her marriage-contract</u> (M. 3:7D-E).

B. Said R. Yosé, "Under what circumstances does this apply?

C. "[It applies] if she accepted the land as [payment of] her marriage-contract.

D. "But if she did not accept the land [as payment of] her marriage-contract--

E. "he has given her what he has given her [as an independant gift] (mh šntn ntn), and her marriage-contract is settled out of what remains [of his estate]."

Yosé qualifies M. 3:7D-E. He says that the woman must agree to accept the land in place of the money which is due her. If she does not the land is simply a gift, and she still is entitled to the settlement.

T. 1:13

A. <u>One who consigns [all of] his property to his slave--[the slave] becomes a free-person, [because the slave, as part of the estate, now owns himself].</u>
<u>If in his consignment the property owner] had retained any land at all--the slave does not become a free-person, [for we assume that the property retained includes the slave]</u> (M. 3:8G-J).

B. R. Simeon says, "Lo, he who says, <u>'Lo, all of my possessions are given to so-and-so, my slave, except for one ten-thousandth part of them'</u> (M. 3:8L), has said nothing [of binding force],

C. "unless he specifies such-and-such a town or such-and-such a field.
D. "and even if he had specified (šm) that very field and that very town, the slave acquires the property and may buy his freedom."
E. And when they said these words in front of R. Yosé, he said, "He who gives a right answer smacks his lips" (Prov. 24:26).

Tosefta (B-C) assigns to Simeon the opposite of his opinion in Mishnah. The property owner must retain a specified piece of land in order to retain control of his slave. Simeon's opinion thus is harmonized with the position that the transfer or retention of land informs us of the intentions of a land owner. The point at D is that even if the owner retains some land he does not retain control of the slave. This is because the slave can buy his freedom with the other property the owner gives to him. E simply asserts that Yosé agreed with this interpretation of Simeon's position.

CHAPTER FOUR
PEAH CHAPTER FOUR

Of the chapter's two thematic units, the first concludes the tractate's treatment of the laws of peah (M. 4:1-5), while the second begins the discourse on gleanings (M. 4:10-11). Because the preceding chapters have regulated the process by which the householder leaves a portion of grain unharvested and then designates it as peah, we now turn to the distribution of this offering. The basic principle of allocation is that each poor person must be allowed free access to claim God's gifts.[1] Neither householders (M. 4:1-2) nor other poor people (M. 4:3-4) may infringe on this right. A householder, for his part, may not control the distribution of peah, because he does not own this produce. He has no right to give it to a specific poor person. Similarly, no one poor person may hoard this food, because he thereby would deprive others of their right to collect it. Each poor person may acquire his share of the offering only by taking possession of the amount he can carry. The unit's final ruling (M. 4:5), a dispute between Aqiba and Gamaliel, says that householders may not prevent the poor from having free access to the peah. The tractate insures the right of free access by specifying that poor people must be allowed to gather the food three times daily.

A short transitional section (M. 4:6-9) bridges the chapter's two main units by making a point common to both peah and gleanings. Only produce owned by an Israelite at the beginning of the harvest is subject to the designation of these two offerings. Hence, grain that gentiles own or that is harvested under the Temple's auspices is exempt from the restrictions of the law.

In the chapter's second main unit (M. 4:10-11), Mishnah's framers define what may be considered gleanings. They proceed from Lev. 19:9's statement that gleanings left "after the harvest" belong to the poor, and interpret this to mean that only grain an Israelite first harvests and claims for himself can be called gleanings. Thus when the householder reaps the individual stalks of produce he initiates the system by which a portion of the grain is set aside for the poor.[2] After the householder has claimed the food, whatever he drops for no apparent reason is deemed gleanings. This produce, set aside entirely at random, is deemed to have been given by God to the poor. The farmer himself has no purposive role in determining which produce becomes gleanings.

If we examine both the laws of peah and gleanings, principles that govern both offerings emerge. These offerings consist of anomalous produce that is owned yet not possessed.[3] What sort of food is this? We speak of grain that grows in a householder's field, but that he never takes. Peah, for example, contains the marginal stalks at the edge of the field. In the ordinary process of reaping his field, the farmer is likely to leave these behind unharvested. Gleanings consist of produce that the farmer reaps, but then drops. Again, he never finally possesses this food. To explain why the poor receive this anomalous food, I offer the following theory. As Israelites living in the Land, the poor are entitled to prosperity and material success.[4] Nonetheless, they have none of the things that the Land ought to give them. So the poor present an anomaly of their own. Their situation as Israelites living in the Land, yet lacking the means to sustain themselves, is resolved by giving to the poor produce that God has taken from wealthy householders. As a result, an Israelite who obeys the laws of gleanings and peah twice restores harmony to the anomalous--first by returning to society all anomalous food, and second by supplying the poor with the nourishment they deserve.

Peah and gleanings also are alike in a second respect. Since the householder never fully takes possession of them, they are not considered his private property. Accordingly, they are exempt from the separation of tithes (see M. 1:6; M. Maas. 1:1).[5] The result is that just as the farmer receives none of the produce designated as peah or gleanings, so too God's priestly representatives receive none. It seems that Mishnah's framers imagine a perfect correspondence between the householder's claim on the crop and God's.

Having established this general theory of gleanings, the chapter now turns to cases of doubt concerning produce's status as gleanings (M. 4:10J-L; 4:11). At issue is how we dispense this food. Do we treat it as gleanings reserved for the poor alone or as ordinary food that the householder may retain? Aqiba (M. 4:10L) and the anonymous ruling at M. 4:11C-D hold that the poor are entitled only to that which unquestionably has the status of gleanings. The householder may keep any produce of ambiguous status, because it never clearly was set aside for the poor. In contrast, Ishmael (M. 4:10K) and Meir (M. 4:11E-F) rule that we must prevent householders from misappropriating food set aside for the poor alone. Farmers must give to the poor all produce of ambiguous status, lest they take for themselves that which God has given to the poor.

4:1-2

A. Peah is designated from [produce that as yet is] unharvested (bmḥwbr lqrq^c).

B. [As regards grape vines[6] that grow] on a trellis, or [the produce of] a palm tree--

C. the householder cuts down [the produce] and distributes [it] among the poor.

D. R. Simeon says, "Also: [The preceding rule, B-C, applies] to [nuts that grow on] smooth nut-trees."

I. E. [In support of the rule at A:] Even if ninety-nine [poor people] say that [the householder should harvest and] distribute [the produce], and [only] one [poor person] says that [the poor should harvest and] take [the produce by themselves],

F. they listen to the latter, [who said that the poor should take the produce],

G. for he has spoken according to the law.

M. 4:1

H. [With regard to grape vines that grow] on a trellis, or [the produce of] a palm tree (B-C), this [rule, E-G,] does not apply.

Peah Chapter Four   73

II. I. [For in the case of a trellis or a palm tree], even if ninety-nine [poor people] say that [the poor should harvest and] take [the produce themselves], and [only] one [poor person] says that [the householder should] distribute [the produce among the poor],

J. they listen to the latter, [who said that the householder should distribute the produce],

K. for he has spoken according to the law.

M. 4:2 (Y. Peah 2:5 [17a]; Sifra Qid. 3:5-6 [Weiss, p. 88a])

Farmers must allow the poor themselves to reap the produce designated as peah (A). Since this food belongs to the poor alone, householders have no right to harvest and to distribute it. This rule has the further effect of preventing farmers from favoring or discriminating against an individual, and so assures all poor people equal access to the offering (see also M. 4:3-5). A separate rule applies to the distribution of peah growing on trees or trellises (B-C+D). In these cases, the poor might damage the householder's property while climbing to gather their food. In order to prevent such a loss, the householder himself may harvest and allocate the fruit.[7] Finally, Mishnah's framers ask whether the poor may decide among themselves who should allocate the produce (E-G and H+J-K). As G and K state, the poor may not specify a distribution process different from the one spelled out in the laws at A-D.

T. 2:7-8

A. Workers who are harvesting (šhyw ʿwśyn) [a field] for a householder may not finish [harvesting] the entire field.

B. Rather, they must leave [standing] sufficient [produce for designation] as peah.

C. But this [produce] is not [in the status of] peah until the householder sets it aside as peah.

T. 2:7

D. A poor person who sees [an amount of standing produce] sufficient [for designation] as peah,

E. whether [he sees] grain or [the produce of] a tree,

F. may not touch it.

G. And [the produce] is forbidden to him under [the law of] robbery,

H. until it is made known to him that it [indeed] is peah.

T. 2:8

Tosefta's central problem (D-H) is that the poor might take grain that looks like, but is not, peah. In order to prevent this, Tosefta rules that the poor may not take produce simply because it appears to be peah. They must wait until they explicitly hear that the food has been designated for them (H). A-C explains how this confusion might arise.

Since peah must be designated from unharvested produce (see M. 4:1), workers must leave enough standing grain for later designation as peah (A-B). They may not designate the produce themselves (B), however, for only the householder who owns the produce has this power.[8]

4:3

A. [If a poor person] harvested a portion of the [produce designated as] peah, and threw it over the remainder [of the produce designated as peah, in order to claim possession of that grain],

B. he is entitled to no part [of the peah that he wrongly tried to claim, although he may keep the grain that he originally picked].

C. [If] he fell upon [the produce designated as peah], or spread his cloak over it, [in order to claim possession of it],

D. they remove it from him.

E. This same [rule] applies to [the collection of both] gleanings and forgotten sheaves.

M. 4:3 (Y. Git. 8:3 [49c]; Y. B.M. 1:4 [7d]; B. B.M. 10a)

Each poor person may acquire peah only by harvesting the produce. By allowing each to gather only the amount of food that he or she can carry, Mishnah's authors assure that all poor people have equal access to this offering (see M. 4:1-2). Accordingly, those who try to gain more than their fair share of the peah (A-B, C-D) have no valid claim on the produce.[9] A secondary issue is that peah, like all movable objects, may be acquired only by drawing it into one's possession.[10] Hence, only by gathering the peah can a poor person establish his claim upon it. The quite separate gloss at E extends the basic principle to other poor-offerings, namely gleanings and forgotten sheaves, because the poor are entitled to free access to these as well.

Let us now pause for a moment, and see how this unit reflects the basic purpose of the law of peah. The law is designated, we recall, to narrow the gap between rich and poor Israelites. Wealthy householders must give up some of their yield so that the poor may receive what they need. In the proper designation of peah, the farmer gives up a portion of his crop by not reaping the produce at all. Instead, the poor person harvests this grain as if he himself were a householder. The complementary roles assigned to the farmer and to the poor person thus reflect the intention of Mishnah's framers to equalize all of Israelite society.

T. 2:1

A. [If a poor person] harvested part of the [produce designated as] peah, and threw [it] over the remainder [of the produce designated as peah, in order to claim ownership of that produce], he is entitled to no part [of the produce designated as peah] (M. 4:3A-B).

B. R. Meir says, "They fine him, by removing from him both that [which he legally gathered] and that [which he attempted to claim]."

Meir asserts that the poor person at M. 4:3A-B is entitled to keep neither the peah that he collected legally nor that which he illegally attempted to claim. The produce that he gathered legally is taken as a penalty for his improper actions.

T. 2:2

I.   A. If a householder designated peah for [certain] poor people,
     B. and a different poor person came along behind their backs, and collected [the produce designated as peah],
     C. lo, this [poor person, who has taken the peah,] has acquired [it].

II. D. If two poor people were fighting over [possession of] a sheaf,
     E. and a different poor person came along behind their backs, and collected [the produce left behind as forgotten sheaves],
     F. lo, this [poor person, who has taken that produce], has acquired it,
     G. because a poor person does not acquire ownership of gleanings, forgotten sheaves, or peah, until it has fallen into his domain.

The point of Tosefta's two parallel rules (A-C, D-F) is at G. A poor person acquires ownership of peah only by physically taking it (see M. 4:3).

4:4

A. [As regards] peah--
B. they may not harvest it with sickles, nor may they uproot it with spades,
C. so that one [poor] person will not strike another.

M. 4:4

Poor people who use garden tools when collecting the produce designated for them might injure each other (C).[11] Accordingly, they may reap this grain only by hand. This procedure has the further effect of assuring that no individual has an unfair advantage over others when gathering the offerings (cf. M. 4:1-2), because all must reap it in the same manner.

4:5

A. [There are] three [periods when the poor may] search [for the produce designated as peah] during each day:
B. (1) in the morning, (2) at noon, (3) and in the afternoon.
C. Rabban Gamaliel says, "They stated [this rule] only so that [householders] would not decrease [the number of times in each day when the poor were permitted to collect peah]."

D. R. Aqiba says, "They stated [this rule] only so that [householders] would not increase [the number of times in each day when the poor were permitted to collect peah]."

E. [The inhabitants] of Bet Namer [permitted the poor] to collect gleanings from each row [of the field, as the field was harvested], and designated peah from each and every furrow.

M. 4:5

The rule that the poor may gather peah three times daily (A-B) sets the stage for Gamaliel's and Aqiba's dispute concerning the purpose of this law (C vs. D). Gamaliel's concern is that the poor have free access to the peah. More than one collection each day should be allowed, in his view, since this permits the poor more readily to collect the food. Aqiba, however, believes the poor should not be bothered to stand at the edge of the field all day waiting for each time the householder allows them to gather peah. Therefore he rules that three collections daily is a maximum. The secondary material at E takes up the case of gleanings, a topic unrelated to the foregoing, so it is separate from the dispute. Nonetheless, in its present context it serves as an illustration of Gamaliel's position. By allowing the poor to gather peah and gleanings after the harvest of each row, the farmers of Bet Namer increased the number of daily searches for this food.

T. 2:5

A. R. Judah says, "[In the] morning the householder must declare, 'Whatever the poor will gather during the binding process (mn h^{c}wmryn), lo, it is ownerless property.'"

B. R. Dosa says, "[He must make this declaration] at evening time."

C. But sages say, "[Produce declared] ownerless under pressure [that the poor otherwise might steal it and consume it without separating the tithes due from it] has not[12] [validly been declared] ownerless property,

D. "since [people are] not responsible for [the actions of] deceivers."

Tosefta takes up a problem left open in M. 4:5's discussion of the distribution of peah. The poor take as peah produce that the householder never designated for them. Under the assumption that this food has the status of peah and is exempt from tithes, the poor eat this produce without separating the required offerings. The issue under dispute between Dosa, Judah, and sages is whether or not this is of concern to the farmer. Judah (A) and Dosa (B) agree that it is. The householder is responsible for ensuring that the poor do not transgress. Sages (C-D) disagree, because the poor have taken what is not theirs. Accordingly, the householder need not scruple on their behalf.

What must be explained now is how the householder might prevent the poor from transgressing. He does this by declaring that any produce the poor take during the binding process is ownerless. Like all ownerless property it is exempt from the separation of tithes and the poor may eat it without culpability. Judah and Dosa dispute when the householder must make such a declaration. Judah holds that before the poor take the produce the householder should declare it ownerless so that at no point will they transgress by eating food still subject to tithing. Dosa, by contrast, holds that the declaration should be made after the poor take the produce. He reasons that the householder cannot declare ownerless all produce that the poor might take; rather, his statement must refer to food that they actually have taken during the day's binding.

<u>T. 2:12</u>

    A.   A householder who designated [unharvested produce as] <u>peah</u> for the poor has no right to say to them, "Take the [edible] seeds [for yourselves] and give [me] the [inedible] stalks of flax," [or] "Take the [edible] dates [for yourselves] and give [me] the [inedible] branches."

    B.   [If the produce] fell and afterward [the householder] separated [the seeds from the stalks of flax],

    C.   the seeds alone are subject to designation as <u>peah</u>.

Tosefta's point is that <u>peah</u> must be distributed as a free gift, not as wages (see M. 4:1-5). The householder therefore may not tell the poor to separate the edible portions of the produce subject to designation from the inedible parts which are exempt (A).[13] By separating the produce, the poor would be working on the householder's behalf and receiving <u>peah</u> as payment for this work. Instead, the poor keep all of the produce, including the inedible portions. On the other hand, if the edible and inedible parts of the produce are separated from each other, the edible portion alone is designated as <u>peah</u> (B-C). The poor have no claim on the inedible part of the crop (see M. 1:4-5).

<u>T. 2:17</u>

    A.   [If] a householder gave to a poor person a small bundle of grain in return for the poor person's drawing water,

    B.   none of [the produce] in [the bundle] is in the status of gleanings, forgotten sheaves, or <u>peah</u>,

    C.   and [the produce in the bundle] is subject to [the separation of] tithes.

Poor-offerings may not be given as wages (T. 2:12). Hence, food given to the poor as payment for their services simply is ordinary produce from which tithes must be separated.

4:6

    A.   [As regards] a gentile who had harvested his field and afterward converted--

    B.   [the produce he had harvested] is exempt from [the restrictions of] (1) gleanings, (2) the forgotten sheaf, and (3) <u>peah</u>, [for at the time of harvest, when the produce would have become subject to designation, the gentile had not yet converted].

C. R. Judah obligates [the convert] to [obey the law of the] forgotten sheaf,

D. since [the law of the] forgotten sheaf applies only after the [conclusion of the] binding [process, which takes place after the gentile has converted].

M. 4:6 (Y. Peah 4:6 [18c]; Sifra Qid. 1:6 [Weiss, p. 87a]; Sifre Deut. #282 [Finkelstein-Horowitz, p. 298])

Only produce owned by Israelites at the time of harvesting is subject to the designation of poor-offerings. This is the moment the householder claims the food for himself, and so is required to set aside a portion for the poor. The gentile at A-B need not designate poor-offerings, because when the produce would have become subject to the law he had not yet converted. Judah (C-D) endorses this basic theory, but disputes a point of fact concerning forgotten sheaves (B2). He notes that the law of the forgotten sheaf takes effect only after the grain is bound into sheaves (see M. 5:8). Since the gentile already has converted by this time, Judah says he must obey the restrictions of the law.

T. 2:9

I. A. [As regards] a gentile who sold his standing [crop] to an Israelite for harvesting--

B. [the produce that the Israelite harvests] is subject to [designation as] peah.

II. C. [As for] an Israelite who sold his standing [crop] to a gentile for harvesting--

D. [the produce that the gentile harvests] is exempt from [designation as] peah.

III. E. [As for] an Israelite and a gentile who share [ownership] of a standing [crop]--

F. the portion that belongs to the Israelite is subject to [designation as] peah,

G. and the portion that belongs to the gentile is exempt from [designation as] peah.

H. R. Simeon says, "[As regards] an Israelite and a gentile who share [ownership] of a standing [crop]--

I. "[the entire crop] is exempt from designation as peah.

J. "Under what circumstances does this apply?

K. "[It applies] if the gentile protests [the designation of part of the field's produce as peah].

L. "But if the gentile does not protest, [the produce of the entire field] is subject to [designation as] peah."

The triplet at A-B, C-D and E-G+H-L clarifies M. 4:6's point that only produce owned and harvested by an Israelite is subject to designation as peah. It is of no concern who plants and tends the crop, whether Israelite or gentile. The quite simple rules at A-B and C-D point toward E-L, which complete the triplet by carrying forward its principle for an ambiguous case concerning an Israelite and a gentile who together own a single field. Two distinct views of joint ownership stand behind the disputing opinions (E-F+G,

H-I+J-L). The first, E-G, holds that the Israelite and the gentile independently have full ownership of distinct parts of the field. In essence the tract of land constitutes two separate fields. For this reason, the produce that the Israelite harvests is subject to designation as <u>peah</u>, while that of the gentile is not. Simeon (H-L) disagrees, claiming that the Israelite and the gentile each are partial owners of the whole.[14] Since he conceives of the entire tract of land as a single entity, all of its produce is part subject and part exempt. Accordingly, none of the produce need by designated as <u>peah</u> if the gentile protests.

T. 2:10

- A. [As regards] a gentile who died, and Israelites divided his property--
- B. he who takes possession of [the unharvested produce] that is attached to the ground is responsible [for designating all offerings for the poor].
- C. [He who takes possession of] the harvested produce is exempt from all [responsibility to designate produce for the poor].
- D. If he took possession of the standing crop, he is exempt from the law of gleanings, forgotten sheaves and <u>peah</u>, but is responsible for the designation of tithes.

A-C again illustrate the principle that produce is subject to designation for the poor only if an Israelite owns and harvests it (see M. 4:6). Ownership alone, however, is not sufficient (C)--the Israelite must harvest the grain. In this context, D makes no sense and should be deleted. It contradicts B, stating that unharvested produce an Israelite claims and harvests is <u>not</u> subject to designation for the poor.

Harmonizing D with B, Lieberman states that these two rules refer to different situations (TK, p. 150). In his view, "attached to the ground" (B) means that the Israelite takes possession of the land along with the produce. In this case, <u>peah</u> must be designated. D merely refers to "standing produce," meaning that the farmer does not claim any land at all. Since he does not own a field, says Lieberman, he need not designate <u>peah</u>, gleanings, or forgotten sheaves. He must designate tithes, however, since one is responsible for this separation whether or not one owns the field in which the produce grew. Lieberman's explanation is not convincing. Elsewhere in Tosefta the phrases "attached to the ground" and "standing crop" are used interchangeably. For example, T. 2:9A-B states that "standing produce" is subject to <u>peah</u>. This is exactly what the present pericope says about produce that is "attached to the ground."

4:7-8

I.
- A. [If] one dedicated [to the Temple] a standing [crop], and then redeemed [that same] standing [crop]--
- B. [the produce he redeems] is subject [to the restrictions of the forgotten sheaf, after it is bound].[15]

II.	C.	[If he dedicated to the Temple a crop that had been bound into] sheaves, and then redeemed [that same crop while it still was bound into] sheaves--
	D.	[the produce he redeems] is subject [to the restrictions of the forgotten sheaf].
III.	E.	[But if he dedicated to the Temple] a standing [crop], and then redeemed [that same crop after it was bound into] sheaves--
	F.	[the produce he redeems] is exempt [from the restrictions of the forgotten sheaf],
	G.	for at the moment [when, under ordinary circumstances, the grain would become] subject [to the restrictions of the forgotten sheaf, the crop] was exempt, [because the Temple owned it].

M. 4:7

I.	H.	Similarly, [as regards] one who dedicated [to the Temple] his produce before it became subject to [the separation of] tithes, and then redeemed it, [again, before the produce was subject to the separation of tithes]--
	I.	[the produce he redeems] is subject [to the separation of tithes].
II.	J.	[If he dedicated to the Temple his crop] after it became subject to [the separation of] tithes, and then redeemed it--
	K.	[the produce he redeems] is subject [to the separation of tithes].
III.	L.	[But if] he dedicated [to the Temple his crop] before it had been processed [i.e., before it reached the point when it normally would become subject to the separation of tithes]^{16}, and then the [Temple]-treasurer processed it, and still later the householder redeemed it--
	M.	[the produce he redeems] is exempt [from the separation of tithes],
	N.	for at the moment [when the produce, under ordinary circumstances, would become] subject to [the separation of] tithes, it was exempt, [because the Temple owned it].

M. 4:8 (M. Ḥal. 3:4; T. Maas. 1:7; Y. Maas. 1:1 [48d], 1:4 [49a], 5:3 [52a]; Y. Ḥal. 2:5 [58a]; B. Men. 66b; Sifre Num. Nasa 5 [Horowitz, p. 8])

Only produce owned by Israelites at the moment of binding can become subject to the law of the forgotten sheaf (M. 4:6). In the first two cases of the triplet before us (A-B, C-D), the farmer owns the produce at this crucial moment when the law of the forgotten sheaf takes effect (see Judah's lemma, M. 4:6C-D).[17] As a result, the grain is subject to the restrictions of the law, despite the fact that the Temple owned it either immediately before or after this time. In the concluding case (E-F+G), however, the Temple possesses the grain when it is bound into sheaves, so that the law never applies. The food cannot fall into the category of forgotten sheaves, even if later redeemed by an Israelite and then forgotten in the field.

A parallel triplet regarding tithes (H-I, J-K, L-M+N) reviews the main principle that only an Israelite's produce is subject to the law. Although this second unit is topically unrelated to the law of the forgotten sheaf, it is included here because it makes exactly the same point.

4:9

A. [As regards a rich] person who picked [some of the produce designated as] peah, and said, "Lo, this is for Mr. So-and-so, who is poor"--
B. R. Eliezer says, "[He] has acquired it for [the poor person]."
C. But sages say, "Let [him] give [the produce] to the first available poor person."
D. Gleanings, forgotten sheaves, and peah, [designated from a field] belonging to a gentile, are subject to [the separation of] tithes,
E. unless [the gentile] has declared them ownerless property.

M. 4:9 (Y. Peah 5:2 [18d]; B. Git. 11b, 47a; B. B.M. 9b)

In the first of two items (A-C, D-E), Eliezer and sages dispute whether or not a householder may acquire peah on a poor person's behalf. This issue is important, as we recall (M. 4:1-2), because householders ordinarily have no right to harvest and allocate produce designated for the poor.[18] Mishnah's authors present us with two distinct viewpoints. If a farmer were to gather some of the peah, he might be viewed as interfering in the distribution process. Accordingly, sages (C) rule that the farmer has no right to take the produce in the first place, and must turn it over to the first poor person who comes along. Eliezer (B), on the other hand, sees the farmer as an agent who may gather on a specific poor person's behalf all produce to which the poor are entitled.[19]

The quite separate rule that follows (D-E) points out an important difference between the poor-offerings of gentiles and Israelites (see M. 4:6). Gentiles are not required to designate poor-offerings at all. Food that they donate to the poor therefore has the status of ordinary produce. Unlike offerings properly designated by an Israelite, therefore, tithes must be removed from a gentile's gift (D).[20] The gloss at E, however, claims that a gentile may renounce ownership of food that he wishes to give to the poor. Like all ownerless produce, of course, such grain is exempt from the separation of tithes (see M. 1:6, M. Maas. 1:1).

T. 2:11

A. Gleanings, forgotten sheaves, and peah [designated from a field] belonging to a gentile are subject to [the separation of] tithes (M. 4:9D).
B. Under what circumstances [is produce that a gentile designates for the poor subject to tithes]?
C. [It is subject] if the gentile protests [when someone other that the poor, to whom he intended to give the produce, takes it]. [In the case the gentile clearly does not consider the produce ownerless, but reserved for the poor alone. Hence, the food remains subject to the separation of tithes.]

D. But if the gentile does not protest, [but allows anyone to take the produce he designated for the poor],
E. the property that a gentile has set aside as ownerless is deemed ownerless property,
F. and is exempt from [the separation of] tithes.

Tosefta qualifies M. 4:9D, by restating the point of M. 4:9E. Produce that a gentile designates for the poor is deemed ownerless only if the gentile allows anyone, rich or poor alike, to take it. But if he attempts to prevent the rich from taking the food, it is not deemed ownerless and so is subject to the separation of tithes.

4:10

A. What [produce is in the status of] gleanings (see Lev. 19:9)?
B. That which falls [to the ground] during the harvest.
C. [If a householder] was harvesting [his field, and] harvested an armful, [or] plucked a handful,
D. [and] a thorn pricked him so that [the produce] fell from his hand to the ground--
E. lo, [this produce] belongs to the householder.
I. F. [Produce that falls from] within the [householder's] hand, or [from] within his sickle, [i.e., that which he already has taken into his possession],
G. belongs to the poor.
II. H. [Produce that falls from] the back of the [householder's] hand, or [from] the back of his sickle, [i.e., the produce fell before the householder took possession of it],
I. belongs to the householder.
III. J. [As regards produce that falls from] the tip of the [householder's] hand, or [from] the tip of his sickle--
K. R. Ishmael says, "[Such produce] belongs to the poor."
L. R. Aqiba says, "[It] belongs to the householder."

M. 4:10 (B. Beṣ. 35b; Sifra Qid. 2:5)

Gleanings are defined as produce that the householder first acquires and then drops completely by accident. That is to say, by grasping or cutting an individual stalk of grain the farmer brings it within the system of the law. Should he then drop this stalk of grain, it enters the status of gleanings. The three segments of the unit before us (A-B, C-E, F-L) clarify this definition, and I take up each in turn.

The broad introduction at A-B limits the category of gleanings to grain dropped during the harvest.[21] As we have seen elsewhere, only the farmer's act in taking the produce can evoke God's complementary claim upon it. This simple rule sets the stage for the two secondary rules that follow.

Grain that the householder is caused to drop by some external force, such as the thorn at C-E, does not fall into the category of gleanings. Rather, only that which falls to

Peah Chapter Four 83

the ground completely by chance is subject to the law.[22] Underlying this rule is the notion that produce that drops due to no identifiable force has been separated for the poor by God. Hence the householder in no way determines what food the poor receive as gleanings, for this category is determined completely at random.[23]

The triplet at F-L goes over the same ground as A-B. Only that which the farmer already has cut with his sickle or grasped with his hand, and then drops, is subject to the law (F-G, H-I).[24] The triplet culminates in the dispute at J-K+L, which arises because it is unclear whether or not the householder had fully acquired the produce before it fell. Ishmael's theory (K) is that the farmer must not misappropriate food designated for the poor. Since any of the grain lying on the ground might have the status of gleanings, he rules that all of it must be given to the poor. Aqiba (L) disputes this point. He holds that the stalks on the ground cannot be gleanings, for the householder never finally established his ownership of them. This grain therefore need not be given to the poor.

T. 2:3

A. [As regards] workers who were harvesting [such that the produce that normally would fall to the ground as gleanings fell instead] into their baskets--

B. lo, [the poor] may remove [the produce that normally would be in the status of gleanings].

Tosefta makes the simple point that farm hands may not perform their chores in a manner that cheats the poor out of what is rightfully theirs.[25]

T. 2:13

I. A. [There are] four[26] gifts [that must be designated for the poor] from [the produce of] a vineyard:
    B. (1) separated grapes, (2) forgotten sheaves, (3) peah, (4) and defective clusters.
II. C. [There are] three [gifts that must be designated for the poor] from grain:
    D. (1) gleanings, (2) forgotten sheaves, (3) and peah.
III. E. [There are] two [gifts that must be designated for the poor] from [the fruit of] a tree:
    F. (1) forgotten sheaves, (2) and peah.
    G. None of these [gifts to the poor] may [be given to a specific poor person] as a favor.
    H. Even a poor Israelite--they take [any] produce [given to him as a favor] from his hand.
    I. But any other gifts, [which are designated for] the priesthood (š'r mtnwt hqhwnh),
    J. such as the shoulder, the two cheeks, and the stomach, [of sacrificial animals, which are unconsecrated, and given as simple gifts] (cf. Deut. 18:3),
    K. may [be given to a specific priest] as a favor.

84 Support for the Poor

L. And the householder may give them to whichever priest he wishes.
M. They may not take a priestly [gift] from a priest [to whom it has been given as a favor], nor a Levitical [gift] from a Levite [to whom it has been given as a favor].

Tosefta introduces the second half of the tractate (M. 4:10-8:9) by listing those offerings that form the topic of discussion in the upcoming chapters: gleanings (M. 4:10-5:6), forgotten sheaves (M. 5:7-7:2), separated grapes (M. 7:3), defective clusters (M. 7:4-9), and poorman's tithe (M. 8:1-9). Accordingly, this pericope is an example of Tosefta as a redactional commentary that views the Mishnah-tractate as a whole.

The lists at A-B, C-D, and E-F, in descending numerical progression (4,3,2), set up the main point of the unit (G-H, I-M). Gifts to the priesthood and to the poor differ from each other in an important way. Gifts to the poor must be distributed entirely at random, as if by God (cf. M. 4:10C-E). This random distribution characterizes all gifts that have a santified status--since God alone determines what produce is sanctified, these offerings must be designated and distributed solely by chance. In the present case, therefore, the householder may not give poor-offerings to chosen individuals because he has no right to influence the distribution process. This is not the case with unconsecrated gifts to the priests. Since these offerings are not holy, they do not require random distribution and the householder may give them to any priest he chooses.[27]

T. 2:14

A. <u>What [produce is deemed to be in the status of] gleanings?</u> That which falls to the ground during the harvest (hqṣyr) (M. 4:10A-B),
B. [and that which falls to the ground] during [random] plucking (htlyšh).
C. R. Yosé says, "Gleanings are produce that falls to the ground during the harvest alone,
D. "as it is stated [in Scripture], 'You shall not collect the gleanings of your harvest (qṣyrkh)'" (Lev. 19:9).

B extends M. 4:10A-B, claiming that produce which falls to the ground during any picking activity is in the status of gleanings. Yosé (C-D) disputes this extension. Since Scripture explicitly refers only to harvesting, only produce which falls during the harvest belongs to the poor.

T. 2:15

I. A. A single [cut] stalk [lying] among the [as yet uncut], standing [crop],
B. lo, it belongs to the householder [i.e., it is not in the status of gleanings] (cf. M. 4:10H-I).
II. C. [A single cut stalk lying] in the [already] harvested area,
D. lo, it belongs to the poor [i.e., it is by definition in the status of gleanings] (cf. M. 4:10F-G).

III. E. [A single cut stalk lying] half in the standing [crop], and half in the [already] harvested area--
F. [the worker] picks it up and throws it behind him [into the already harvested area as a gleaning] (cf. M. 4:10J-K),
G. for [produce concerning which there is] a doubt about its status as gleanings [in fact is deemed to be in the status of] gleanings (šspq lqṭ lqṭ).

Tosefta's triplet goes over the same ground as M. 4:10F-L. It adjudicates the dispute between Ishmael and Aqiba (M. 4:10J-L) in favor of Ishmael. Produce in an ambiguous status must be given to the poor in order to prevent others from misappropriating this food (G).

4:11

A. [As regards] ant-holes in the midst of a standing [crop]--
B. lo, [grains of produce that the ants carry into them][28] belong to the householder, [because they are not deemed to be gleanings].
C. After the harvesters [have gone through the field],
D. the [grains of produce at the] tops [of the ant-holes] belong to the poor, while the [grains of produce at the] bottoms [of the antholes] belong to the householder.
E. R. Meir says, "All [grains of produce found in ant-holes after the harvesters have gone through the field] belong to the poor,
F. "for [all produce concerning which there is] a doubt about its status as gleanings [in fact is deemed to be in the status of] gleanings (šspq lqṭ lqṭ)."

M. 4:11 (B. Ḥul. 134a; Sifra Qid. 3:7; Sifre Deut. 283 [Horowitz, p. 300])

Produce that ants carry off is not in the status of gleanings (A-B) because the farmer neither harvested nor dropped it (see M. 4:10A-E). This straightforward rule draws in its wake the dispute at C-D vs. E-F. On one hand, produce found in ant-holes after the harvest has been completed may have been brought there by the ants, and so be exempt from designation as gleanings. On the other hand, during the harvest the householder himself may have dropped the grain, so it should be given to the poor as gleanings.[29] This case of doubt sets the stage for two theories, already familiar from M. 4:10J-L. First, C-D hold that only produce that unquestionably is gleanings need be given to the poor (cf. Aqiba's lemma, M. 4:10L). This grain is found at the tops of ant-holes where the harvester dropped it. Food located at the bottoms of the ant-holes, by contrast, must have been carried off by the ants and is exempt. Second, Meir (E-F) claims that all produce found in ant-holes could have been dropped by the householder. In order to prevent misappropriation of this food, any of which might in fact have the status of gleanings, all of it must be given to the poor (cf. Ishmael's lemma, M. 4:10K).[30]

T. 2:16

A. [Grain carried by ants into] ant-holes is forbidden [to the poor under the law of] robbery (M. 4:11A).
B. But if the householder declares such produce ownerless property, it is permitted [to the poor] with respect to [the law of] robbery.
C. R. Simeon b. Eleazar says, "If [it is likely that the poor will] damage[31] [the field while they collect the produce from the ant-holes],
D. "[the produce is] forbidden [to the poor under the law of] robbery."

T. 2:16

Tosefta takes up a separate issue with regard to grain found in ant-holes (M. 4:11). Produce that the ants take belongs to the householder. The poor may not take it because this would constitute robbery (A). Nonetheless, produce that the householder declares ownerless (B) is legally accessible to the poor, as is all ownerless property.

Simeon's lemma (C-D) is included here because it too treats the issue of robbery. Interpreted in context, it rules that the poor must not damage the field when collecting ownerless property because this would be considered robbery.

CHAPTER FIVE
PEAH CHAPTER FIVE

The tractate's discussion of gleanings continues in the opening unit (M. 5:1-2) by addressing a fundamental problem. What happens if food in the status of gleanings becomes mixed with ordinary produce, so that we cannot tell which stalks of grain should be given to the poor? One possible answer, presented at M. 5:1A-C and 5:2G, is that the farmer must give to the poor all produce in a doubtful status. By giving the poor all such grain, householders take care not to misappropriate for themselves food that has been set aside exclusively for the poor. According to this theory, gleanings are analogous to sanctified offerings. That is to say, grain in the status of gleanings is materially reserved for the poor, just as the substance of heave-offering, eo ipse, is consecrated for the priests alone.[1] An alternative is offered at M. 5:1D-E and 5:2H-L. Here the poor have no claim upon those particular stalks of grain that fell to the ground as gleanings. Instead, the farmer may give them any food of equal value, that is, a similar quantity of grain that is exempt from the separation of tithes. The governing analogy for gleanings, according to this theory, is presented by second tithe, which the farmer may exchange for other produce of equal value.[2]

The discussion of gleanings is closed by a short section (M. 5:3-6) that reiterates the point of M. 4:1-5. All poor people must have equal access to the produce set aside for them by God. Poor field-owners therefore may not collect the offerings that are set aside from their own fields while they harvest. This would deprive others of their right to a fair portion of the food. In context, this section also functions as a transition. By shifting the discussion to a topic applicable to all poor-offerings, it prepares for the chapter's final unit (M. 5:7-8).

The law of the forgotten sheaf (M. 5:7-7:2) is based on Deut. 24:19, "When you reap your harvest in your field, and have forgotten a sheaf in the field, you shall not go back to get it. It shall be for the sojourner, the fatherless, and the widow." Mishnah's framers here focus their attention on two issues, the definition of forgetting and of a sheaf. M. 5:7 makes the point that if anyone involved in harvesting and binding the grain remembers that a sheaf remains in the field, by definition it cannot enter the category of the forgotten sheaf. The poor are entitled only to what all forget. Moreover, the law does not apply to sheaves that the householder leaves behind because the poor have hidden them. Since the farmer and his workers are constrained to forget such sheaves, they cannot be deemed subject to the law. The underlying notion, familiar from the laws of gleanings (cf. M. 4:10), is that the poor have a claim only upon what is left behind entirely by chance. If some identifiable force causes the householder to forget a sheaf, we need not give the grain to the poor. This is because the sheaf was set aside not by God, but by some other cause (in this case, by the poor themselves). M. 5:8 completes the picture, clarifying the definition of a sheaf. Farmers bind loose stalks of grain into sheaves for easy transportation to the threshing floor.[3] Once at the threshing floor, however, they break apart these sheaves for storage or threshing. Only during the span of time between the conclusion of the binding process and the beginning of threshing does the produce fall into the category of sheaves. Only at this time, therefore, can the produce become subject to the law of the forgotten sheaf. An exception to this rule (M. 5:8A-D) concerns a householder who binds produce into sheaves, but does not yet wish to take the bundles to the threshing floor. Rather, he intends to use them in the field. Since he purposely leaves these sheaves behind and does not forget them, of course the law does not apply.

Let us now place this unit of law within the unfolding structure of the tractate as a whole. In the previous discussions, we have learned that peah and gleanings consist of produce that the farmer owns, but never takes into his possession. This principle also underlies the law of the forgotten sheaf. In this case, the farmer has claimed a quantity of grain for himself by binding it into sheaves. Nevertheless, some of these sheaves remain outside his possession for he forgets to bring them to his threshing floor. This produce is set aside through no conscious act of the farmer, but at random. Only that which he forgets entirely by accident must be given to the poor. Like peah and gleanings, therefore, forgotten sheaves share an anomalous status, owned but not possessed. This food must be given to the poor, those under God's special care.

5:1

A. [As regards] a heap [of grain piled in the field, such that gleanings] have not been collected underneath it (šl' lqṭ tḥtw), [that is, before the grain was piled, some gleanings remained uncollected in the field, so that now there is a doubt whether the produce at the bottom of the heap is gleanings left from before the grain was piled, or common produce from the grain-heap]--
B. whatever [grain] touches the ground,
C. lo, this belongs to the poor.
D. [As regards] wind that [breaks apart and] scatters [over an area from which gleanings have not yet been collected] sheaves [from which gleanings have already been removed, once again creating a doubt concerning the status of all of the produce in the field]--
E. they estimate the amount [of gleanings the field] is likely to produce, and give [this amount of food] to the poor.
F. Rabban Simeon b. Gamaliel says, "One gives to the poor [the amount of grain] needed to sow [the entire field] (kdy npylh)."[4]

M. 5:1 (Y. Sheq. 1:2 [46a]; B. B.M. 105b)

An ambiguity arises if gleanings that remain uncollected in the field become mixed together with ordinary produce. In the two cases before us, this happens when the householder piles common grain on top of the gleanings (A-C), or when the wind scatters

Peah Chapter Five

some ordinary produce throughout an area containing gleanings (D-E). All of the grain lying on the ground now has a doubtful status, because the poor might have a claim on each individual stalk. Hence, it is unclear what part of the mixture the poor should receive as gleanings. The two parallel cases present distinct answers to this problem. At A-C the poor are entitled to receive both the gleanings themselves and any other produce in a doubtful status. At D-E, by contrast, they receive ordinary grain that has the same value as the gleanings, but they do not receive the very stalks lost in the mixture. How do we account for these two inconsistent solutions to a single dilemma? One possibility, presented by Y. 5:1[18d], is that the cases in fact refer to two different situations. The householder at A-C acted improperly, by piling his grain on top of the poor's gleanings. Since he thereby prevents the poor from easily gathering their food, he is penalized and must hand over to the poor all grain in an ambiguous status. At D-E, however, the wind, not the householder, causes the mixture of produce. We need not penalize the farmer because at all times he acted properly. Accordingly, he gives to the poor only the amount of food that they lost in the mixture.

If we closely examine the language of these rules, however, a further possibility presents itself. The cases formally are dissimilar and so probably express two different principles. We note that neither the protases (A, D) nor apodoses (B-C, E) share common syntactic traits or repeat phrases. It thus seems likely that the two cases present different conceptions of the character of produce in the status of gleanings. On the one hand, this grain might be materially consecrated for the poor alone (A-C). If so, the poor must receive precisely those stalks that fell to the earth as gleanings. To assure that they get this particular food, the householder must give them both the gleanings themselves and any produce in an ambiguous status. Since any of the grain underneath the heap at A-C might be gleanings, all of it must be given to the poor. According to this theory, gleanings are entirely analogous to sanctified offerings, which physically are reserved for the priests alone. In the case at D-E, on the other hand, only the value of the stalks that were lost is reserved for the poor. The gleanings themselves need not be given to them.

Simeon's lemma (F) explains how much food the householder must give to the poor, as specified at D-E. He claims that the poor must receive as gleanings the amount of grain needed to sow the field, 1/45 of the yield.[5] Presumably, this represents the amount of grain that the average harvester drops while reaping a field.

5:2

A. [As regards] a single stalk [of unharvested grain that stands] in [an area of land that already has been] harvested,

B. the top of which [single stalk] is as tall as the standing [crop next to it, so that the stalk perhaps appears to be part of the standing crop],

C. if [that stalk] is harvested at the same time as the standing [crop],

D. lo, it belongs to the householder, [that is, it is not deemed a gleaning].

E. But if [the stalk is] not [harvested at all, but remains standing after the harvest of the entire field is completed],

F. lo, it belongs to the poor, [that is, it is deemed a gleaning].

G. [As regards] a single stalk [of grain that is in the status of] gleanings [such that it belongs to the poor and is exempt from the separation of tithes], that was mixed with a heap [of grain that is not in the status of gleanings, and so is subject to the separation of tithes]--

H. [with the goal of returning to the poor person that one lost stalk, the householder must follow this procedure: He takes two other stalks of grain from the pile, and sets aside one for the poor. From the second, he] designates the tithes [required for the first] stalk, and then gives [that first stalk, now exempt from the separation of tithes], to a poor person. [This assures that the poor receive in exchange for the original stalk in the status of gleanings the proper amount of grain, one full stalk from which tithes need not be separated].[6]

I. Said R. Eliezer, "But how can this poor person [receive] anything in exhange for [something that] had not yet come into his possession, [namely, the original stalk in the status of gleanings]?

J. "Rather, one transfers to the poor person [partial ownership of] the entire heap [of grain, so that now the poor person owns the stalk that was mixed in]. [Since he has acquired ownership of the gleaning, he now may trade it for a stalk of common produce.

K. [To this end, the householder must follow the procedure outlined at G.] He designates the tithes [required for] one stalk [of grain], and then gives [another stalk to a poor person].

M. 5:2 (M. Ed. 2:4; Sifre Deut. #283 [Horowitz, p. 300])

The two distinct units redacted together treat a common topic, cases of ambiguity regarding a single stalk of grain. Since they raise different issues, however, let us consider each separately. At A-E, we deal with a single stalk that the harvester has passed by and left uncut. This stalk now stands near the remaining, unharvested portion of the crop. This poses a problem, for the stalk shares some, but not all, of the features of gleanings. On the one hand, the farmer accidentally has left it behind just like produce in the status of gleanings (cf. M. 4:10C-E). On the other hand, the stalk never was cut and claimed, and so cannot be subject to the law (cf. M. 4:10F-L). The contrasting rules at C-D and E-F make the point that the harvester's actions resolve the doubtful status of this grain.[7] If he cuts the stalk along with the other produce standing nearby, it is deemed part of that crop and the poor have no claim upon it.[8] But if, when reaping the remainder of the field, the householder still does not take the stalk for himself, the poor may take it as a gleaning.[9]

The second unit (G-K) focuses upon a single stalk in the status of gleanings that becomes mixed into a pile of common produce, a situation familiar from M. 5:1. This stalk imposes a doubtful status upon the entire heap, because we no longer can tell which stalk is the gleaning that belongs to the poor. How do we assure that the poor receive what is due them? The dispute at G-H vs. I-K presents two opposing theories. The first

(G-H) claims that the poor need not receive the original stalk in the status of gleanings. Rather, the farmer may give them another stalk of equal value (cf. M. 5:1D-E). The poor therefore must receive a full stalk of grain that is exempt from the separation of tithes like the stalk which they lost in the pile. Accordingly, as outlined at H, the householder must separate tithes from one stalk on behalf of a second, and give the second, full stalk to the poor. Eliezer (I-K) objects to this solution. He claims that the original stalk in the status of gleanings is reserved exclusively for the poor (cf. M. 5:1A-C). As a result, the householder has no right to claim it for himself and to substitute other grain for it. Because the farmer does not know which particular stalk belongs to the poor person, he must transfer to him partial ownership of the entire grain-heap. Once the poor person has acquired partial ownership of the entire pile, including the gleaning that was lost, he may trade the stalk for ordinary produce on behalf of which tithes already have been separated. Once again, this assures that the poor person receives fair value for the stalk in the status of gleanings that fell into the grain pile.

T. 2:19

A. "From what point in time do they burn the stubble that lies in the field?
B. "In a shadeless field (śdh lbn) [they burn the straw] until Passover.
C. "but in orchard, [they burn the straw] until the New Year,
D. "In a field dependent on irrigation (Jastrow, II, p. 1580, s.v. slḥ iii) they may burn the straw immediately," the opinion of R. Judah.
E. But sages say, "In a shadeless field [they burn the straw] until Pentecost.
F. "In an orchard, [they burn the straw] at New Year,
G. "because of the robbery of men and cattle.
H. "In a field dependent on irrigation, [they burn the straw] immediately."

Tosefta here represents a case in which the householder should act generously, by letting the poor take any straw that remains in his field after the harvest. At issue is how long the farmer must wait for the poor to take this produce before he burns the entire field in preparation for planting the next year's crop. Judah (B-E) and sages (F-I) dispute the appropriate time for different types of fields. Judah claims that the farmer must wait until he is ready to plough the field; only then may he prepare the land by burning the stubble. This gives the poor ample opportunity to gather the straw. Sages claim that the farmer must allow the poor access to the straw for a longer period of time, until Pentecost. This prevents the householder from "stealing" the sustenance provided by the straw from the poor and from the animals who graze in the fields.

T. 2:21

A. Single stalks [that remain unharvested] among stubble [in an area that already has been harvested] or in fields [that already have been harvested] (cf. M. 5:2A)--

92   Support for the Poor

- B. lo, these belong to the householder.
- C. Said R. Aqiba, "With regard to this [sort of produce] householders usually are generous, [with the result that they usually leave the stalks for the poor].

Tosefta claims that single stalks that remain unharvested by definition belong to the householder (cf. M. 5:2A-C). The grain cannot enter the status of gleanings, because the worker neither harvested nor dropped it. Aqiba (C) agrees in principle, but not in practice. Although the stalks do not fall into the category of gleanings, he claims that householders should give them to the poor as a generous gift.

5:3

- A. "They may not turn a water wheel[10] [in order to irrigate a field, until after the poor have collected their produce]," the opinion of R. Meir [This is because irrigation will make the field so muddy that the poor will have difficulty collecting their produce.][11]
- B. But sages permit [irrigation before the poor have collected their produce], because it [still] is possible, [though difficult, for the poor to gather what is theirs].[12]

M. 5:3 (M. Par. 6:1)

This dispute focuses on whether or not a farmer may tend his field in a manner that makes it difficult for the poor to collect their offerings. Meir (A) holds that the poor possess an inviolable right to gather the food without difficulty. The farmer thus is forbidden to irrigate until they have finished collecting the poor-offerings. Sages (B), by contrast, rule that the farmer may perform any agricultural activity so long as he does not make it impossible for the poor to take their grain. He therefore is allowed to irrigate, for this poses no insurmountable obstacle to the poor.

T. 2:20

- A. One who irrigates his field before[13] the poor have entered it [to collect the produce designated for them] (cf. M. 5:3)--
- B. if the damage [that the water will cause] to [the householder's produce] is greater than [the damage to the produce that] belongs to the poor, [the irrigation] is permitted.
- C. But if the damage [that the water will cause to the produce that] belongs to the poor is greater than [the damage to the householder's] own [produce, the irrigation] is forbidden.
- D. R. Judah says, "Either way (byn kk wbyn kk),
- E. [the householder] must collect the produce that belongs to the poor, and set it on the fence,
- F. "and the poor person comes and takes that which belongs to him."

Irrigation poses a problem not dealt with in Mishnah, in that the water damages and rots produce remaining in the field. Tosefta's point is that this damage must not fall disproportionately to the poor. Thus, irrigation is permitted only if the householder is willing to suffer a greater loss to his own produce than that which he causes to the poor's produce (A-C). Judah (D-E) solves this problem in another way. In line with M. 4:1-2, he allows the householder to interfere in the distribution of poor-offerings to prevent damage to his own property. The householder simply moves the poor's produce to a dry place and then irrigates, preventing damage both to their produce and to his field.

5:4

A. "[As regards] a householder who was travelling from one place to another,

B. "and [because he had no money with him] he needed to collect gleanings, forgotten sheaves, peah, or poorman's tithe,

C. "let him collect [what he needs].

D. "But when he returns to his home, he must repay [the amount of produce he took as a poor person]," the opinion of R. Eliezer.

E. But sages say, "[He need repay nothing, because] he was a poor person when [he collected produce designated for the poor]."

M. 5:4 (B. Hul. 130b)

At issue is how we determine who is entitled to collect poor-offerings. Do we consider a person's total wealth, or only the assets he has available at the moment he collects the produce? Eliezer (A-C+D) holds that the householder's net worth is decisive. By this criterion, the farmer is not poor and is not entitled to take the food for free. He must repay whatever he legitimately collects because of temporary need, as if it were a loan. Sages (E) dispute this claim. In their view we consider only the householder's immediately available assets. He was a poor person when he collected the poor-offerings, and so need never pay for this food. The pericope belongs in Chapter Eight, which contains the tractate's definition of a poor person. I cannot account for its inclusion at this point in the tractate.

5:5

A. One who trades [untithed produce for food in the status of poor-offerings owned by] poor people (hmḥlyp ^{c}m h^{c}nyym)--

B. that which [the rich man acquires from the poor remains in the status of poor-offerings and] exempt [from the separation of tithes].[14]

C. And that which the poor [acquire from the rich man remains private property and] subject [to the separation of tithes].

D. [As regards] two [poor men] who [independently] contracted to sharecrop [separate halves of a single] field, [and so become partial owners of those parts of the field respectively]--

E. one of them may give to the other the poorman's tithe [from his part of the field], and this other person may give to the former the poorman's tithe [from his part of the field].

F. One who contracts to harvest a field
G. is forbidden [to take for himself] gleanings, forgotten sheaves, peah, or poorman's tithe, [designated from that field].
H. Said R. Judah, "Under what circumstances does [the rule at F-G] apply?
I. "[It applies] if [the laborer] contracted with [the householder to harvest the field and be paid] one-half, one-third, or one-fourth [of the entire yield]. [In these cases, the harvester becomes a partial owner of the entire crop, and so may not gather its produce as poor-offerings.]
J. "But if [the householder] said to him, 'A third of [the produce] that you harvest [and bring to the threshing floor] shall belong to you [as your payment],'
K. "[the laborer] is permitted [to take for himself] gleanings, forgotten sheaves, and peah, [designated from that field]. [Since these offerings never are brought to the threshing floor, the worker has no claim of ownership upon them.]
L. "But he is forbidden [to take for himself] poorman's tithe [designated from that field, since this is designated at the threshing floor]. [This produce, of course, is partly owned by the worker.]

M. 5:5 (Y. Peah 2:5 [17b])

Two units (A-C, D-L) deal with various ways in which ownership might determine how the laws of poor-offerings apply. Since they present entirely different principles, however, we take them up separately. In the first case (A-C) grain in the status of poor-offerings has been given by the poor to a rich person. We wish to know whether the food now becomes subject to the separation of tithes like other produce owned by ordinary householders. The matched pair at B and C claim that the food retains its status as gleanings, peah, or forgotten sheaves, even though the poor no longer own it. It therefore remains exempt from the separation of tithes. That is, once the poor have claimed the offerings they may do anything with them that they wish, even sell them to the rich. Since the produce remains exempt from the separation of tithes, the poor gain a monetary advantage. The food they sell is worth more in the market place.

The principle underlying the second unit (D-L) is that a poor person may not collect poor-offerings designated from a field that he owns in whole or in part.[15] This assures that poor people neither can hoard these offerings nor can prevent others from having fair access to them (cf. M. 4:1-4). Two distinct cases (D-E, F-G+H-L) present this principle. The first concerns a sharecropper who receives a fixed portion of the entire crop he contracts to harvest.[16] Since he now claims partial ownership of the entire field, he may not collect poor-offerings designated from it. If, however, two sharecroppers harvest separate halves of a field (D-E), they may exchange poorman's tithe. Each will receive produce that grew in a field he does not own. This is permitted. A second case (F-G), independent of the first claims that any poor worker is forbidden to gather poor-offerings from a field that he harvests, whether or not he has a partial claim on the field. Such a harvester would have an unfair advantage over others because he could gather the offerings for himself while he harvested on the householder's behalf. In its present context, however, this rule sets up Judah's gloss at H-L, which returns us to the issue of ownership. The contractor at I is paid a fixed portion of the crop and so becomes partial owner of the entire yield. He thus cannot gather poor-offerings from that field. What happens if he has arranged to receive a portion only of that which he actually reaps and brings to the threshing floor (J-K)? In this case, he has no claim of ownership on offerings that remain in the field, such as peah, gleanings, and forgotten sheaves. Therefore he may gather them for himself. Only poorman's tithe would be forbidden to him (L). This offering is designated at the threshing floor from grain that the contractor partially owns because he has returned it to the householder.

T. 2:4

A. A householder may not take [for himself] gleanings from the poor,
B. [even if he makes] the provision [that, in place of the gleanings, he will let them] collect [the produce that falls to the ground] during the binding process.

The householder at A wishes to exchange gleanings for common produce (cf. M. 5:5 A-C). He wants to collect the grain that falls as gleanings for himself, and in its place he would give the poor that which falls during the binding process. This trade would allow the householder to harvest his field without the obstacle of the poor people collecting gleanings (Lieberman, TZ, p. 64). He cannot do this, however, for he thereby would misappropriate what God has set aside for the poor alone. Furthermore, the poor would receive produce subject to the separation of tithes. Such food has less value than the gleanings themselves, which are exempt from the separation of tithes.

T. 3:1b

A. [If in the field] there are some poor people who have no right to collect [gleanings, e.g., because they are part owners in the crop (cf. M. 5:5D-L)]--
B. if the householder is able to protest [their presence] immediately (bydn),
C. he may protest, [and recover that which the ineligible poor people take].
D. But if [the householder] cannot [protest immediately],
E. he should let them be,
F. in the interests of peace.

Tosefta supplements M. 4:10-5:6's discussion of gleanings. Its point is made obvious through contrasting a case in which a farmer can protest with a case in which he cannot, B vs. D.

5:6

A. One who sells his field--
B. [after the property has been transferred], the seller, [if he is a poor person], is permitted [to collect from that field produce designated for the poor].

C. But the buyer, [who now owns the field], is forbidden [to collect the poor-offerings] (cf. M. 5:5).
D. A person may not hire a worker [who agrees to work only] on condition that his son collect [gleanings] behind him.
E. (1) One who does not allow the poor [freely] to collect [gleanings], (2) or who allows one [poor person] but not another, (3) or who assists [only] one of them,
F. lo, that person robs the poor.
G. With regard to that person it is stated, "Do not remove the landmark of the poor," (gbwl ^{c}wlym).[17] [This is a play on words for Prov. 22:28, which states, "Do not remove the ancient landmark" (gbwl ^{c}wlm).]

M.5:6 (B. B.M. 12a; Sifre Deut. #284 [Horowitz, p. 301])

Three distinct rules illustrate the principle that the poor must have free access to their food. A poor field-owner (A-B) may not hoard the offerings for himself (cf. M. 5:5D-L). Former owners, like all other poor people, should have freedom to collect this produce (C). In the separate case at D a worker wishes to keep all of the poor-offerings for his own family. Since this would deprive others of the food, it is not allowed. Finally, the list at E-F and the prooftext at G reiterate the main point. Impinging on the right of the poor to gather their offerings is tantamount to robbery.

T. 3:1a

A. <u>He who receives a field to harvest--his son may not collect gleanings behind him</u> (M. 5:6D).
B. R. Yosé says, "His son may collect gleanings behind him."
C. But [with regard to] (1) sharecroppers,[18] (2) [those who] rent fields,[19] (3) or one who sells his standing [crop] to his neighbor to harvest--
D. his son may collect gleanings behind him.[20]

The two rules at B and C-D each refer to M. 5:6D, but are independent of one another. First, Yosé (B) contradicts A. He reasons that a son does not receive his father's wages. If the son is a poor person in his own right, therefore, he may collect gleanings even from a field that his father owns. The list at C-D treats cases in which a worker does not own the portion of the crop designated as gleanings. He is allowed to collect gleanings (cf. M. 5:5J-K, M. 5:6A-B), and obviously his son also is allowed.

T. 3:3c

A. They do not hire gentile workers [to harvest],
B. for [gentile workers] do not scruple with regard to [the laws of] gleanings.
C. They do not designate poorman's tithe for poor gentiles,
D. but as a favor [householders] give [poor gentiles] common [produce] that has been properly prepared [by having tithes separated on its behalf].

Tosefta's two independent rules (A-B, C-D) take up a single topic, proper relations with gentiles. A-B are straightforward. A householder must hire workers who act in accord with the restrictions of the law. In the second case, the householder may not give poorman's tithe to a gentile, because by definition this produce is set aside for poor Israelites (Deut. 14:25-29). If the householder wishes to give aid to poor gentiles, he may give them common produce as a gift. He first must separate tithes, however, because he must assume that the gentiles will not.

5:7

A. [As regards] a sheaf that (1) workers forgot, but the householder did not forget, (2) that the householder forgot, but the workers did not forget,

B. or (3) in front of which poor people stood, or (4) if they covered it with straw, [thereby hiding the sheaf from sight so that the householder and his workers would leave it behind]--

C. lo, the [sheaf] is not [subject to the restrictions of the] forgotten sheaf (cf. Deut. 24:19).

M. 5:7 (B. Sot. 45a; Sifre Deut. #282 [Horowitz, p. 299])

We now begin Mishnah's discussion of the law of the forgotten sheaf (M. 5:7-7:2). The discourse begins at the logical foundation of the matter, by explaining what constitutes forgetting. In this regard, the list at A-B+C makes two quite separate points. First, a sheaf is deemed forgotten only if all those involved in the harvest forget that it remains in the field (A). A sheaf that is remembered by some workers is not subject to the law, even if others no longer keep it in mind. A point of secondary interest here is that Mishnah treats the workers as agents of the householder. They too are capable of remembering a sheaf on his behalf, and so must be considered in determining which sheaves are subject to the law. The list's second major point is that if the poor hide a sheaf from sight it cannot enter the category of forgotten sheaves (B). The farmer and his workers in this case are forced by external constraint to leave the grain in the field. Since there is no forgetting involved, the law cannot apply. This rule also assures that God alone, through processes of random chance, determines what falls into the category of forgotten sheaves. As with other poor-offerings (cf. M. 4:10), only that which is set aside for no apparent reason is deemed subject to God's claim on behalf of the poor.

T. 3:1d

A. A householder who was standing in town said, "I know that the workers [will] forget a sheaf in such-and-such a place"--

B. [if] the workers do forget [the sheaf],

C. [the sheaf] is not[21] [subject to the restrictions of the] forgotten sheaf (cf. M. 5:7A).

98   Support for the Poor

D. (Delete this entire stich, which repeats the substance of E-G; see Lieberman, TK, p. 160.) R. Simeon b. Judah says in the name of R. Simeon, "Even if [the only ones who do not forget a sheaf are] others passing by in the road [who] see the sheaf that [the workers] forgot, [the sheaf] is not [subject to the restrictions of the] forgotten sheaf."

E. R. Simeon b. Judah says in the name of R. Simeon, "Even if [the only ones who do not forget a sheaf are] others passing by in the road [who] see the sheaf that the worker forgot,

F. "it is not deemed a forgotten sheaf,

G. "unless everybody has forgotten it."

A-C illustrate M. 5:7A1. Since the householder has not forgotten the sheaf, it is not subject to the restrictions of the law. The fact that the householder is in the city, not in the field, is of no importance. Simeon b. Judah's point (E-G) is that so long as any householder, worker, or even a passer-by remembers that a sheaf remains in the field, the sheaf cannot enter the category of a forgotten sheaf.

5:8

I. A. One who binds [produce] into (1) stack-covers,[22] (2) stack-bases,[23] (3) temporary stacks,[24] or (4) [small] sheaves, [all of which will be used in the field itself][25]--

B. [any of this bound produce that he leaves in the field] is not [subject to the restrictions of the] forgotten sheaf, [because the farmer never intended to remove it from the field].

C. [If at some later time this bound produce is brought] from [the field] to the threshing floor,

D. [any sheaves that he leaves behind] are [subject to the restrictions of the] forgotten sheaf, [for by bringing the produce to the threshing floor, the farmer indicates that he no longer wants it in the field]. [Hence we may assume that sheaves left behind were forgotten.]

II. E. He who binds [sheaves that will be placed in a] grain-heap [near the threshing floor, for storage until they will be broken apart and threshed][26]--

F. [any bound sheaves that he leaves behind in the field] are [subject to the restrictions of the] forgotten sheaf, [for the farmer did not intend to keep them in the field, but rather to store them near the threshing floor]. [Hence we may assume that sheaves left behind were forgotten.]

G. [If at some later time the sheaves are brought] from [the grain-heap] to the threshing floor,

H. [any sheaves that he leaves behind in the grain-heap] are not [subject to the restrictions of the] forgotten sheaf, [for this produce remains in storage, and was not forgotten].

I. This is the general principle:

I. J. All who bind sheaves [for storage] at a place where processing will be completed[27] [e.g., at a grain-heap near a threshing floor]--
K. [any bound sheaves that he leaves behind in the field] are [subject to the restrictions of the] forgotten sheaf, [because it is clear that the farmer wishes to remove the sheaves from the field and process them].
L. [If at some later time the sheaves are brought] from [the storage place, where processing is to be completed] to the threshing floor,
M. [any sheaves that he leaves behind] are not [subject to the restrictions of the] forgotten sheaf, [for they remain in storage].
II. N. [But if the sheaves are bound for use in the field, that is] at a place where processing will not be completed,
O. [any sheaves that the farmer leaves in the field] are not [subject to the restrictions of the] forgotten sheaf, [for he clearly wants to keep them in the field].
P. [If at some later time the produce is brought] from [the field] to the threshing floor,
Q. [any sheaves that he leaves behind in the field] are [subject to the restrictions of the] forgotten sheaf, [for now the farmer wants all of the produce at the threshing floor]. [What he leaves behind, therefore, must have been forgotten.]

M. 5:8

At several stages in processing grain, a farmer may leave behind a sheaf. For example, when he transports produce from the field to the grain-heap, or from the grain-heap to the threshing floor, some of the sheaves may remain behind. Similarly, when he binds produce for temporary use in the field, he leaves the bound produce there. At issue is how we distinguish sheaves that he purposely leaves behind from those that he actually has forgotten, for only the latter are subject to the law. As we shall see, the contrasting cases at A-D and E-H, matched by the two-part general rule at I+J-M and N-Q, present a single theory. The farmer's actions indicate whether or not the sheaves fall into the category of what has been forgotten. Accordingly, we determine the status of the sheaves that remain behind by observing what he does with those that he has removed. If he takes some sheaves away from the field, to the threshing floor, for example, we assume that what he leaves behind has been forgotten. But if he does not intend to remove the sheaves from the field, none of the produce that remains in the field is subject to the law. The category of forgotten sheaves, therefore, is defined solely in terms of the Israelite's actions and intentions. With the main principle of the unit in hand, let us turn to the specifics of the rules before us.

The simplest case (E-F, J-K) involves a farmer who binds produce into sheaves for immediate transportation to the grain-heap near the threshing floor. When he begins to remove these sheaves from the field, we may assume that any he leaves behind have been forgotten. The law therefore applies to them. Sheaves that are stored in the grain-heap are another matter. The householder brings these a few at a time to the threshing floor for processing (G-H, L-M). Those that he leaves in the grain-heap do not fall into the category of forgotten sheaves, because they simply remain in storage.

A more complex situation arises if the farmer uses some of the bound produce as part of a stack in the field (A-B, N-O). By using the sheaves in this manner, he indicates that, at this time, he has no intention of taking them to the threshing floor. Since he leaves this produce behind purposely but does not forget it, the law does not apply. Eventually, however, the farmer will begin to carry these bundles to the threshing floor for processing (C-D, P-Q). This action indicates that he no longer wishes to use the sheaves in the field. From this point on, whatever he leaves behind is forgotten and subject to the restrictions of the law.

T. 3:1e

    A.   R. Judah says, "He who binds [all of the produce in] his field into sheaves, [placing them in a temporary heap, but with no intention later to rebind them] (cf. M. 5:8A),

    B.   "his binding of them is like binding [sheaves which will be placed] in a grain-heap (cf. M. 5:8E), [and so the sheaves are subject to the law].

    C.   "[That is,] the temporary stack (ḥrrh) is like a grain-heap ."[28]

Tosefta claims that sheaves in a temporary heap share the same rule as sheaves in a grain-heap (cf. M. 5:8A3). The farmer intends to bring them directly to the threshing floor, and so the restrictions of the law of forgotten sheaves apply to any produce he leaves behind.

CHAPTER SIX
PEAH CHAPTER SIX

The role of human intention in determining which sheaves must be left as forgotten produce for the poor forms the central problem of this entire chapter. The issue is introduced by a series of Houses-disputes (M. 6.1-2) that ask about the status of a sheaf the farmer leaves behind with the clear intention to collect it at some later time. The Shammaites consistently hold that such sheaves are exempt from the law. If the farmer binds an unusually large quantity of produce into a single sheaf (M. 6:1F), or places an ordinary sheaf in a special location (M. 6:2I), he indicates that he intends to retrieve the grain. The Shammaites consider decisive the intention revealed through this act. Hence, they rule that the produce does not enter the status of forgotten sheaves. Hillelites (M. 6:1G, 6:2J) have a different view. They claim that the fact of the farmer's leaving the sheaves behind is decisive. Since we cannot be certain that the householder ever will retrieve the sheaves, all grain left in the field, even those sheaves that he might have set aside for later collection, immediately enter the category of the forgotten sheaf.

The bulk of the chapter (M. 6:3-9) takes up the position advocated by the Shammaites: by definition, sheaves that a householder purposely leaves in the field do not fall into the category of the forgotten sheaf. But how might a farmer indicate through his action that he intends to retrieve the sheaves at a later time? Mishnah's authorities propose three possible methods. First, the householder may place the sheaves in a specific pattern in the field, or near an object to which he certainly will return (M. 6:3). His act of arranging these sheaves for later collection shows that he has not forgotten them. Second, he can leave a large amount of produce in the field, as if in temporary storage (M. 6:5-7). Since we assume that he would not forget so great a quantity of food, his action of leaving it behind again makes it clear that he intends to retrieve the sheaves. Finally, the farmer may leave sheaves near unharvested produce (M. 6:8). When he returns to reap the standing crop, he also will gather any sheaves left nearby.

The chapter concludes with two units that illustrate and reiterate the main points of the law. First, produce that never is bound into sheaves, such as animal fodder, by definition cannot enter the category of forgotten sheaves (M. 6:10). Second, a short essay on intention and the law of the forgotten sheaf (M. 6:11) restates the chapter's underlying point: sheaves that the householder leaves behind but intends to gather at some later time do not enter the category of forgotten produce.

Two rules (M. 6:4, 6:9) stand outside of the chapter's overall theme, but are included here because they provide relevant, if secondary, information. First, a general principle (M. 6:4) states that a worker may not return to gather sheaves once he has passed them by. This rule, derived from Deut. 24:19, is presented as the Scriptural basis for the entire law of the forgotten sheaf. Second, the framers of M. 6:7-8 apply the restrictions of the forgotten sheaf to a patch of unharvested grain. We speak of a case in which a householder harvests and binds part of a crop, but leaves the rest standing. If he does not reap this remaining grain forthwith but leaves it behind, it takes on the status of forgotten produce. The underlying theory is that the farmer's action in binding one portion of the field immediately renders the whole crop subject to the law. This rule is noteworthy because it stands in sharp contrast to the bulk of the tractate, which holds that the law applies only to produce already bound into sheaves (see above, M. 5:7-8).

6:1-2

A. The House of Shammai say, "[Property that is declared] ownerless [exclusively] for [the benefit of] the poor [fully enters the status of] ownerless property."

B. But the House of Hillel say, "[Such produce] has [the status of] ownerless property only if it is declared ownerless also for [the benefit of] the rich,

C. "as is the case with [produce that grows during a year of] release." [During the Sabbatical year, all produce growing in fields is deemed ownerless, and may be taken by rich and poor alike.]

D. [If] every sheaf in a field [contains] a single qab [of grain], but one [sheaf contains] four qabs, and [the householder] left behind[1] [this big sheaf]--

E. the House of Shammai say, "It is not [subject to the restrictions of the] forgotten sheaf."

F. But the House of Hillel say, "[It is subject to the restrictions of the] forgotten sheaf."

M.6:1

G. [As regards] a sheaf near (1) the stone fence [at the edge of the field], (2) a grain-heap, (3) oxen, or (4) farm tools, and [the householder] left [this sheaf] behind--

H. the House of Shammai say, "It is not [subject to the restrictions of the] forgotten sheaf."

I. But the House of Hillel say, "[It is subject to the restrictions of the] forgotten sheaf."

M. 6:2 (M. Ed. 4:3-4; Y. Peah 1:5[16c], 5:1[18d], 6:5[19c], 7:1[20a]; Y. Sheq. 1:2[46a]; Y. Ket. 8:1[32a]; B. Ned. 7a; B. B.M. 30b)

The pericope deals with two distinct topics, produce in the status of ownerless property (A-C) and produce in the status of forgotten sheaves (D-F, G-I). I turn first to the latter materials, for they alone address the subject of the entire chapter. These two disputes, at D-E vs. F and G-H vs. I, focus on sheaves that have distinctive characteristics,[2] either large size (D-F) or special location (G-I). Such sheaves present an ambiguity, because when left behind, they seem to be forgotten. Yet their distinguishing features suggest that the farmer remembers them and intends to retrieve them. The Hillelites (F, I) rule that the sheaves are subject to the law. In their view, all produce that a householder leaves behind in the fields immediately enters the category of forgotten sheaves. The fact that he might later remember the food is of no account, because he left the sheaves behind. The Shammaites (E, H) take the alternative view. Because of the special features of the sheaves in question, it is a distinct possibility that the householder will remember and retrieve them. Accordingly, they do not fall into the category of the forgotten sheaf and are exempt from the law.

A formally separate dispute (A vs. B-C) addresses the category of ownerless property. Here the farmer has declared some food ownerless, yet intends that the edibles be used by the poor alone. In the view of the Hillelites (B-C) the farmer's wishes are unimportant. His act of declaring the food ownerless defines his intention, so that the food belongs to all, rich and poor alike.[3] The Shammaites (A), by contrast, rule that the farmer's intention does define the category of ownerless produce. What he sets aside in this case is reserved for the poor; yet, like all ownerless produce, it is exempt from the separation of tithes.

The pericope thus brings together two superficially unrelated topics and, in so doing, addresses a single larger issue: What is the role of human intention in defining categories such as "forgotten sheaves" and "ownerless property?"[4] For the case of forgotten sheaves, we wish to know which of the sheaves that a householder leaves behind are subject to the law. Does this include those that he clearly intends to retrieve? So too, we ask whether or not a farmer may declare some of his produce ownerless, yet stipulate that he intends that the food be taken only by poor people. In both cases we wish to know whether or not the farmer's will is decisive. The Hillelites, for their part, consistently claim that the farmer's stated intent cannot affect the definitions of "forgotten sheaves" or of "ownerless property." His actions alone determine what enters these categories. The householder is presumed to intend the natural consequences of his actions. Hence that which he leaves behind is forgotten; that which he declares ownerless belongs to all. In striking contrast, the Shammaites claim that the ordinary farmer's intentions place all things in their proper categories. The phrases "forgotten sheaf" and "ownerless property" therefore acquire meanings only in light of the farmer's wishes. According to this theory, human intention takes precedence over action. What the farmer wishes is more important than what he actually does. As at M. 3:1-5, only the Shammaites' view is carried forward in the material to follow. The tractate's framers apparently deem this view to be authoritative.

T. 3:1f

A. The House of Shammai and the House of Hillel agree that if [one] declares [produce] to be ownerless

B. for [the benefit of] man but not beast,

C. for [the benefit of] Israelite but not gentile,

D. [that which has been declared ownerless indeed is] ownerless property (cf. M. 6:1A-D).

Tosefta indicates the limits of M. 6:1A-D's dispute. Both the Shammaites and the Hillelites agree that a householder may reserve for Israelites but not gentiles produce that he declares ownerless (C). Similarly, he may state that his ownerless property is reserved for humans but not for animals (B). The Houses disagree only concerning the distribution of ownerless property within the Israelite world. The Shammaites hold that the householder may reserve such produce for a specific segment of Israelites. The Hillelites, by contrast, hold that all Israelites must have equal access to property declared ownerless.

6:3

A. [As regards sheaves that the householder has left at] ends of rows [on one side of his field]--

B. [the presence of] a sheaf on the opposite side [of the field] proves [that the sheaves referred to at A are not forgotten]. [While harvesting the field, zig-zagging up and down the rows, the householder has arranged the sheaves at the end of each row for latter collection. We therefore know that he has not forgotten them.]

C. [As for] a sheaf that [the householder] had picked up,[5] in order to take it to the city [for sale], and that he then left behind [in the field]--

D. the [Hillelites] concede [to the Shammaites][6] that [the sheaf] is not [subject to the restrictions of the] forgotten sheaf. [By his deed, the farmer already has indicated that he intends to take the sheaf with him later when he goes to the city.]

M. 6:3 (Sif. Deut. #283 [Horowitz, p. 300])

Sheaves that a farmer leaves behind but fully intends to retrieve appear no different from those that he has forgotten. At issue here is how we know whether or not the farmer in fact remembers this produce. The two formally distinct rules (A-B, C-D) before us express a single solution, that the householder's actions indicate his intentions (see M. 6:1-2).[7] By arranging the sheaves at A-B in a distinctive pattern, for example, the farmer has made it clear that he remembers them. The law therefore does not apply to sheaves left at the edge of the field. When the householder has finished harvesting, he will pass up and down the edge of the field, gathering the sheaves. Similarly, the farmer who picks up the sheaf at C-D indicates that he will take it with him at some later time. He has not forgotten it, even though he leaves it in the field. It remains only to note that C-D are phrased to conclude the series of Houses-disputes at M. 6:1-2. Both Houses here are assigned the view previously given the Shammaites alone, that the farmer's intention determines which sheaves fall into the category of the forgotten sheaf.

T. 3:2

A. Said R. Ilai, "I asked R. Joshua, 'Over which sheaves did the House of Shammai disagree [with the House of Hillel that such sheaves are subject to the restrictions of the forgotten sheaf]?'

Peah Chapter Six   105

B. "He [i.e., Joshua] said to me, 'By the Torah! This [dispute refers to those] sheaves that are near the picking ladder, grain-heap, or farm tools, and which the householder left behind (M. 6:2H-J).[8] [The Shammaites hold that sheaves near fixed locations] are exempt from the law, while the Hillelites hold that they are subject.]

C. "But when I came and asked R. Eliezer[9] [which sheaves the Houses disputed], he said to me, '[The Houses] agree that these [sheaves near fixed locations are[10] [subject to the restrictions of] the forgotten sheaf. With regard to what did they disagree? [They disagree] with regard to a sheaf which [the householder] picked up in order to take it to the city [for sale], and [which he] placed near the fence and then left behind (M. 6:3C).

D. "'For the House of Shammai say [that such a sheaf] is not [subject to the restrictions of] the forgotten sheaf, because the householder had taken possession of it [= the position taken by both Houses at M. 6:3D]. But the House of Hillel say [that such a sheaf] is [subject to the restrictions of] the forgotten sheaf.' [The Hillelites are assigned a position consistent with their opinion throughout M. 6:1-2. Human intention later to retrieve the produce is not determinative. Since the sheaf is left behind in the field, the law applies.]

E. "And when I came and recited these matters before R. Eleazar b. Azariah, he said to me, 'By the Torah! These matters were spoken at Sinai.'"

Ilai's report addresses a problem raised by the divergent positions assigned to the Hillelites at M. 6:2 and at M. 6:3. As we recall, the Hillelites first hold (M. 6:2H-J) that human intention is unimportant in determining whether or not a sheaf is subject to the law of the forgotten sheaf. At M. 6:3, however, they agree with the Shammaites that the farmer's wishes are decisive. That pericope claims that, by taking full possession of a sheaf, the farmer indicates his intention later to take it to the city. Accordingly, the law does not apply. Joshua (B) introduces this problem by reiterating the Hillelites' and the Shammaites' positions. Eliezer (C-D) resolves the contradiction between the two pericopae by assigning to the Houses opinions consistent with their veiws at M. 6:2. Eleazar b. Azariah (E) supports this harmonization as authoritative.

T. 3:3

A. [As regards] a sheaf that [the householder] picked up [in order] to take it to the city [for sale] (M. 6:3C),

B. and that he set on top of another [sheaf] (hbrw), and then left behind both [the top and the bottom sheaves]--

C. the bottom [sheaf] is [subject to the restrictions of] the forgotten sheaf, and the top [sheaf] is not [subject to the restrictions of the] forgotten sheaf.

D. (Delete: The bottom [sheaf])[11]

E. R. Simeon says, "Neither [sheaf is subject to the restrictions of the] forgotten sheaf,

F. "(Add: The bottom)[12] [sheaf is exempt]--because it is covered [and so removed from sight] (see M. 5:7A3-4).
G. "The top [sheaf is exempt]--because he had picked it up."

Tosefta's two-part rule (A-C, E-G) supplements M. 6:3C-D, cited at A. The farmer picks up a sheaf, thereby indicating that he wishes to retrieve it later and rendering it exempt from the law. He then places it on top of another sheaf. We wish to know whether or not this action is sufficient to indicate his intention later to gather the bottom sheaf. At A-C sages hold that it is not. The householder did nothing to the bottom sheaf in order to indicate his intention. Merely covering it is not enough. As in Mishnah's rules of acquisition, the farmer must act directly upon an object in order to indicate his intention in its regard.[13] In this case, since the farmer never touched the bottom sheaf, the law of the forgotten sheaf applies. Simeon's lemma (E-G) responds to the same situation, but reads in a different issue.[14] For him the status of the bottom sheaf is determined by its being covered (cf. M. 5:7A3-4), not by the farmer's indications that he will return to gather it. He holds that the sheaf was hidden from sight, but never actually forgotten. The sheaf therefore is exempt from the law.

T. 3:4a

A. [As regards] a field the [produce of which has not yet been bound into] sheaves, [and so the produce still is] scattered [over the field][15]--
B. [if the householder] bound and then left behind one of the sheaves,
C. the law of the forgotten sheaf does not apply.
D. [This is the case] until he binds all [other produce] in the vicinity.

Tosefta illustrates the principle of M. 6:3 with an obvious case. The farmer at A leaves behind a sheaf during the binding process. Since he has not yet finished binding the grain, we know that he intends to return and to gather any sheaves he bound. The law therefore does not apply (C). If the farmer has finished binding (D), however, there is no indication that he will collect sheaves left behind in the field. Hence, these sheaves fall into the category of forgotten produce, and must be left for the poor.

T. 3:4b

A. <u>[As regards sheaves that the householder has left at] ends of rows [on one side of his field]--[the fact that he picks up] a sheaf on the opposite side [of the field] proves [that the sheaves left on the first side of the field are not forgotten]</u> (M. 6:3A-B).
B. How [can this procedure prove that sheaves left at ends of rows are not forgotten]? [This is a problem because M. 6:3 assumes that the householder may return to the field in order to collect sheaves that he earlier arranged for collection. Deut. 24:19, however, expressly forbids him to return.]

Peah Chapter Six

C. [The problem is solved by the case of] one who owned [a field of] ten rows,[16] such that [the entire field contains enough produce to comprise] ten sheaves [i.e., each row's produce will be bound into a single sheaf],

D. and he bound one of the sheaves [comprised of produce growing in a row oriented] from north to south, and he [left it, apparently] forgotten [at the end of the row]--

E. the law of the forgotten sheaf does not apply.

F. This is because [the case] concerns [a householder who moves] from east to west. [That is to say, after the harvest, when gathering sheaves laid out for collection, the householder travels along the edge of the field, perpendicular to the rows. Since he travels from east to west, he does not return and retrace his earlier path. Since he does not violate Deuteronomy's injunction, he is allowed to gather the sheaves.]

At issue is a contradiction between M. 6:3A-B, cited at A, and Deut. 24:19. As we recall, M. 6:3 allows the farmer to return to the field in order to gather sheaves he earlier arranged for collection. Deut. 24:19, however, forbids this. C-F resolves the problem. When the householder gathers the sheaves he does not retrace his exact path up and down the rows, but moves along the edge of the field. Because he moves in a different direction, this does not fall into the category of "returning," and so is not forbidden.

6:4

A. And these are [the rules that apply to] ends of rows [in a field]:

B. [As regards] two men who began [to collect sheaves] from the middle of a row, one facing north and the other facing south,[17]

C. and they left behind [sheaves both in the areas that were] in front of them [i.e., between their starting locations and the edges of the field] and [in the areas that were] behind both of them [i.e., the area between the points where they started harvesting]--

D. [a sheaf that they left behind] in front of [either one of] them [i.e., between either of their starting locations and the edge of the field] is [subject to the restrictions of the] forgotten sheaf, [for one of the harvesters passed by the sheaf, but did not take it].

E. But [a sheaf that they left in the field] behind them [i.e., in the area between their starting locations] is not [subject to the restrictions of the] forgotten sheaf, [for neither worker passed by the sheaf]. [Neither worker, then, left it behind.]

F. An individual who began [to collect sheaves] from one end of a row, and left ungathered [a sheaf either] in front of himself [i.e., in an area through which he has not yet passed] or behind himself [i.e., in an area he already had worked]--

G. [a sheaf that he left] in front of himself is not [subject to the restrictions of the] forgotten sheaf, [for he has not yet left it behind].

H. But [a sheaf that he left in the field] behind him is [subject to the restrictions of the] forgotten sheaf,

I. because it is governed by [the Scriptural law], "[When you reap your harvest in your field, and have forgotten a sheaf in the field,] you shall not go back [to get it]" (Deut. 24:19).

J. This is the general principle:

K. Whatever [sheaf] is governed by [the law], "You shall not go back," [i.e., any sheaf that the workers already have left behind while passing through the field], is [subject to the restrictions of the] forgotten sheaf.

L. But that which is not governed by [the law], "You shall not go back," is not [subject to the restrictions of the] forgotten sheaf, [for the workers never passed it and never left it behind].

M. 6:4 (B. B.M. 11a)

The main point is that a sheaf can enter the system of the law only after the harvester has passed it by and left it behind. By definition, a worker cannot have forgotten to collect a sheaf that he has not yet passed. The farmer's actions in passing the produce and in leaving it uncollected thus precipitate the process whereby food is set aside for the poor. The two cases at A+B-D and E-H+I, as well as the general principle at J+K-L, thus claim that sheaves lying in areas that the harvesters have not yet worked are exempt from the law.

6:5

I. A. Two sheaves [of grain that are left side-by-side in a field] are [subject to the restrictions of the] forgotten sheaf.

B. But three [sheaves left side-by-side in a field] are not [subject to the restrictions of the] forgotten sheaf.

II. C. Two piles of olives or carob [that are left side-by-side in a field] are [subject to the restrictions of the] forgotten sheaf.

D. But three [such piles left side-by-side in a field] are not [subject to the restrictions of the] forgotten sheaf.

III. E. Two stalks of flax [that are left side-by-side in a field] are [subject to the restrictions of the] forgotten sheaf.

F. But three [stalks left side-by-side in a field] are not [subject to the restrictions of the] forgotten sheaf.

IV. G. Two [individual] grapes [that separate from a vine, and lie on the ground side-by-side] are [subject to the law of] the separated [grape] (Lev. 19:9-10).

H. But three [grapes lying side-by-side] are not [subject to the restrictions of] the separated [grape].

V. I. Two stalks [of grain that fall to the ground during the harvest and lie side-by-side] are [subject to the restrictions of] gleanings.

J. But three [stalks lying side-by-side] are not [subject to the restrictions of] gleanings.

K. These [rulings] accord with the opinion of the House of Hillel.
L. But concerning all of them, the House of Shammai say, "Three [measures of produce left in the field] belong to the poor, but four [measures of produce] belong to the householder."

M. 6:5 (B. Shab. 113b; B. B.B. 72b; B. San. 88a; Sifre Deut. #283 [Horowitz, p. 299])

A large amount of produce left at one place in a field is exempt from the law of the forgotten sheaf. The distinctively large amount of grain suggests that the householder in fact remembers the sheaves (see M. 6:1D-F). Accordingly, the law applies to two measures of produce that remain in the field, but not to three.[18] Three parallel rules work out this principle for sheaves of grain (A-B), the fruit of trees (C-D), and flax (E-F). Two further statutes (G-H, I-J) repeat the formal construction, and apply the principle to laws discussed elsewhere in the tractate. The law of the separated grape (Lev. 19:9-10; see M. 7:3) states that single grapes that fall from the vine must be left for the poor. Three such grapes are exempt from the law, however, because they probably did not separate from the vine individually, but fell as a bunch (G-H). At I-J the law of gleanings (see M. 4:10-5:2) is limited within the clearly established pattern. Two stalks that fall to the ground during the harvest are subject to the law. Since the householder probably would not drop three stalks at once, however, the law in this case does not apply.

K-L provide attributions for the foregoing and a dispute. The rules as explained are attributed to the Hillelites. The Shammaites dispute a minor point. In their view three measures of produce are subject to the law while four are exempt.[19] The difference between the two views seems to me inconsequential.

T. 3:5a

I. A. "Two distinct bundles (hmwbdlwt zw mzw) are [subject to the restrictions of the law of] the forgotten sheaf.
   B. "Three bundles are not [subject to the restrictions of the law of] the forgotten sheaf.
II. C. "Two distinct sheaves are [subject to the restrictions of the law of] the forgotten sheaf.
   D. "Three sheaves are not [subject to the restrictions of the law of] the forgotten sheaf (M. 6:5A-B).
III. E. "Two distinct vines are [subject to the restrictions of the law of] the forgotten sheaf.
   F. "Three vines are not [subject to the restrictions of the law of] the forgotten sheaf.
IV. G. "Two single grapes are [subject to the restrictions of the law of] the separated grape.
   H. "Three single grapes are not [subject to the restrictions of the law of] the separated grape (M. 6:5G-H).

V. I. "Two stalks which lie [on the ground] in their normal fashion are [subject to] the law of gleanings.
    J. "Three stalks are not [subject to] the law of gleanings."
    K. These are the words of the House of Hillel (M. 6:5I-K).

Tosefta goes over the same ground as M. 6:5. It adds only the notion that the different measures of produce need not be piled on top of each other, but may be separated. The distinct sheaves nonetheless comprise an amount of produce large enough for the householder easily to remember.

6:6

A. A sheaf that contains two seahs [of grain], and [that the householder] left behind,
B. is not [subject to the restrictions of the] forgotten sheaf.
C. [As regards] two sheaves that [together] contain two seahs [of grain, e.g., each sheaf contains one seah]--
D. Rabban Gamaliel says, "[They belong] to the householder."
E. But sages say, "[They belong] to the poor."
F. Said Rabban Gamaliel, "Now as the number of sheaves [that are left together in a field] becomes larger (see M. 6:5), does the strength of the householder's [claim on the sheaves] increase, or [does it] decrease?"
G. [Sages] said to him, "The strength [of his claim] increases."
H. He said to them, "Now if with regard to one sheaf that contains two seahs [of grain], and that [the householder] left behind, [we rule that it] is not subject [to the restrictions of the] forgotten sheaf [see A], [when we deal with] two sheaves that [together] contain two seahs, is it not logical that they also are not [subject to the restrictions of the] forgotten sheaf?"
I. They said to him, "No! For if you say that one sheaf [containing two seahs] has the status of a grain-heap, [and so is exempt from the restrictions of the forgotten sheaf], would you [not] say that two [smaller] sheaves are equivalent to bundles, [which do enter the status of forgotten sheaves when left behind]?"

M. 6:6 (B. B.B. 72b; Sifra Deut. #283 [Horowitz, p. 299])

When a farmer leaves behind a large amount of produce, namely, more than two seahs, the grain does not enter the status of forgotten sheaves (cf. M. 6:5). The distinctively large quantity of food remaining in the field suggests that the farmer purposely left it there in temporary storage, and has not forgotten it. This point (A-B) generates a dispute (C-D) and debate (F-I) between Gamaliel and sages. Must each sheaf separately contain more than two seahs of grain in order to be exempt from the law, or do several small sheaves that combine to form two seahs also gain exemption?[20] Gamaliel (D) claims that all grain left behind by the householder forms a single mass. By leaving so large a quantity, the farmer indicates that he has not forgotten it. Sages (E), by contrast, claim that each bundle of grain that the householder binds separately constitutes a distinct entity. Since each of these sheaves contains less than two seahs, each falls into the category of forgotten produce. In the debate that follows at F-I, Gamaliel reiterates M. 6:5's point that the greater the number of sheaves left together in a field, the more likely the farmer is to remember them.[21] We therefore may assume that he will retrieve the two sheaves left in the field. Sages (I) reject this argument. They claim that since the sheaves appear to be distinct entities, they must be considered separately. Hence, they fall into the category of forgotten sheaves.

6:7-8

A. [A patch of] standing [grain that remains unharvested in a field that the householder already has begun to reap, and] that comprises two seahs [of produce],
B. and that [the householder] left behind,
C. is not [subject to the restrictions of] the forgotten sheaf. [Since the farmer leaves behind such a large amount of food, it is clear that he could not have forgotten it, but intends later to return and harvest the grain.]
D. [If the standing grain, at this point in its growth] contains less than two seahs, but [when fully grown] is likely to produce two seahs [of grain],
E. even if [the grain] is inferior barley (tph),[22] [which produces a low yield],
F. they view it as if it were a high-yielding [type of] barley.[23] [Since virtually all budding crops, whether high- or low-yielding barley, have the potential to produce two seahs of grain, such crops cannot enter the status of forgotten produce, see A-B.]

M. 6:7

G. [The presence of] a standing [crop like that mentioned at A above, namely, one that contains at least two seahs,] prevents a sheaf or other standing [produce[24] nearby from becoming subject to the restrictions of the forgotten sheaf].[25] [Since a large crop of unharvested grain does not fall into the category of forgotten produce, we may assume that the farmer will return to reap it. At that time he will gather any other produce left behind.]
H. [The presence of] a sheaf [that remains in the field] prevents neither a sheaf nor standing [produce nearby from becoming subject to the restrictions of the forgotten sheaf]. [The householder might have forgotten the sheaf itself; accordingly, we do not assume that he will return and gather produce he has left near it.]
I. What sort of standing [produce] prevents a sheaf [from becoming subject to the restrictions of the forgotten sheaf]?
J. Any [standing grain] that [does not fall into the category of forgotten produce],
K. even a single stalk of grain.

M. 6:8 (Y. Peah 5:2[18d]; Sifre Deut. #283 [Finkelstein-Horowitz, p. 300])

Mishnah's framers now apply the familiar principle that large quantities of produce are exempt from the law (M. 6:5-6) to several cases (A-C, D-F, G, H, I-K) concerning an unharvested crop. Before discussing the substance of these rules, however, let us consider the theory that underlies the unit as a whole. These pericopae assume that the law of the forgotten sheaf takes effect long before the householder finishes binding the entire crop (cf. M. 5:7-8). In fact, the householder activates the process whereby a portion of the crop enters the status of forgotten sheaves as soon as he begins to harvest and bind any part of the yield. By claiming one portion of the grain for himself (through binding some of the grain into sheaves), he renders the whole crop subject to the restrictions governing forgotten sheaves. Whatever he leaves behind, including a patch of unharvested grain, immediately takes on the status of the forgotten sheaf. This notion, that standing grain can become subject to the law of the forgotten sheaf, contradicts the tractate's dominant theory. As we recall, M. 5:7-8 explicitly state that only produce that actually has been bound into sheaves can enter the system of the law.[26] This is because the householder establishes his claim upon the sheaves by binding them. Only his act of tying together each sheaf can precipitate the poor's complementary claim upon that which he forgets.[27] Before the householder binds the grain, by contrast, he has not established any claim on it at all. Accordingly, in the bulk of the tractate, the law does not apply to standing grain.

We now turn to the details of the rules before us. The general principle that the restrictions of the forgotten sheaf can apply to standing crops is introduced at A-C. As at M. 6:5-6, we assume that a farmer who leaves behind more than two seahs of grain fully intends to retrieve the food and has not forgotten it. The poor therefore have no claim upon these edibles. A secondary rule, D-F, takes up a problem generated by the foregoing. A farmer forgets an unharvested crop at an early stage in its growth. The restrictions of the forgotten sheaf should govern this crop, for it has not yet produced the two seahs that would render it exempt from the law (as at A-C). As the grain continues to grow, however, it almost certainly will yield far more than the requisite amount. Does this crop fall into the category of forgotten produce? The contrasting language at E and F asserts that the crop's potential to produce more than two seahs, not its actual yield, decides the issue. Since virtually all budding crops, both low- and high-yielding varieties, have the potential to produce more than two seahs, they do not enter the status of forgotten produce.

The pair of rules at G-H present the case of a householder who leaves a sheaf near a standing crop of large size, so as to indicate that he has not forgotten this bundle of produce (so MR). The sheaf at G does not enter the status of forgotten produce, for it is clear that the farmer will retrieve it when he returns to reap the unharvested grain. In the complementary case at H, a householder places a sheaf near other produce in order to indicate that he has not forgotten these other edibles. Nonetheless, the farmer easily might forget this sheaf because it possesses no distinctive features, such as large size. Its presence in the field therefore cannot serve to indicate that he will return and gather other produce left nearby. Accordingly, the restrictions of the law govern any food remaining in the field.

Peah Chapter Six

These rules draw in their wake explanatory material at I-K. We now wish to know how the presence of a standing crop indicates that the householder intends to return to the field. This is a problem, we recall, for A-C rules than an unharvested crop itself might become subject to the law. As a result, the farmer may have forgotten the standing grain, having no thought of returning to reap it or to gather sheaves left nearby. Mishnah's authorities solve this problem by asserting that the rule at G speaks only of unharvested grain that the farmer in fact does remember. When he returns to harvest even a single stalk of standing grain (E), it is clear that he will gather any sheaves left nearby. Hence, these sheaves do not enter the status of forgotten produce.

T. 3:5c

A. In what circumstances did they rule that <u>a standing [crop] protects a [nearby] sheaf [from becoming subject to the restrictions of the forgotten sheaf]</u> (M. 6:8A)?

B. [The rule applies to a case] in which the [standing crop] was not harvested before [the poor came to collect the forgotten sheaves] (mbntym).[28]

C. But if the [standing crop] was harvested before [the poor came to collect the forgotten sheaves],

D. lo, this [standing crop that has been removed] does not prevent [a sheaf from becoming subject to the restrictions of the forgotten sheaf].

E. "A standing [crop] of a particular [type] protects [a sheaf] of a different [type from becoming subject to the law of the forgotten sheaf] (qmt ḥbyrw mṣlt ^{c}l šlw).

F. "[For example], (1) [a standing crop] of wheat [protects a sheaf] of barley [from becoming subject to the law of the forgotten sheaf], and (2) [a standing crop] belonging to a gentile [protects a sheaf] belonging to an Israelite [from becoming subject to the law of the forgotten sheaf]," the opinion of R. Meir.

G. But sages say, "[A standing crop] protects [a sheaf] only of its own type [from becoming subject to the law of the forgotten sheaf], and [a standing crop of a particular] species [protects a sheaf] only of its own species [from becoming subject to the law of the forgotten sheaf]."

Tosefta's two rules (A-D and E-G) both concern the effect of placing a sheaf near a standing crop (cf. M. 6:8A). Since they are substantively and formally distinct, however, I treat each of them in turn. We recall that a sheaf near a standing crop is not subject to the law of the forgotten sheaf (M. 6:8A). Its distinctive location indicates that the farmer intends to retrieve it when he returns to harvest the rest of the standing crop. The two contrasting doublets at A-B and C-D ask what happens if workers harvest the standing crop, leaving the sheaf alone in the field. That is to say, despite the farmer's earlier indication that he would gather the sheaf when he reaped the standing produce, the sheaf now lies alone in the field, apparently forgotten. Since the workers did not gather the sheaf when they completed harvesting the field, the poor are entitled to take it. In the absence of indications to the contrary, they may assume that the sheaf has been forgotten and has not been purposely left in the field.

At issue in the separate dispute at E-F vs. G is whether or not a standing crop of one type can prevent a sheaf of another type from becoming subject to the law of the forgotten sheaf (cf. M. 6:8A; M. Hal. 4:1). In order to understand this subtle issue, let us spell out the details of the two distinct cases presented in the gloss at B. The farmer at B1 owns a crop of wheat and a crop of barley. His wheat crop ripens first, and he harvests and binds it as usual. He gathers most of the sheaves of wheat, but one remains in the field near the barley crop. We now can identify the area of ambiguity. On the one hand, the farmer probably would not leave a sheaf of wheat to be gathered with the barley crop, and so it seems to have been forgotten. On the other hand, when the householder returns to harvest the barley, he will see the sheaf of wheat and collect it. It therefore is not clear whether the law applies. The case at B2 focuses on the issue of ownership. Produce owned by a gentile is not subject to the law of the forgotten sheaf at all (cf. M. 4:9). We wish to know whether or not such a standing crop, itself outside the system of the law, can protect a sheaf belonging to an Israelite from becoming subject to the law. Predictably, Meir and sages dispute this grey area. Meir (A-B) holds that the law of the forgotten sheaf applies to any sheaf and standing crop, regardless of species or ownership. Any sheaf placed by a standing crop appears to the poor to have been placed there purposely, and not forgotten. Sages (C), by contrast, hold that the farmer would not leave a sheaf of one type to be collected with a standing crop of another. The law applies because the poor assume that the householder simply forgot the sheaf.

T. 3:6

A. R. Simeon b. Gamaliel says, "Just as <u>a standing [crop] protects a sheaf [from becoming subject to the law of the forgotten sheaf]</u> (M. 6:8A),

B. "so too a sheaf protects a standing [crop from becoming subject to the law of the forgotten sheaf] (contra M. 6:8B).

C. "And it is a matter of logic:

D. "If [it is the case that] a standing [crop], on which the householder[29] has a weak claim [i.e., because it has not yet been harvested, the crop contains produce that will be designated as <u>peah</u>, gleanings, and forgotten sheaves],

E. "lo, such a [standing crop] prevents a sheaf [from becoming subject to the law of the forgotten sheaf],

F. "a sheaf, on which the householder has a strong claim [i.e., because it has already been harvested, and so no longer is subject to the designation of <u>peah</u> or gleanings, but only of forgotten sheaves],

G. "is it not logical that this [sheaf] protects a standing [crop from becoming subject to the law of the forgotten sheaf]?"

H. They said to him, "Rabbi, [if it is the case that] a standing [crop] protects a sheaf [from becoming subject to the law of the forgotten sheaf], because the householder has a strong claim [on the sheaf],

Peah Chapter Six 115

I. "can [a sheaf] protect a standing [crop from becoming subject to the law of the forgotten sheaf], [even though] the poor have a stronger claim [on the standing crop]?" [No. Hence Gamaliel's restatement of M. 6:8A-B, cited at A-B, is rejected.]

Gamaliel contradicts M. 6:8A-B. Both a sheaf and a standing crop are treated under a single rule. If the farmer will return to the field, all grain, whether harvested or unharvested, is not subject to the law of the forgotten sheaf. Gamaliel's reasoning for this position is at B-F. It relies on a distinction between the strength of a poor person's claim on a standing crop and on a sheaf. On the one hand, a standing crop contains produce that will be designated as (1) peah, (2) gleanings, and (3) forgotten sheaves. A sheaf, on the other hand, is subject only to the law of (1) the forgotten sheaf. It does not contain produce to be designated as peah or gleanings, for these were designated during the harvest. In this respect, Gamaliel holds that the poor have a stronger claim on the standing crop than they have on a sheaf. On the basis of this distinction, Gamaliel presents a conclusion a minori ad maius: A standing crop, on which the poor have a strong claim, can save a sheaf from being subject to the law. Analogously, since the householder's claim on a sheaf is stronger than the poor's, it also can prevent grain nearby from entering the status of forgotten produce.

Sages (G-H) reject Gamaliel's argument. They state that a standing crop prevents a sheaf from being subject to the law only because the poor have a weak claim on the sheaf. Since the poor have a stronger claim on the standing crop, a sheaf cannot protect it from becoming subject to the law.

T. 3:7

A. The poor have a stronger claim on a standing [crop] than [they have] on a sheaf, yet [in another respect they have a stronger claim] on a sheaf than on a standing crop.

B. For a standing [crop] contains [produce that will be designated as] gleanings, forgotten sheaves, and peah, which is not the case for a sheaf. [Since the produce in a sheaf already has been harvested, the sheaf is subject to designation only as a forgotten sheaf, but not as peah or gleanings. In this respect, the poor have a stronger claim on a standing crop than they have on a sheaf.]

C. [But as regards] a sheaf which contains less than two seahs of produce[30]--

D. the law of the forgotten sheaf applies,

E. unless [the sheaf actually] contains [a full] two seahs [of grain]. [This contrasts with a standing crop, which is exempt from the law if it has the potential to comprise two seahs of grain (cf. M. 6:7C-E). Since almost all standing crops in potential comprise this amount of produce, few ever are deemed subject to the law of the forgotten sheaf. The poor's claim in this respect is stronger on the sheaf than it is on the standing crop.][31]

As I have explained at B and E, the pericope clarifies T. 3:6's statement that the poor have a stronger claim on a standing crop than they have on a sheaf. Nonetheless, I treat it separately, because it is formed as an independent unit. That is to say, its formal balance, both the poor and the householder having a stronger claim on both a standing crop and on a sheaf (A), in no way is determined by T. 3:6. Rather, Tosefta here spins out its own concerns, supplying information relevant to its general topic of discussion.

6:9

A. A seah of uprooted produce and a seah of produce that is not uprooted,
B. and similarly, [picked and unpicked fruit of a single] tree,
C. or garlic and onions,[32]
D. [these pairs] do not join together[33] [to form the minimum] two seahs [of produce that are exempt from the law of the forgotten sheaf, as specified at M. 6:7A-B].
E. Rather [if one seah of each type of produce listed in each pair is forgotten in the field, adding to two seahs total], the [two lots of produce] belong to the poor.
F. R. Yosé says, "If [produce] that belongs to the poor [i.e., a forgotten sheaf] lies [on the ground] in between [two sheaves that normally would join together to form two seahs not subject to the law],
G. "[the two sheaves] do not join together.
H. "But if [produce belonging to the poor] does not [lie on the ground in between two sheaves that normally would join together],
I. "lo, these [two sheaves] do join together [to form the requisite two seahs of produce]."

M. 6:9 (Y. Peah 5:2[18d])

At issue is whether or not two batches of produce that are alike in some ways, yet different in others, combine to form an amount of food exempt from the law of the forgotten sheaf (see M. 6:6-7). In particular, at A and B we speak of a single crop of produce, part of which the householder has reaped, and part of which he has not. In the slightly different case at C, we consider garlic and onions, which belong to a single genus,[34] yet comprise two distinct species. In resolving these cases of ambiguity, Mishnah's framers rule that we must give primary consideration to differences exhibited by these pairs. The physically separate elements of each pair listed at A-C thus cannot join together to form the requisite two seahs, even though in some ways they are alike.

Yosé's lemma takes up a related issue, but is separate in both form and substance.[35] He claims that two sheaves join together only if they may be viewed as separate parts of a single storage heap. Accordingly, if produce belonging to the poor lies on the ground in between the sheaves (E-F), the bundles do not combine to form the minimum two seahs. Since the sheaves are separated by produce that the poor own, they cannot comprise a single grain pile. On the other hand, if the farmer in fact owns all of the produce in the area, the sheaves join together to form the requisite two seahs and are exempt from the law (G-H).

T. 3:5b

A. R. Yosé says, "Hananiah, R. Joshua's nephew, says, 'All cases in which the property of the poor is between [two measures of produce which otherwise combine to form an amount of grain not under the law of the forgotten sheaf] (M. 6:9E),

B. "'for example, [a field of] grain or a vineyard, [both of these contain gleanings or separated grapes on the ground between the sheaves],

C. "'[the two measures of produce] do not combine [to form an amount exempt from the law of the forgotten sheaf] (M. 6:9F).

D. "'But in all cases in which the property of the poor is not between [two measures of produce] (M. 6:9G),

E. "'for example, the fruit of a tree, [which is not separated by produce that belongs to the poor, for no poor-offerings remain on the tree; instead, they fall to the ground],

F. "'lo, these [two measures] do combine [to form an amount not under the law of the forgotten sheaf]'" (M. 6:9H).

Tosefta glosses Yosé's lemma (M. 6:9E-H), attributing it to Hananiah at A, and providing examples of the situations at B and E.

6:10

A. Produce intended (1) for use as fodder, or (2) for binding sheaves [i.e., produce that never will be bound into sheaves],

B. and similarly (3) small bundles of garlic, or (4) small bundles [containing both] garlic and onions [i.e., produce that only later will be bound into full sheaves],

C. these are not [subject to the restrictions of] the forgotten sheaf.

D. And [concerning] all tubers [that farmers store] in the ground,

E. such as (1) arum, (2) garlic, and (3) onions--

F. R. Judah says, "These are not [subject to the restrictions of] the forgotten sheaf."

G. But sages say, "They are [subject to the restrictions of] the forgotten sheaf."

M. 6:10 (Y. Peah 6:3[19c]; Y. Soṭah 9:2[23c]; Y. B.Q. 6:7[5c]; B. Soṭah 45a; Sifra Emor 10:4; Sifre Deut. #283 [Finkelstein-Horowitz, p. 299])

The opening unit (A-C) illustrates the point that the law applies only to produce bound into sheaves (see M. 5:8).[36] Accordingly, grain used as fodder or for binding other sheaves (A1-2) cannot enter the status of forgotten sheaves. Similarly, the law of the forgotten sheaf takes effect only after the completion of the binding process. Thus small bundles of garlic and onions (B), which have not yet been bound into sheaves, cannot enter the status of forgotten produce.

118   Support for the Poor

The dispute at D-E vs. G carries forward the discussion of garlic and onions, the subject of B. An ambiguity arises because these and other tubers often are left in the ground for storage after they ripen. On the one hand, this food is left behind, apparently forgotten. Yet, tubers stored in the ground are not bound together as sheaves. Judah (F) considers the latter fact decisive. Since the edibles are not bound together, they are not subject to the restrictions of the forgotten sheaf. Sages (G), by contrast, hold that the tubers must be given to the poor. Since the householder has left them behind, they immediately fall into the category of forgotten produce.

T. 3:8a

A. He who cuts apart [small] bundles [of grain], which he [intends] in the future to bind into sheaves,
B. and similarly, small bundles of garlic, or small bundles [containing both] garlic and onions [i.e., produce which only later will be bound into full sheaves],
C. these are not [subject to the restrictions of] the forgotten sheaf (M. 6:10B-C).
D. One who binds [his grain into sheaves in order to prevent damage caused by an approaching] fire, or [an overflowing] irrigation ditch--
E. these [sheaves that he binds] are not [subject to the restrictions of] the forgotten sheaf,
F. for [he intends] in the future to search [for them].

Tosefta's two formally distinct rules (A-C, D-F) together reinforce the point that we take account of the farmer's intention in applying the law of the forgotten sheaf. This is indicated by the operative language at A and at F, "for he intends in the future to...." Let us turn to each in order to see how it makes this point.

A-C repeats M. 6:10A-C verbatim, except for the variation at A. The point of this new stich is that any produce which the farmer has yet to bind into full sheaves is not subject to the law of the forgotten sheaf. In line with M. 5:8 the law applies only from the time the sheaves are bound until they are broken apart. If the farmer still intends to bind the grain, the law cannot yet apply.

At D-F the farmer has bound produce into sheaves in order to quickly remove it from the path of oncoming fire or water. If, in his hurry, the farmer leaves behind some of these sheaves, the law does not apply. As stated at F, we fully assume that the farmer intends to return to his field after the fire or flood in order to see if any of the produce remains (so Lieberman, TK, p. 169). This indicates that he never forgot the produce, and so the law does not apply.

6:11

A. (1) One who harvests [a field] at night, or (2) who binds [produce into sheaves at night],[37] or (3) who is blind [and harvests and binds sheaves]--
B. [the produce that he harvests and binds yet leaves behind] is [subject to the restrictions of] the forgotten sheaf.

C. But if [a farmer][38] intended to collect [only] the largest sheaves,
D. [the smaller sheaves[39] that he purposely leaves in the field for later collection] are not [subject to the restrictions of the] forgotten sheaf.
E. If [a farmer] said, "Lo, I harvest on condition that whatever I forget I later will collect"--
F. [despite his statement, those sheaves that he leaves behind] are [subject to the restrictions of the] forgotten sheaf.

M. 6:11 (Y. Peah 5:6[19a])

The role of the householder's intention in the law of the forgotten sheaf forms the focus of these three rules. The basic point is that sheaves he intends to gather immediately, but nonetheless leaves behind, fall subject to the law. For example, the worker at A-B harvests and binds grain at night, or is blind, and so is constrained to leave some sheaves uncollected.[40] Nonetheless, by beginning to harvest despite his inability to see the sheaves, the worker indicates that his intention is to accept the possibility of forgetting some of the bundles. Whatever he leaves behind therefore falls into the category of the forgotten sheaf. The rule at C-D further illustrates the power of the farmer's intention. We now consider a person who, at this time, wishes to remove only the large sheaves from the field (C-D). Since he intentionally leaves behind the small sheaves, but does not forget them, the law cannot apply. Finally, at E-F we take up a case in which human intention is of no effect. Here a worker proposes a condition that would overrule Scripture's law[41] regarding forgotten sheaves. Accordingly, his intention-- namely, to declare that any sheaves he forgets actually are not subject to the law--is irrelevant to the application of the law. Whatever he leaves behind must be given to the poor.

T. 3:8b

A. A certain righteous man (ḥsyd) forgot a sheaf in the middle of his field. He said to his son, "Go and offer in my behalf a bullock as a burnt-offering and a bullock as a whole-offering."[42]
B. [His son] said to him, "Daddy, why do you (mh r'yth) rejoice [for performing] this commandment [i.e., the forgotten sheaf] more than all other commandments set forth in the Torah?"
C. [The father] said to him, "The Omnipresent has given us all of the commandments mentioned in the Torah [such that we perform them] intentionally (ld^ctynw). But this [one commandment] he gave to us [such that we perform it] unintentionally. For if anyone purposely performs [this commandment] before the Omnipresent, [i.e., he purposely left a sheaf in the field, but did not genuinely forget it], he has not performed this commandment."
D. [His son] said to him, "Lo, [Scripture] says, 'When you reap the harvest of your field, and have forgotten a sheaf in the field, you shall not go back to get it; it shall be for the sojourner, the fatherless, and the widow (Deut. 24:19).' Thus

Scripture sets forth a blessing [for the unintentional performance of the commandment].

E. "Is not the matter to be reasoned <u>a minori ad maius</u>? If one who did not intend to acquire merit [by performing the commandment], but nonetheless did acquire this merit (<u>l' ntkwwn lzkwt wzkh</u>) is deemed as one who has acquired merit [by performing it], how much more should he who [in fact] intends to acquire merit [by performing the commandment], and does acquire this merit [be deemed to have acquired merit]!

F. "Similarly, [Scripture states], 'If anyone sins, doing any of the things which the Lord has commanded not to be done, though he does not know it, yet he is guilty and shall bear his iniquity. He shall bring to the priest a ram without blemish out of the flock, valued by you at the price of a guilt-offering, and the priest shall make atonement for him for the error which he committed unintentionally, and he shall be forgiven (Lev. 5:17-18).'

G. "Is not this matter [also] to be reasoned <u>a minori ad maius</u>? If someone who did not intend to transgress, yet in fact does transgress[43] is deemed to have sinned, how much more should he who intends to transgress and then does transgress [be deemed guilty of sinning]!"

The short narrative has no direct relationship to Mishnah, but takes up an interesting issue with respect to the law of the forgotten sheaf. This commandment, as the righteous man at A states, cannot be performed intentionally. That is to say, one cannot purposely forget a sheaf. His intention to leave the sheaf behind implies that it always remains in mind. The man's son presents two cases of exegesis <u>a minori ad maius</u> (B-E, F-G), in order to show his father that one can intentionally fulfill the commandment of the forgotten sheaf. In both cases, he reasons that what one does intentionally deserves the same treatment as that which one does unintentionally. If one is praiseworthy for inadvertently leaving sheaves in the field, he certainly is to be praised if he purposely leaves them for the poor.

CHAPTER SEVEN
PEAH CHAPTER SEVEN

Mishnah's framers systematically apply the rules of various poor-offerings to two special crops: olive trees (M. 7:1-2) and vineyards (M. 7:3-8). These types of produce warrant special consideration within Mishnah's system of poor-offerings, because Scripture explicitly applies its rules to these species (cf. Lev. 19:10, Deut. 24:20-21).

The opening unit applies the law of the forgotten sheaf to the fruit left behind on olive trees. Its main point is that olives growing on trees with distinctive features cannot fall into the category of forgotten produce (M. 7:1-2). Because these trees exhibit special characteristics, householders almost certainly will not forget to harvest them. We thus assume that the farmer has purposely left behind fruit remaining on these trees. This principle is familiar from M. 6:1, which claims that sheaves with distinguishing features cannot become subject to the law at all.

We next turn to a comprehensive review of the offerings designated from vineyards: separated grapes (M. 7:3), defective clusters (M. 7:4-5, 7:7-8A-G), and forgotten produce (M. 7:8F-I). The law of the separated grape, Lev. 19:10, holds that individual grapes that fall during the harvest must be left for the poor. Mishnah adds an important qualification to Scripture's injunction. Only those grapes that fall for no apparent reason are subject to the law (M. 7:3). If a cluster becomes entangled in the vine, for example, that which falls does not take on the status of separated grapes. The householder was constrained to drop this fruit, so that the poor are not entitled to it. As with gleanings (M. 4:10), only that which falls completely at random is subject to God's claim in behalf of the poor.

Deut. 24:21 states that defective grape clusters must be given to the poor. Through a series of ambiguous cases (M. 7:4E-F, G-K, and L-N), Mishnah's framers refine this definition. Well-formed grape clusters possess a conical shape; that is to say, they have either a shoulder or a pendant. Bunches that lack both of these features are deemed defective, and so belong to the poor. As with peah, gleanings, and forgotten sheaves, the underlying theory is that God has set this produce aside for consumption exclusively by the poor. By creating the clusters defectively, God indicates his desire that the poor receive a portion of the crop. With this broad definition in hand, the sages ask a fundamental question: At what point in the growing season does the law of defective clusters take effect (M. 7:6-8)? Mishnah's authorities advance two separate possibilities. Meir (M. 7:5C) and the anonymous rule at M. 7:8A-D claim that the law takes effect as soon as defective clusters appear on the vine. According to this theory, once these bunches have begun to grow the householder must treat them as the property of the poor. Hence, he may neither prune the defective clusters nor dedicate this fruit to the Temple. The alternative view, presented by Judah (M. 7:5E) and Yosé (M. 7:8E), is that the law applies only after the farmer begins to harvest. Accordingly, the poor have no claim on the defective clusters until the farmer claims the well-formed bunches for himself. Thus before he starts reaping, he may trim or dedicate to the Temple all clusters in his vineyard, including those that are defective.

A single rule, M. 7:8F-I, applies the restrictions of forgotten produce to vineyards. In line with Deut. 19:24, Mishnah's framers rule that the householder may not return to gather produce he already has passed by. Accordingly, he may collect bunches of grapes so long as he need not retrace his steps (see M. 6:4).

One minor interruption breaks the flow of the chapter. At M. 7:6 the Houses compare and contrast the rules that apply to the produce of a four-year-old vine (see Lev. 19:24) with those that govern food in the status of second tithe. This unit appears verbatim in M. M.S. 5:3, and seems to have been included here only to complete the chapter's list of offerings designated from vineyards.

7:1

A. [The fruit of] any olive tree that is distinguished (šyš lw šm) [from the other trees] in its field,

B. such[1] as an olive tree [that is famous because its fruit] exudes [much oil] (hntwph) when it is ripe (bš‘tw),[2]

C. and that [the householder] left [unharvested],

D. is not [subject to the restrictions of] the forgotten sheaf.

E. In what case does this apply?

F. [It applies to a tree distinguished by] (1) its reputation [based on past years' production of oil], (2) its production [of oil during this year], or (3) its location.

G. (1) [With regard to] its reputation [based on past years' production of oil]--

H. [the tree] was [known to have been] a heavy producer (špkwny) or a dry one (byšny).[3]

I. (2) [With regard to] its production [of oil during this year]--

J. [the tree] produces more [oil than usual for that particular tree].

K. (3) [With regard to] its location--

L. [the tree] is situated near the wine-press or near the gate [of the fence surrounding the orchard].

M. But [as regards] all remaining olive trees, [which are not distinguished by such traits]--

N. [the fruit of] two [such trees left unharvested] is [subject to the restrictions of the] forgotten sheaf.

O. But [the fruit of] three [trees left unharvested] is not [subject to the restrictions of the] forgotten sheaf.

P. R. Yosé says, "The [restrictions of the] forgotten sheaf do not apply to olive trees [at all]."

M. 7:1 (Y. Peah 6:2[19b], 7:1[20a])

Olive trees that possess distinctive features stand out in the householder's mind, with the result that he cannot easily forget them. Accordingly, their fruit does not enter the category of forgotten produce, even if it is left unharvested (see M. 6:2). This rule, phrased at D, sets the stage for secondary expansions at E-L, which merely spell out three types of distinctive characteristics. The rules at M-O balance the foregoing by taking up the case of olive trees without distinctive features. As at M. 6:5, we assume that the amount of fruit contained on three such trees is great enough that the farmer will remember to reap it, even it he has left the trees unharvested. However, a farmer who leaves behind the fruit of only two trees probably will not remember this small amount of food. Olives that he leaves unharvested thus enter the category of forgotten produce.

Yosé (P) rejects this entire discussion. He claims that olive trees simply are not subject to the rules of forgotten sheaves. That is to say, since their fruit is not grain and cannot be bound into sheaves, the law by definition does not apply.

7:2

A. [The fruit of] an olive tree [that is completely surrounded by other olive trees, for] it stands in the middle (byn) of three rows [of trees, that mark off] two rectangular [plots of grain],[4]

B. and that [the householder] left [unharvested],

C. is not [subject to the restrictions of the] forgotten sheaf. [This is because of the tree's distinctive location (see M. 7:1K-L).][5]

D. An olive tree upon [the branches of] which remain two seahs [of unpicked olives],

E. and that [the householder] left [unharvested],

F. is not [subject to the restrictions of the] forgotten sheaf.

G. Under what circumstances does this (D-F) apply?

H. [It applies] so long as [the farmer] has not yet begun [to harvest the tree].

I. But if he had begun [to harvest] it,

J. even if it is an olive tree [the fruit of which] exudes [much oil] when it is ripe (cf. M. 7:1B),

K. and that [the householder] left [unharvested],

L. it is [subject to the restrictions of the] forgotten sheaf.

M. So long as [the restrictions of the forgotten sheaf] apply to [the olives that have fallen and lie] under the tree,

N. [the restrictions of the forgotten sheaf also] apply to [the olives that remain unpicked on the crown of the tree.

O. R. Meir says, "[This ruling, M-N, applies only] after the [worker] has gone by with a harvesting rod."

M. 7:2 (Sifre Deut. #284 [Finkelstein-Horowitz, p. 301])

Three distinct rules (A-C, D-F+G-L, M-O) now conclude the discussion of the law of the forgotten sheaf and olive trees. The first (A-C) illustrates M. 7:1K-L's principle that a tree distinguished by its location is not subject to the law. Since the tree under discussion is located in an unusual place, the householder certainly will remember its fruit. The second rule (D-L) repeats verbatim M. 6:7 for the case of olive trees (D-L). The householder is likely to remember a tree containing more than two seahs of fruit, and so the law does not apply (D-F). G-L add an important qualification. Once the householder has begun to harvest a tree, we may assume that he intends to collect all of its olives forthwith. Thus, whatever he does not gather immediately falls into the category of forgotten produce.[6] This is the case even if the tree possesses some distinctive feature, which normally would render its fruit exempt from the law (J). A final rule (M-N) claims that all of a tree's fruit, both those olives that have fallen to the ground and those that remain on its branches, are subject to a single law. I can make sense of this rule only in light of Meir's explanation (O) that the householder already has begun to reap the tree with a harvesting rod. According to this interpretation, the farmer already has claimed both the produce on the tree and that on the ground below. If he leaves some of this produce behind, then the fruit (both that on the tree and that on the ground) becomes subject to the restrictions of the forgotten sheaf.

T. 3:9

A. Any olive tree which is distinguished (šyš lw šm) [among the other trees] in its field,

B. as an olive tree [which is famous because of its fruit] exudes [much oil] (hntwph) when it is ripe (bš^{c}tw),

C. and [the worker] left it [unharvested],

D. [the tree] is not [subject to the restrictions of the] forgotten sheaf (M. 7:1A-D).

E. Under what circumstances does this (A-D) apply?

F. [It applies] so long as [the farmer] has not yet begun [to harvest the tree].

G. But if he has begun [to harvest] it,

H. and he left [some fruit] behind,

I. it is [subject to the restrictions of] the forgotten sheaf (M. 7:2G-I+K-L).

J. [This applies] unless [the tree] contains two seahs [of olives].

Tosefta conflates M. 7:1A-D and 7:2G-L, merely rearranging familiar materials. The point of the construction before us is that if a householder has begun to harvest a tree, that which he leaves behind is subject to the law. This is the case even if the tree possesses distinctive features, such that the law normally would not apply. Of course, if the farmer leaves behind more that two seahs of olives (J), this fruit is exempt from the law. As at M. 6:5-7, this amount is deemed too large for the farmer to forget.

T. 3:10

A. An olive tree [which is completely surrounded by other olive trees, for] it stands in the middle of three rows [of olive trees], which [mark off] two plots [of grain],

B. and which [the householder] left [unharvested],
C. is not [subject to the restrictions of] the forgotten sheaf (M. 7:2A-C with variations).
D. Under what circumstances does this apply?
E. [It applies] if [the farmer] does not recognize [the tree as having distinctive features].
F. But if [the farmer] does recognize [the tree as having distinguishing characteristics],
G. [the farmer may] run back and harvest it [i.e., he may return, for we assume that he never actually forgot the tree, due to its special features].
H. [This is the case] even if [the householder has passed by the tree and gone a full] one hundred cubits.

Tosefta appears to provide an explanation of M. 7:2, cited at A-C. As Lieberman, TK, p. 173, has noted, however, the explanation, D-H, does not respond to A-C at all (see also Y. 7:1[20a]). A-C treats only an olive tree which is distinguished in its location, and so not subject to the law. D-H, though, distinguish between trees that do and do not display distinctive characteristics, and supply distinct rules for each. The rhetorical question at D, therefore, is merely a redactional device used to connect these two entirely separate units.

Although D-H do not respond to M. 7:2, their point is clear. The farmer may return to harvest a tree that possesses distinctive characteristics, for the law does not apply to this tree at all (cf. M. 7:1). On the other hand, if the tree possesses no special features, the law of the forgotten sheaf applies as soon as the farmer passes it. In line with Deut. 24:19, the householder may not return (E).

7:3

A. What [produce is subject to the law of the] separated grape (prṭ), [with the result that it belongs to the poor]?
B. [Individual grapes] that fall [to the ground] during the harvest.
C. [If a householder] was harvesting, [and] cut an entire cluster,
D. [and] it became entangled in the leaves [of the vine],
E. [so that the cluster] fell from his hand to the ground, and separated [into individual grapes],
F. lo, [the individual grapes, together with the remaining cluster], belong to the householder, [since the fruit fell due to some external contraint]. [Only produce that falls to the ground at random, for no apparent reason, enters the category of the separated grape (see M. 4:10).]
G. One who places a basket under the vine while he harvests, [in order to catch the grapes that separate and fall, so that they will not enter the status of separated grapes],

H. lo, that man steals from the poor.
I. Concerning him it is stated, "Remove not the landmark of the poor," (gbwl ʿwlym). [This is a play on words on Prov. 22:28, which reads, "Remove not the ancient landmark," (gbwl ʿwlm) (see M. 5:6).]

M. 7:3 (Sifra Qid. 3:2)

The law of the separated grape arises from Lev. 19:10, which states, "You shall not gather the fallen grapes of your vineyard; you shall leave them for the poor and for the sojourner." The opening rule, A-B, paraphrases Scripture, by claiming that all grapes that fall during the harvest must be given to the poor. This simple statement sets the stage for the main emphasis of the pericope, cases of ambiguity and secondary developments of Scripture's injunction (C-F, G-I).

The harvester at C-F drops a cluster of grapes because it becomes entangled in the vine. Mishnah's authorities claim that this bunch does not enter the status of separated grapes, even though it fell during the harvest. The theory that underlies this ruling is familiar from the laws of both gleanings and forgotten sheaves (see for example M. 4:10, 5:7, and T. 2:13). Grapes that fall due to an external constraint and not completely at random cannot enter the status of poor-offerings. Rather, only that which falls to the ground through no identifiable cause is deemed subject to God's claim in behalf of the poor. In the present case the vine caused the worker to drop some of the grapes, so the poor have no claim upon the fruit.

A final rule and prooftext, G-H+I, assert that householders may not misappropriate produce that rightfully belongs to the poor. Accordingly, householders may not attempt to catch grapes as they fall to the ground because this action would constitute theft (H-I).

7:4

A. What [produce is subject to the law of] the defective cluster (ʿwllt), [such that it belongs to the poor]?
B. Any [cluster of grapes] that has neither a shoulder [i.e., a wide upper-part] nor a pendant [i.e., a cone-shaped lower-part].
C. If[7] [a cluster of grapes] has either a shoulder or a pendant, [or both],
D. it belongs to the householder, [for it is deemed well-formed].
E. If it is uncertain [whether a cluster has at least one of these two definitive features, a shoulder or a pendant],
F. [it is deemed a defective cluster and belongs] to the poor.
G. [As regards] a cluster [that appears to be] defective, [for it grows] on the [portion of the vine that] lies [on the ground] ('rkbh),[8] [such a cluster cannot hang down, and so appears to have neither a shoulder nor a pendant, even though in fact it may possess these features]--
H. if [the cluster] is harvested along with the [normal] clusters,
I. lo, it belongs to the householder [i.e., it is deemed a well-formed cluster].
J. But if [the cluster] is not [harvested with the normal clusters],
K. lo, it belongs to the poor [i.e., it is deemed a defective cluster].

L. [As regards] a single grape [i.e., one that does not grow within a cluster]--
M. R. Judah says, "[It is deemed] a [normal] cluster, [and belongs to the householder]."
N. But sages say, "[It is deemed] a defective cluster, [and belongs to the poor]."

M. 7:4 (Sifra Qid. 3:3; Sifre Deut. #285 [Finkelstein-Horowitz, p. 302])

The law of the defective cluster is based on Deut. 24:21, "When you gather the grapes of your vineyard, you shall not return to gather the defective clusters." Mishnah's framers open their discussion of this law by defining a well-formed cluster as one that possesses either a shoulder or a pendant (C-D). Bunches of grapes that lack both of these characteristics are deemed defective, and therefore must be left for the poor (A-B). These two contrasting rules are followed by a typical case of doubt (E-F) in which the farmer cannot tell if some of the clusters are well-formed. These bunches must be left behind as defective clusters, lest the householder misappropriate produce that might actually belong to the poor (see M. 4:11).

These three units draw in their wake two further cases of ambiguity, G-K and L-N, which I take up in turn. The vine at G-K runs along the ground,[9] so that a bunch of grapes growing on it cannot hang down. Since its pendant and shoulder are not clearly visible, this cluster appears to be defective, even though it may be well formed. The pair of rules at H-I and J-K claim that the farmer's actions in harvesting such a bunch determines its status. If he reaps it along with the normal clusters, it is deemed well-formed. The householder may keep it. But if the farmer treats the grapes as a defective bunch by leaving them behind when reaping the other, well-formed clusters, they enter the status of a defective cluster. The poor may take them.

A separate case of ambiguity (L-N) concerns the status of a single grape that grows on the vine, completely distinct from any cluster. Does the law that governs whole clusters also apply to this single grape? This issue is the focus of the dispute at L-M+N. Sages (N) claim that a single grape possess neither a shoulder nor a pendant. Hence, it falls into the category of defective clusters and must be left for the poor. Judah (M), by contrast, rules that a single grape is not a cluster at all. Hence, by definition the grape cannot fall into the category of a defective cluster. The householder need not give the grape to the poor.

T. 3:11a

A. [As regards] one who declared his vineyard to be ownerless--
B. rich people may gather the normal clusters,
C. and poor people may gather both the normal and defective clusters.

Defective clusters are reserved for the poor alone. This is the case even if the householder declares them to be ownerless (C); since he does not own or control this food, his declaration regarding it is null. Normal clusters which are declared ownerless, of course, are available for both rich and poor to take (B).

T. 3:11b

A. What [produce is subject to the law of the] defective cluster, [such that it belongs to the poor]?
B. Any [cluster of grapes] which has neither a shoulder [i.e., a wide upper part] nor a pendant [i.e., a cone shaped lower part] (M. 7:4A-B).
C. [If a cluster] has a shoulder but no pendant, or a pendant but no shoulder,
D. lo, it belongs to the householder.
E. But if [the cluster has] neither [of these identifying characteristics],
F. lo, it belongs to the poor (M. 7:4C-D with variations).
G. What is [the definition of a] shoulder?
H. [A shoulder consists of] sprigs attached to the main stalk [of a cluster] one over the other, [such that they form a wide top].
I. [What is the definition of a] pendant?
J. [A pendant consists of] grapes attached [directly] to the main stalk [of the cluster], such that they hang down.

Tosefta clarifies M. 7:4, cited at A-F, by spelling out the formations which comprise the definitive features of a well-formed cluster, a shoulder (G-H) and a pendant (I-J).

7:5

A. [As regards] "One who thins [some of the stalks of his grape] vines [in order to improve the growth of the entire vineyard]--
B. "just as he [is allowed] to thin his own [produce, i.e., the well-formed clusters], so may he thin [the defective clusters] that belong to the poor," the opinion of R. Judah.
C. R. Meir says, "He is permitted to thin his own [produce], but he is not permitted [to thin the defective clusters] that belong to the poor."

M. 7:5 (Y. Peah 5:3 [19a]; B. M.Q. 4b)

Householders periodically prune poorly developed clusters from their vines, in order to improve their vineyards' yield, and so increase their profits.[10] This procedure poses a problem, however, for by thinning and throwing away defective clusters, the farmer deprives the poor of that which is rightfully theirs. The issue of whether or not the farmer may prune his vines depends upon when the restrictions governing defective clusters take effect.[11] Judah (B) holds that produce becomes subject to the law only after the householder begins to reap the field as a whole. Earlier in the season, the poor have no claim on the grapes, and so the farmer may prune them as he likes. As with all other poor-offerings, the householder's act of claiming the produce for himself generates the poor's complementary claim on a part of the crop. Meir (C) has a different theory of when the restrictions of defective clusters take effect. He claims that the law begins to apply as soon as the defective clusters appear on the vine. One who thins these grapes misappropriates produce belonging to the poor, which is forbidden. Underlying Meir's view, I discern a subtle theory. Defective clusters are designated by their very nature; the householder, for his part, plays no role in determining which grapes must be left for the poor. Similarly, Meir rules, the householder should have no part in determining when the law takes effect. The poor may take the defective clusters immediately after they form, without waiting for the householder to begin to reap his vineyard.

T. 3:12

I. A. [As regards] a gentile who sold his vineyard to an Israelite for harvesting--
    B. [the produce of the vineyard] is subject to [the law of] the defective cluster, [for when the law takes effect, at the beginning of the harvest, an Israelite owns the vineyard].[12]
II. C. And [as regards] an Israelite who sold his vineyard to a gentile for harvesting--
    D. [the produce of the vineyard] is exempt from [the law of] the defective cluster, [for when the law takes effect, a gentile owns the vineyard].
III. E. [As regards] an Israelite and a gentile who jointly own a vineyard--
    F. [the produce that grows in] the part [of the vineyard] owned by the Israelite is subject [to the law of the defective cluster],
    G. and [the produce that grows in the part of the vineyard] owned by the gentile is exempt [from the law of the defective cluster].
    H. R. Simeon says, "[As regards] in Israelite and a gentile who jointly own a vineyard [= E]--
    I. "[all of the produce that grows in the vineyard] is exempt from [the law of] defective clusters."

T. 3:12

The law of the defective cluster takes effect at the beginning of the harvest (cf. M. 7:5B).[13] The first two rules in Tosefta's triplet (A-B, C-D) make the point that only produce which Israelites own at harvest time is subject to the law. These two cases set up a predictable ambiguity, a field jointly owned by an Israelite and by a gentile (E-G+H-I). Our view of joint ownership determines whether or not the law applies. If each of the owners individually possesses a distinct portion of the vineyard (E-G), the half of the vineyard that belongs to the gentile is exempt from the law and the Israelite's half is subject. The alternative view, taken by Simeon (H-I), holds that a jointly owned vineyard is a single entity. All of its produce is owned equally by both the gentile and the Israelite. Since all of the food is partly owned by the gentile, Simeon reasons, none of it is subject to the law.

7:6

A. [As regards] a vine[14] in its fourth year [of growth, the fruit of which must be eaten only in Jerusalem, just as is the case with produce in the status of second tithe (cf. Lev. 19:24)]--

130 Support for the Poor

B. the House of Shammai say, '[If the owner converts this produce to his own coin, which he will bring to Jerusalem, the cash] is not [subject to the law of] the added-fifth[15] (see M. M.S. 4:3),

C. and, [moreover, if the produce remains in one's home after Passover of the fourth and seventh years of the Sabbatical cycle],[16] it is not [subject to] removal (see M. M.S. 5:6)." [The laws of the added-fifth and of removal do apply to produce in the status of second tithe. The Shammaites thus claim that although both types of produce, the fruit of a four-year-old vine and food in the status of second tithe, must be consumed only in Jerusalem, the two types of food are not analogous to each other in these respects.]

D. The House of Hillel say, "[The produce of a vine in its fourth year of growth] is subject to the laws [of the added fifth and removal, for the fruit is deemed fully analogous to food in the status of second tithe]."

E. The House of Shammai say, "[Unlike produce in the status of second tithe, the fruit of a four-year-old vine is subject to both the law of] the separated grape and [the law of] the defective cluster. [Second tithe is deemed holy, and so poor-offerings need not be designated from it. As at B-C, the Shammaites claim that the grapes of a four-year-old vine are not governed by the rules that apply to second tithe.]

F. "[Since poor-offerings must be separated from the produce of a four-year-old vine, it is] the poor [who] redeem [the produce they receive as separated grapes and as defective clusters] for themselves, [and they bring the cash to Jerusalem, and use it to buy other food]." [All food in the status of second tithe, by contrast, is redeemed by the householder, for the poor have no claim on it (see D).]

G. But the House of Hillel say, "[In contrast to E-F], all [of the produce of a vine in its fourth year of growth is to be taken by the householder] to the wine-press." [Just as with second tithe, the householder is the one who must prepare the wine, and then take it to Jerusalem.]

M. 7:6 (M. M.S. 5:3; M. Ed. 4:5; T. M.S. 5:17; Sifra Qid. 3:7; Y. M.S. 4:2[55a]; B. Qid. 54b; B. B.M. 55b)

Both the fruit of a four-year-old vine and produce in the status of second tithe must be consumed in Jerusalem (cf. Lev. 19:24, Deut. 14:22-27). These facts, taken from Scripture, provide the background for the two Houses-disputes before us (A-B vs. C, D-E vs. F). At issue is whether or not these two types of produce are subject to precisely the same rules in all other respects. That is to say, since they share one law, do they share all other laws as well? The Hillelites claim that the two types of food are entirely analogous. Hence, all laws that apply to second tithe also govern produce that grows on a four-year-old vine. The alternative view, taken by the Shammaites, is that the two sets of food are subject to precisely opposing rules. The laws that govern second tithe do not apply to the produce of a vine in its fourth year of growth. The only exception, in their view, is Scripture's injunction that both types of food be eaten in Jerusalem. With these two opinions broadly outlined, I now review the specifics of these two units.

The first dispute, A-B vs. C, concerns the laws of the added-fifth and removal. The law of the added-fifth applies when a householder wishes to redeem second tithe for his own cash. We assume that the farmer will attempt to convert the second tithe to coin at a low rate, and so will not properly deconsecrate all of the produce. In order to prevent this from occurring, Lev. 27:31 specifies that he must add an additional 25% to his purchase price. The law of removal, Deut. 26:12-13, states that before Passover of the fourth and seventh years of the Sabbatical cycle the householder must remove from his home all consecrated produce, such as first and second tithe. At this time, these offerings must be distributed to their appropriate recipients. As I explained above, the Hillelites claim that these two restrictions, which apply to produce in the status of second tithe, also govern the fruit of a four-year-old vine. The Shammaites, on the other hand, claim that only produce in the status of second tithe must be treated in accord with these rules. In their view, the fruit of a vine in its fourth year of growth is not governed by the analogy of second tithe, and so is exempt from removal and from the law of the added-fifth.

A second dispute (D-E vs. F) asks whether or not the quite familiar laws of the separated grape (M. 7:3) and of defective clusters (M. 7:4) apply to second tithe and the produce of a four-year-old vine. Only the formulations of the Houses' opinions require explanation. The Shammaites hold that the poor are entitled to separated grapes and defective clusters from a four-year-old vine. Since this produce must be eaten only in Jerusalem, the poor must take these offerings, or their equivalent in cash, to that city (E). The Hillelites claim that the produce of a four-year-old vine is exempt from the laws of separated grapes and defective clusters, for the entire vineyard's yield already is sanctified in accord with Scripture.[17] Accordingly, the householder is the one who must handle and redeem second tithe, and likewise, the grapes of a four-year-old vine. He must take the grapes "to the winepress" in order to increase the value of the produce to be eaten in Jerusalem (so T. M.S. 5:19).[18]

7:7

A. [As regards] a vineyard [the produce of which] entirely is defective clusters--

B. R. Eliezer says, "[The fruit] belongs to the householder [i.e., the clusters do not fall into the category of defective clusters because the norm in that vineyard is clusters that are not well formed]."

C. R. Aqiba says, "[The fruit] belongs to the poor, [i.e., the clusters are deemed defective, because they lack the definitive characteristics of well-formed clusters]."

D. Said R. Eliezer, "[Scripture states], 'When you harvest the grapes of your vineyard, you shall not return to gather the defective clusters' (Deut. 24:21).

E. "If there is no harvest [of normal clusters, because the entire yield is defective], how can there be defective clusters [left after the harvest]?"

F. Said to him R. Aqiba, "[Scripture also states], 'And you shall not gather defective clusters' (Lev. 19:10).

G. "[This verse indicates that the law applies] even if [the] entire [produce of the vineyard] is defective clusters, [such that there is no harvest of normal clusters].

H. [Aqiba continues:] "[If that is the intent of Lev. 19:10], why does [Scripture] state, 'When you harvest the grapes of your vineyard, you shall not return to gather the defective clusters' (Deut. 24:21)?

I. "[This verse, i.e., Deut. 24:21, teaches that] the poor may not claim the defective clusters before the harvest, [for the law of defective clusters takes effect only when the farmer claims the normal bunches of grapes for himself, by harvesting them]. [Before this time, none of the grapes can enter the status of defective clusters.]"

M. 7:7 (Sifra Qid. 3:1; Sifre Deut. #285
[Finkelstein-Horowitz, p. 302])

We now consider a case in which all of a vineyard's yield possesses the characteristics of defective clusters. At issue is whether or not this whole crop must be given to the poor. The answer depends upon our fundamental conception of the law of defective clusters. By "defective" we might refer to the objective standard for the shape of well-formed clusters presented at M. 7:4. In line with this view, Aqiba (C) rules that all bunches that lack both shoulders and pendants must be left for the poor. It is of no concern whether the householder must give to the poor a few clusters of grapes or his entire vineyard's yield. The alternative view, presented by Eliezer (B), is that the category of defective clusters is relative, defined only by the norm within a single field. Since most of the grape clusters within the vineyard at A have neither shoulder nor pendant, Eliezer reasons that they are well-formed. Accordingly, the poor have no claim on them.[19]

In the secondary material at D-I, the two authorities attempt to show how their views may be derived from Scripture. Deut. 24:21, cited by Eliezer (D-E), refers both to harvesting normal clusters and to defective clusters that are left after the harvest. Since the farmer at A-B never harvests any normal clusters, the entire law of defective clusters cannot apply. Aqiba's prooftext, Lev. 19:10, never refers to harvesting normal grape clusters, but only to the prohibition against gathering defective ones. The law should apply, he says, even if the entire field is composed of defective clusters. At H-I Aqiba provides an alternative interpretation of Eliezer's prooftext, Deut. 24:21. According to Aqiba, the reference to the harvest teaches that the poor may not claim the defective clusters until after the householder begins to reap his vineyard.

7:8

A. [As regards] one who dedicates his vineyard's [yield to the Temple], before the defective clusters within it appear--

B. the defective clusters [that form after the dedication] do not belong to the poor, [because they are owned by the Temple] when they first form, i.e., when the law takes effect (cf. M. 1:6)].

Peah Chapter Seven   133

C. [If he dedicated his vineyard's yield to the Temple] after the defective clusters appear--

D. the defective clusters belong to the poor, [since the law applies from the moment they form]. [From this time on, the householder has no control over the defective clusters, and therefore his dedication of them is null.]

E. R. Yosé says, "If so,[20] [i.e., if one dedicated his vineyard's yield to the Temple after the defective clusters appeared, the poor] must give to the Temple the value of that part of the defective clusters that [appears and] grows [after the vineyard is dedicated].[21] [But they may keep the portion of the produce that had grown before the vineyard's yield was dedicated]."

F. What [sort of grape cluster growing on a] trellis is subject [to the restrictions of] forgotten produce?

G. That which [the worker passes by, and cannot collect merely] by reaching [behind him] with his hand. [That is to say, if the worker must retrace his steps in order to take the grapes, the fruit is deemed forgotten produce.]

H. And with regard to [produce growing on] vines that run along the ground [what fruit is subject to the restrictions of forgotten produce]?

I. [All produce becomes subject] when [the harvester] passes by it.

M. 7:8 (Y. Pes. 4:9[31b]; Sifre Deut. #285 [Finkelstein-Horowitz, p. 302])

In the first of two entirely separate units (A-E, F-I), a farmer has dedicated to the Temple a vineyard containing defective clusters. The validity of his dedication is in question, however, for it is unclear whether or not he has the right to consecrate the defective clusters. The two contrasting rules at A-B and C-D assert that the issue is decided by whether the dedication occurred before or after the defective clusters appeared. This is because the law of the defective cluster takes effect only after the poorly formed bunches have appeared on the vines. Before such clusters appear, the farmer has full control of his vineyard. His dedication of its produce, including any defective clusters yet to form, is valid (A-B). Accordingly, he must give the defective clusters to the Temple priests. Once the defective cluters have formed, however, the householder may validly dedicate only his own produce. The poor already are deemed the owners of the defective clusters, and so the householder's dedication cannot apply to this fruit (C-D).

Yosé (F) raises a subtle issue regarding the foregoing. As at C-D, we deal with a farmer who dedicates his vineyard after the defective clusters have appeared. But what happens if, after the dedication, still more defective clusters form on the vines? Such bunches belong to the Temple, yet probably will be given to the poor with the other defective clusters. In order to prevent the Temple from being cheated, Yosé rules that the poor are entitled only to that portion of the defective clusters that grew before the farmer dedicated the vineyard. They must give to the Temple the value of that which appeared and grew after the dedication.[22]

The second unit applies the laws of forgotten produce to the case of vineyards.[23] Two parallel rules (F-G, H-I) affirm Deut. 24:19's injunction that one may not return to gather forgotten produce. Grapes that the householder has a chance to harvest, yet passes by, immediately fall into the category of forgotten produce. The restrictions of forgotten produce therefore apply to fruit he can reach only by retracing his steps (see M. 6:4).

T. 3:13

A. One who dedicates [the produce of] his vineyard [to the Temple],
B. may not dedicate the defective clusters [growing within it],
C. for a person may not dedicate something that he does not own.

Once defective clusters appear on the vines, the householder no longer has control over this produce (cf. M. 7:8C-D). He therefore is not permitted to dedicate these grapes.

T. 3:14

A. A Levite to whom grapes were given [as tithes],[24]
B. and within [this gift] were some defective clusters,
C. need not scruple that the defective clusters might actually belong to the poor.

It is the responsibility of the householder alone to assure that defective clusters are not misappropriated. A Levite who receives some defective clusters therefore need not consider the possibility that the householder has cheated the poor.

T 3:15

A. One who plants a vineyard [with the intention later] to dedicate [its fruit to the Temple]--
B. [the fruit of such a vineyard] is exempt from the laws of orlah and from the laws of a four-year-old vine. [These rules hold that the yield of a tree or a vine during its first four years of growth is sanctified, and may not be used for ordinary purposes (cf. Lev. 19:22, M. M.S. 5:1-3).]
C. But [the fruit of the vineyard at A] is subject to the laws of the Sabbatical year.
D. From what stage [of a vineyard's growth] is a person permitted to harvest the vineyard?
E. [One is permitted to harvest] from the time when he knows the character of the fruit [i.e., as soon as the clusters can be identified as normal or defective].
F. For [at this point in time, the fruit of] the vineyard already is subject [to the law], because of the growth of defective clusters.

Peah Chapter Seven   135

Tosefta's two units (A-B+C, D-E+F) provide additional information regarding poor-offerings designated from vineyards, the topic of M. 7:3-8. The first rule makes the point that the farmer's intention determines the status of his produce. Vines that he plants with the full intention to dedicate to the Temple therefore are treated as if they already were dedicated. Just as produce owned by the Temple is exempt from the laws of orlah and of a four-year-old vine, so too produce that the farmer intends to dedicate is exempt (A-B). On the other hand, the law of the Sabbatical year applies even to produce that the householder intends to dedicate (C). All food grown in the Land of Israel during the Sabbatical year is deemed ownerless, and may not be cultivated.

The householder at D-F may not harvest his vineyard until he knows which clusters are defective. This assures that he will not unknowingly misappropriate produce that belongs to the poor.[25]

T. 3:16

	A.	What [produce within a vineyard is subject to the law of] forgotten produce?
I.	B.	With regard to a large trellis--
	C.	that which [the worker passes by, and cannot collect] by reaching [behind him] with his hand (M. 7:8G).
II.	D.	[And] with regard to a small trellis--
	E.	[a cluster is subject to the law of forgotten produce] as soon as [the farmer] has passed by it (M. 7:8I with variations).
III.	F.	[And] with regard to grapes on an espalier or the produce of a date palm--
	G.	as soon as [the farmer climbs] down, [the law of forgotten produce applies to that which he has left behind on the tree].
IV.	H.	[And as regards] all other types of trees--
	I.	[the law of forgotten produce applies] as soon as the householder turns and walks away [from the tree].
	J.	Under what circumstances does this apply?
	K.	[It applies] so long as the farmer has not begun [to harvest the tree].
	L.	But if he had begun [to harvest the tree], and then forgot [the produce remaining on it],
	M.	the law of forgotten produce does not apply,
	N.	until he has harvested all of the surrounding [trees].

Each of the four rules (B-C, D-E, F-G, and H-I) makes the same point as M. 7:8. Once the householder has passed by produce in a vineyard or on a tree, he may not return to collect it. These straightforward rules set up J-N, an important qualification. The prohibition against returning to gather produce applies only if the farmer has not yet begun to reap the tree or vine. Once he begins to harvest a tree, on the other hand, we may assume that he intends to complete its harvest.

Lieberman, TK, p. 177, points that this explanation contradicts much of the tractate's earlier material. Mishnah and Tosefta commonly hold that the law of forgotten produce applies only after the farmer has begun to harvest (see, for example, M. 7:2G-L and T. 3:9E-I). In order to bring J-N into line with these similar rules, Lieberman would like to read at K-L:

K. [The law applies] once the farmer has begun to harvest the tree.

L. But if he had not begun to harvest the tree, the law would not apply.

Lieberman, however, is unable to find textual evidence to support this reading, and so suggests the explanation I have provided above.

CHAPTER EIGHT
PEAH CHAPTER EIGHT

This chapter completes the systematic review of the harvest and of those offerings designated for the poor, a fitting conclusion to the entire tractate. Its core (M. 8:1-4) focuses on the status of poor-offerings after the poor have gathered them. This is followed by a brief discussion of two types of charity given after the harvest, poorman's tithe and community charity (M. 8:5-7). The final unit (M. 8:8-9) defines a poor person, an issue of central importance to the application of the law. Since these three sections are distinct, I shall examine each in turn.

After the poor have had an opportunity to collect the produce designated for them, two important issues arise. First, what is the status of produce set aside for the poor, but which they never take? Perhaps that which the poor do not take remains exclusively reserved for them and may not be taken by others. According to this view, poor-offerings would be seen as sanctified for the poor just as priestly offerings are consecrated only for priests. Mishnah, however, rejects this possibility (M. 8:1). Instead, produce that the poor do not collect within a reasonable time is deemed ownerless, available to rich and poor alike. This assures that the yield of the Land of Israel is not wasted. The second issue complements the first, turning to those offerings which the poor have taken and now wish to sell (M. 8:2-4). Poor-offerings, we recall, are exempt from the separation of tithes (cf. M. 1:6, 5:5), unlike common produce. The poor therefore benefit by claiming that all produce they sell has the status of poor-offerings exempt from tithing, even if this is a lie. By doing this, they can command a higher price for their goods because the householder who buys the goods will be able to use all of the produce. But this creates a problem for householders who purchase food from the poor. Under what circumstances should they believe that this produce in fact is exempt from the separation of tithes? The basic notion is that a poor person's statement is deemed credible only when circumstances suggest that it might be true. That is to say, farmers can assume that their purchases are exempt from tithing only during the proper season or year for the distribution of poor-offerings (M. 8:2A-B), and only with regard to the sorts of food that usually are given as poor-offerings (M. 8:2D+8:3-4).

The chapter's second unit concerns types of charity given after the completion of the harvest. First, as part of the normal tithing process, farmers designate poorman's tithe (cf. Deut. 14:28-29) during the third and sixth years of the Sabbatical cycle (M. 8:5-6). The basic rule is that a fixed amount of poorman's tithe must be given to all poor individuals. This assures, first, the equitable distribution of this produce, and second, that householders do not interfere in the distributive process. The unit's rules then describe the two basic institutions for the support of a community's poor throughout the year, from one harvest season to another. The soup-kitchen (M. 8:7G) provides food for those in immediate need, who have less than one full day's supply of food. The community fund, by contrast, provides long-term, monetary support for the indigent (M. 8:7H).

The tractate as a whole concludes with a quite practical concern: Who is deemed poor? The framers define poverty as the inability to support oneself from one harvest season to the next. Thus anyone without enough liquid assets for a full year, that is, two hundred zuz, is poor. He may gather poor-offerings from this year's crops in order to sustain himself until the next harvest when poor-offerings again are distributed. A person whose money is utilized as capital, by contrast, is not deemed poor. The interest earned by investing this money will be enough to support him, even if he has substantially less than two hundred zuz. These definitions are followed by a short passage of Scriptural exegeses (M. 8:9J-U), which marks the end of the chapter and tractate.

8:1

A. After what time [of year] are all people, [rich and poor alike], permitted [to gather] gleanings[1] [that the poor have not yet taken]?

B. [All are permitted] after the aged-poor (nmwšwt)[2] go [through the field in order to collect this produce, for by this time, we may assume that all poor people have had a chance to gather their share of the gleanings].

C. With regard to separated [grapes] and defective clusters, [when is any person, rich or poor, permitted to take the food]?

D. [All are permitted] after the poor go through the vineyard [to collect the produce designated for them], and have come [a second time, to gather the grapes they earlier passed over].

E. And with regard to olive trees, [when is any person permitted to collect the fruit left behind as forgotten produce]?

F. [All are permitted] after the time of the second rainfall.[3]

G. Said R. Judah, "But are there not some [farmers] who pick their olives only after the time of the second rainfall? [These householders would not yet have begun to harvest for themselves, and so could not have left any produce behind for the poor. Clearly, the olives should not be available for others to take.]

H. "Rather, [the proper ruling for olive trees is that all are permitted after] a poor person goes out [to the orchard to collect the produce designated for the poor], and cannot return with four issars [worth of olives]."

M. 8:1 (B. Taan. 6b; B. B.M. 12a, 21b)

Produce left for the poor, but never taken by them, has an ambiguous status. God has set aside this food for the poor alone so that others should not be allowed to gather it. Nevertheless, the poor seem to have foregone their exclusive right to collect this food because they never actually took it. Mishnah's framers resolve this ambiguity by asserting that edibles the poor have not taken are deemed ownerless. Rich and poor alike may take them. In the units before us, the sages address a secondary issue, the point in time when people may gather these unclaimed poor-offerings as ownerless produce. The basic principle is that after the poor have had ample opportunity to take the foodstuffs set aside for them, whatever they leave behind should be deemed ownerless. This rule assures that the poor are able to gather all the food they need[4] and has the further effect of assuring that produce of the Land of Israel will not go to waste. That which the poor leave behind almost certainly will be taken by others.

With the main point in mind, we now turn to the details of the law. Distinct rules apply to grain (A-B), grapes (C-D), or olives (E-F+G-H) that are left as poor-offerings yet remain uncollected. This is because each species of produce is harvested in a different manner and at a different time in the harvest season. Gleanings (A-B) that have not been collected by the time the oldest and slowest poor people have gone through the field immediately become available for all to take (A-B). At this point householders may assume that all of the poor have taken what they wish. Separated grapes and defective clusters (C-D) are deemed ownerless only after the poor have come to the vineyard twice. This assures that poor people have ample time to take this valuable fruit. Finally, olives designated for the poor (E-F+G-H) become available to all after the second rainfall. The poor will take their portion of the fruit before these rains commence, because heavy rain damages any olives left on the trees (Maimonides, Commentary). Judah (G-H) disputes the foregoing rule, claiming that by the time of the second rainfall farmers in some parts of the country have not yet harvested their olive trees. These householders could not yet have left behind any olives for the poor. Accordingly, others certainly should not be allowed to take the fruit remaining on the trees. Instead, Judah rules that when most of the olives set aside for the poor have been gathered, all are permitted to collect those remaining. Thus if a poor person who goes out to the field can collect no more than four issars worth of olives, those left in the field are deemed ownerless.

T. 2:18b

    A.   And [the portion] of the poor-offerings that [remains] in the fields,
    B.   to which the poor pay no attention--
    C.   lo, this [produce] belongs to the householder.

In contrast to M. 8:1A, Tosefta claims that produce which the poor do not take never becomes ownerless. Rather, since the householder designated this food for the poor from his own produce, he alone is entitled to that which they do not gather.

8:2-4

    A.   [Poor people who sell produce in their possession] are believed [if they claim that they received this food as] gleanings, forgotten sheaves, or peah,
    B.   [only if they are selling this produce] during the proper time [of year for the designation of these offerings] (bš'tn). [Thus during harvest season, when the poor collect these offerings, a poor person is deemed trustworthy when he claims that food he sells is in the status of poor-offerings. Accordingly, this produce is exempt from the separation of tithes (see M. Hal. 1:3).]

- C. And [poor people who sell produce also are believed if they claim that the food was received as] poorman's tithe,
- D. [so long as it is] the proper year [for the designation of this offering]. [Poorman's tithe is designated during the third and sixth years of the Sabbatical cycle. During these years alone a poor person is deemed trustworthy if he claims that the food he sells has the status of poorman's tithe. As at A, such produce would be exempt from further separation of tithes.]
- E. But, a Levite [who sells produce, and claims that the food has the status of first tithe] is believed during all [years of the Sabbatical cycle] (l^c wlm). [Since first tithe is designated every year, the Levite's claim prima facie always is credible.]
- F. But [the poor's claim that produce they sell is in the status of poor-offerings or was received as poorman's tithe] is believed only with regard to [the sort of] foodstuff (dbr) that people usually [leave for them]. [Thus we trust a poor person's claims only with regard to unprocessed food, for by definition this is what farmers usually leave behind or designate for the poor.]

M. 8:2

I.
- G. [The next five cases illustrate the point of F.] [The poor] are believed [if they claim that] wheat [that they sell was received as poor-offerings, and so is exempt from the separation of tithes],
- H. but they are not believed with regard to flour or a loaf [of bread]. [We assume that, when designating poor-offerings or poorman's tithe, householders ordinarily do not leave processed food for the poor. Further, we may assume that the poor person himself could not afford to process any grain he found in the field. Hence the flour or bread could not have derived from poor-offerings or poorman's tithe.]

II.
- I. They are believed with regard to panicles of rice,
- J. but they are not believed [with regard to husked rice], whether raw or cooked.

III.
- K. They are believed with regard to beans,
- L. but they are not believed with regard to bean-grits, whether raw or cooked.

IV.
- M. They are believed with regard to oil, [if they] say that [the oil] is in the status of poorman's tithe, [because this is what farmers usually designate for the poor].[5]
- N. But they are not believed with regard to [oil, if they] say that [the oil] derives from olives [that were forgotten on the] crown [of a tree].

M. 8:3

V.
- O. They are believed with regard to raw vegetables.
- P. But they are not believed with regard to cooked [vegetables],
- Q. unless [the poor person] has a small amount [of the cooked vegetables].
- R. For it is the custom of householders to take [a small amount] out of the stew-pot,[6] [and to give it to the poor as part of the poorman's tithe].

M. 8:4 (Y. Dem. 6:8[25d])

Poor people who sell their produce to householders might claim that all of the food they sell, including common produce, is in the status of poor-offerings or poorman's tithe. Deceiving buyers in this way would be to the poor person's advantage because householders who believe that they need separate no further tithes from the edibles would be willing to pay a higher price. The problem at hand is how a farmer knows whether or not the produce he buys truly has the status of poor-offerings or poorman's tithe. Mishnah's framers assert that a poor person's claim is deemed credible so long as the circumstances surrounding the transaction do not indicate that he is lying.

This general principle gives rise to two units, A-D and F+G-P, that specify circumstances in which the poor may be believed. First, if a poor person claims to sell poor-offerings (A-B) or poorman's tithe (C-D) when this produce is not available, the farmer can assume that the poor person is taking advantage of him. These edibles are subject to the separation of tithes because the poor person could not have received them as poor-offerings. Second, the householder should not believe a poor person who sells a type of produce that is not usually left for the poor (F). Five formally parallel rules (G-P) clarify this point by asserting that poor people ordinarily receive only unprocessed, uncooked food as poor-offerings.[7] Poor people who sell other types of produce should not be deemed credible.

Two glosses now require our attention. The rule at E takes up the case of a Levite, who receives tithes during every year of the Sabbatical cycle. When he sells this produce, therefore, his claims regarding its status always are deemed credible. This contrasts with the poor person at C-D, who can be trusted only during the third and sixth years of the Sabbatical cycle when poorman's tithe is distributed. Finally, Q-R assert that farmers often give to the poor small amounts of cooked vegetables as part of poorman's tithe. Accordingly, one may believe their claims that such food is exempt from further separation of tithes even though it already has been processed.

T. 4:1

A. R. Judah says, "[In] a place where [householders] press [the grapes on] defective clusters, [and give the resulting wine to the poor],
B. "a poor person is believed if he claims (1) 'This wine is in the status of defective clusters, [and so no tithes need be separated from it].'
C. "[A poor person also is believed if he claims], (2) 'My brothers, relatives and I gathered these gleanings.'
D. "But he is not believed if he claims, (1) 'I purchased [this food] from Mr. Smith, a gentile [who claimed that the produce had the status of gleanings],' or (2) 'I purchased it from Mr. Jones, a Samaritan [who claimed that it had the status of gleanings].'"
E. Poor Samaritans are deemed equivalent to poor Israelites, [and so are deemed credible under all circumstances in which Israelites are believed]. [This is in direct contradiction to D2.][8]
F. But [as regards] poor gentiles--we do not believe their claim about any matter.

Judah (A-B) argues that the poor should be deemed credible only with regard to the sorts of food that householders usually give them as poor-offerings (cf. M. 8:2D). This sets the stage for two contrasting rules, C and D, also attributed to Judah.[9] An Israelite's statements about the status of produce are deemed trustworthy (C), while those made by gentiles and Samaritans are regarded as false (D). A formally and substantively separate pair of rules (E-F) contradicts D. They claim that poor Samaritans, just like poor Israelites, are believed about the status of produce in their possession. Gentiles, by contrast, never are trusted (cf. D1), because they are assumed to cheat Israelite farmers.[10]

8:5-6

A. [When dispensing poorman's tithe] they may give to [each of] the poor people at the threshing floor no less than:

B. (1) one-half qab of wheat,

(2) one qab of barley, [but] R. Meir says, "One half qab [of barley],"

(3) one and one half qabs of spelt,

(4) one qab of dried figs, or one maneh of fresh figs, [but] R. Aqiba says, "One half (prs) [of a maneh of fresh figs],"

(5) one half loq of wine, [but] R. Aqiba says, "A quarter [of a loq of wine],"

(6) a quarter loq of oil, [but] R. Aqiba says, "An eighth [of a loq of oil]."

C. And [as regards] all other types of produce--

D. said Abba Shaul, "[They must give to each poor person] enough [produce] so that he may sell it [and use the revenue] to buy food for two meals."

M. 8:5

E. This measure [for each type of produce, specified at A-D], applies [when distributing poorman's tithe to poor] priests, Levites, and Israelites.[11]

F. [If a householder wished to] save [for his own poor relatives the produce he designated as poorman's tithe],

G. he may take only half [of the poorman's tithe for his own relatives], but must give [the remaining half to other poor people].[12]

H. If he had [only] a small amount of any type [of produce, i.e., less than the measure for poorman's tithe specified at M. 8:5],

I. he places [the produce] before [the poor], and they divide it among themselves.

M. 8:6 (Sifre Deut. #110 [Finkelstein-Horowitz, p. 171], #303 [Finkelstein-Horowitz, p. 321]; B. Erub. 29a; Y. Erub. 3:1[20d]; Y. Peah 8:5[21a])

Mishnah's framers now turn their attention to the amount of food that must be given to each poor person as poorman's tithe, an offering first discussed in the previous pericope (M. 8:2-4). The basic rule, A-B, states the proper measures for several common crops of the Land of Israel.[13] Mishnah itself does not explain the rationale behind the amounts specified in the list or of those provided in the glosses at B2, 4, 5 and 6. Nonetheless, Abba Shaul's lemma (C-D), a secondary rule governing all other types of food, may provide an indication of the authors' reasoning. Abba Shaul claims that each poor person must be given produce to trade for a full day's supply of food, one meal in the morning and one meal at night. On the basis of this lemma, B. Erub. 29a and most later exegetes claim that the measures at A-B also provide the poor person with precisely the amount of food needed for two meals.[14]

These two rules introduce a series of secondary considerations at E, F-G and H-I, concerning the proper distribution of poorman's tithe. First, each poor person must receive the same amount of poorman's tithe regardless of his status as a priest, Levite, or Israelite (E). This is the case even though poor priests and Levites derive additional income from first tithe and heave-offering. A second rule takes up the case of a householder who has poor relatives and wishes to distribute the poorman's tithe to them alone (F). This act, however, would deprive other poor people of their fair portion of the food. In order to ensure that the farmer distributes the grain equitably, he may retain at most half of the poorman's tithe for his own family, and must give the remainder to others (G).[15] Finally, Mishnah's authors consider a case in which a farmer does not have enough poorman's tithe to give each person a proper share as specified at M. 8:5B (H-I).[16] In order to prevent the householder from favoring one poor person over another, the framers rule that the poor themselves should divide this small amount of food (as at M. 4:1).

T. 2:18a

A. [As regards] poor people who are making the rounds of threshing floors (hmḥzryn byn hgrnwt)--

B. [if a householder wishes to distribute the poorman's tithe from his home, he need not give the poor any poorman's tithe at the threshing floor. Rather he must] designate tithes [from some common produce] and give them [this grain as a gift].

C. [And] decent people (ṣnw^{c}ym)[17] bring out in their hand food [worth a small amount of] money,

D. and give [a poor person] this trifle, so that he will [have something to] eat before he reaches the city.

Tosefta takes up the case of a householder who wants to distribute poorman's tithe from his home, rather than at the threshing floor (cf. M. 8:5A-B). The householder benefits by waiting to tithe his produce, for he is permitted to make a random snack of the untithed food.[18] Thus when he finally does process the food, upon his arrival home, he has less total produce from which to separate a fixed percentage as tithes. While the householder has the right to distribute poorman's tithe from his home, he should not send the poor away from the threshing floor empty-handed. Rather he must separate tithes from a small amount of ordinary produce and give this grain to the poor (A-B). It also is considered proper to give the poor some extra food for the trip home (C-D).

T. 4:2-7

A. During[19] the proper year for dispensing poorman's tithe, they may give to the poor no less than (1) one-half qab of wheat, or (2) a qab of barley (M. 8:5B1-2 with variations).
B. Under what circumstances does this apply?
C. [It applies if the householder distributes the produce] at the threshing floor.
D. But if he distributes produce from his own house, he may give to the poor any amount, and need not scruple [that he has given them less than the required amount].
E. But as regards the remainder of gifts [distributed at the threshing floor, namely those] given to the priesthood and to the Levites, he may give any amount, and need not scruple [that he has not given enough].
T. 4:2a

F. [As regards] priests and Levites who stand by the threshing floor [waiting to be given the gifts due them, heave-offering and first tithe],
G. and other priests came, and stood [there for a short time only],
H. [the priests who came by later] may not take [the priestly gifts] out of the hands [of the priests who were there first].
I. Said Rabban Simeon b. Gamaliel, "[Rich] priests used to be generous, and in order not to send out their [poor] brothers empty-handed, they used to take a handful [of the food they had collected as heave-offering] and give it to them."
J. Rabban Simeon b. Eleazar says, "If [some priests] came [to the threshing floor after the householder had given out one round of offerings, but] before he had given out the second round (^{c}d šl' thzwr ḥlylh),[20] they must stand at the end of the line, and take [the offerings only in turn]."
T. 4:3

K. As regards the wives or slaves [of priests][21]--
L. they may not apportion them [priestly offerings] at the threshing floor.
M. But [if dispensing this produce from the house], they may give them priestly or Levitical gifts as a favor.
T. 4:4

N. Rabban Simeon b. Gamaliel says, "Just as, [when produce is] distributed at the threshing floor, [a person's receiving] heave-offering is prima facie evidence [that he is a member] of the priesthood, so too, [when produce is] distributed at the threshing floor, [a person's receiving] first tithe is prima facie evidence [that he is one] of the Levites."

Peah Chapter Eight   145

O. [But when] distributing through the agency of a court [an inheritance containing produce in the status of tithes that never was given to priests, a person's receiving a portion of the food]²² is not prima facie evidence [that he is a member of the] priesthood, [because this produce can be given, by the court, to anyone].

T. 4:5

P. [There are] two [matters that constitute] prima facie evidence [that a person is a member of] the priesthood:
Q. within the Land of Israel--
R. (1) raising one's hands [during the priestly benediction], and (2) receiving [heave-offering] at the threshing floor.
S. And in Syria, up to the place where the messenger [who tells of the new] moon reaches²³--
T. (1) Raising one's hands [during the priestly benediction], but (2) [they do] not receive [heave-offering] at the threshing floor.
U. And Babylonia [is in the same status] as Syria.
V. R. Simeon b. Eleazar says, "Also Alexandria [had the same status as Syria], during the early times, when there was a court there."

T. 4:6

W. A more stringent rule applies to holy things of the Temple than applies to holy things of the provinces (kdšy gbwl).
X. (Delete with E: And a more stringent rule applies to holy things of the provinces than applies to holy things of the Temple.)²⁴
Y. [As regards] the holy things of the provinces--
Z. (1) minor [priests] may partake of them,
   (2) unclean [priests] may partake of them,
   (3) they may divide them in conditions of uncleanness,
   (4) and they may measure out an equivalent amount [of common food to be used in place of the holy things].
AA. [As regards] the holy things of the Temple--
BB. (1) [priests] are charged with the responsibility of caring for them,
    (2) and [with the responsibility] to bring them to the Temple building.
CC. [As regards] holy things of the provinces--
DD. they give them to any associate [merely as a gift].
EE. But [as regards] holy things of the Temple--
FF. they give them only to members of the [present] priestly watch.

T. 4:7

Tosefta distinguishes between giving out poorman's tithe at the threshing floor (cf. M. 8:5A-B) and at the home. Only that which is distributed in public, at the threshing floor, must be of a specified minimum quantity. Produce given at the home, merely as a gift, may be of any quantity (A-D). The rule at E extends this principle to other gifts distributed at the threshing floor, the priestly and Levitical offerings. These offerings also may be of any size (cf. M. Ter. 4:3).

E draws in its wake a spree of free associations regarding priests and Levites. To clarify them, let us review the principles underlying this section. First, the priestly offering must be distributed in an orderly fashion (F-J). Those priests who have waited the longest at the threshing floor should get the tithes first. Second, a priest's wife or slaves may not collect tithes at the threshing floor, lest it appear that this produce has been distributed improperly (K-M). Instead, they are given produce from the house as a favor. Third, receiving heave-offering and first tithe at the threshing floor constitutes prima facie evidence that the recipient is a priest or Levite (N-O). This discussion is followed by a fourth unit (P-V), a list of prima facie evidence that one is a priest applicable inside and outside of the Land of Israel. Finally, we contrast the holy things of the Temple in Jerusalem with those of lesser sanctity, the holy things of country shrines (W-FF). The major difference between these two types of holy things is that in the Temple holy things must be maintained and not exchanged for common produce. Holy things of lesser sanctity, on the other hand, may be exchanged for ordinary food.

T. 4:2b

A. If he wishes, he may reserve half [of the poorman's tithe for his own relatives' use] and give half [to other poor people] (M. 8:6F-G).
B. Abba Yosé b. Dosithai says in the name of R. Eliezer, "If he wishes, he may give [to the other poor people] a third [of the poorman's tithe], and give two thirds (šty ydwt)[25] to his own relatives.

Abba Yosé b. Dosithai glosses M. 8:6F-G, merely providing different proportions for the householder's relatives and the other poor people.

8:7

A. They give to a poor person travelling from place to place no less than a load [of bread] worth a <u>dupondius</u>, [made from wheat that costs at least] one <u>sela</u> for four <u>seahs</u>.
B. [If such a poor person] stayed overnight,
C. they must give him enough [food][26] for a night's lodging.
D. [If the poor person] spends the Sabbath,
E. they must give him food for three meals (see M. Shab. 16:2-3).
F. Whoever has sufficient food for two meals, [i.e., one day's food-supply], may not take food from a soup-kitchen (tmḥwy).[27]
G. [Whoever has sufficient] food for fourteen meals, [i.e., one week's supply of food], may not take [money] from the communal fund (qph).
H. [Money for] the communal fund is collected by two [people], and distributed by three [people].

M. 8:7 (Y. Erub. 3:1[20d]; B. Shab. 118a; B. B.M. 8b-9a; B. San. 17b)

Peah Chapter Eight 147

The community as a whole is responsible for providing poor people within their midst with a sufficient amount of food. This principle gives rise to two formally distinct units (A-E, F-G+H) which I take up in turn. Poor people passing through a town (A) should be given a load of high-quality bread.[28] This satisfies their immediate need for food, and permits them to continue their journeys. By contrast, individuals who remain in the locale for longer periods of time, whether overnight (B-C) or for the Sabbath (D-E), should be supplied with additional food for their stay.

Two community-wide charitable institutions, the soup-kitchen (F) and the communal fund (G), again provide for the short- and long-term needs of a town's poor. The soup-kitchen provides a single meal for those who are in immediate need of sustenance because they have less than a day's supply of food. In addition, long-term, monetary support for the indigent is supplied by the communal fund. Accordingly, only those people who possess less than one week's food supply are eligible to collect this money. The gloss at H takes up two issues with regard to the collection and distribution of the communal fund. First, this money must be gathered by two people because no single individual can represent the community as a whole (see M. Sheq. 5:2). Second, the communal fund must be distributed by three citizens. This is because decisions regarding who receives this money are deemed analogous to monetary cases in a court, which require three judges (see M. San. 1:1).[29]

T. 4:8

    A.   <u>They give to a poor person travelling from place to place no less than a loaf [of bread] worth a dupondium,</u> [made from wheat which costs at least] <u>one sela for four seahs.</u>

    B.   [If such a poor person] stayed overnight,

    C.   they must give him enough [food] for a night's lodging (M. 8:7A-C),

    D.   [namely, they give him] oil and beans.

    E.   [If such a poor person] spends the Sabbath,

    F.   they give him food for three meals (M. 8:7D-E),

    G.   [namely, they give him] oil, beans, fish, and a vegetable.

    H.   Under what circumstances does this apply?

    I.   [It applies] so long as [the town's people] do not recognize the poor person.

    J.   But if they recognize him, they even provide clothing for him.

    K.   [If a poor person] went from door to door, [begging for food from each family],

    L.   they are not obligated to him in any way, [because he should receive money from the communal fund, not by bothering individuals].

Tosefta provides further details (D, G) regarding the amount of food that must be given to the transient poor (cf. M. 8:7A-E). These glosses set the stage for an important distinction, H+I-J. The townspeople have a minimal responsibility toward strangers, and so are required only to provide food for these people. The citizens have a further obligation to poor people whom they know, those of their own town. Thus, clothing as well as food must be supplied for the local poor.[30] The pericope is concluded at K-L by an entirely separate case. We speak of a poor person who wishes to collect charity for himself, not through the agency of the communal fund. In order to assure the equitable distribution of the community's resources, however, this is not allowed.

T. 4:9

- A. The soup-kitchen [provides enough food] for a full day,[31] but the communal fund gives [sufficient food to last] from one week to the next.
- B. The soup-kitchen [provides food] for anybody, but the communal fund [gives support only] to the poor of that locale.
- C. If [a poor person] dwelt there for thirty days, lo, he is considered to be in the status of resident of the locale for [purposes of receiving assistance] from the communal fund.
- D. But [to receive] shelter, [he must have dwelt there] for six months.
- E. And to be liable to the town-tax (psy h^{c}yr),[32] [he must have been a resident] for twelve months.

Tosefta contrasts the soup-kitchen (M. 8:7F) and the communal fund (M. 8:7G-H). The soup-kitchen provides a small amount of food for anybody in immediate need. The communal fund, for its part, provides long-term support, and is limited to poor people who are residents of the town (A-B). The rules at C-E take up a question left open at B: How do we determine who is a resident? Thirty days is deemed sufficient to establish residency for purposes of receiving support from the communal fund (C). A six-month term, by contrast, is required to be eligible for community-funded shelter (D). Finally, to ease the burden on new citizens, municipal taxes are not assessed until a full year of residency has passed (E).

T. 4:10-11

I.
- A. [As regards] a poor person who, [like any other citizen], gave a <u>perutah</u> to [support] the communal fund or a piece of bread[33] to [support] the soup-kitchen--
- B. they may take [the money or food] from him.
- C. But if he did not contribute, they do not force him to give.

II.
- D. If they gave [to a poor person] new clothes [from the communal fund], and he exchanged [his] worn out clothes [in partial payment]--
- E. they may take [the clothes] from him.
- F. But if he did not exchange [his worn out clothes], they do not force him to give.

I.
- G. [If] he used to wear fine wool[34] [before he became poor],
- H. they supply him with [clothes of] fine wool.

II.
- I. [If he used to receive] a coin [as a salary before he became poor],

Peah Chapter Eight   149

	J.	they give him a coin.
III.	K.	[If he used to eat] dough [before he became poor],
	L.	they give him dough.
IV.	M.	[If he used to eat] bread [before he became poor],
	N.	they give him bread.
V.	O.	[If they used] to spoon feed him [before he became poor],
	P.	they spoon feed him.

Q. [These five rules all accord with] what is written [in Scripture], "You shall open your hand to [the poor person], and provide him sufficient for his need, whatever it may be" (Deut. 15:8).

R. [This refers to providing] even a slave or a horse, [if this is deemed his need].

S. "For his need (lw)" (Deut. 15:8)--this refers to [providing him with] a wife, as it is written [in Scripture], "Then the Lord God said, 'It is not good that the man should be alone. I will make a helper for his need (lw)'" (Gen. 2:18).

T. Hillel the elder once gave (so ed. princ.; V, E: took) to a certain poor person, a member of a good family, a horse for the man to ride for exercise, and a slave to be the man's servant; [this provides a precedent for the ruling at R].

U. The people of Galillee each day would send to a certain old man a pound of meat [according to the weights used in] Sephoris.[35]

T. 4:10

I.	V.	[If a poor person] was used to using golden utensils,
	W.	he must sell them, and use silver ones.
II.	X.	[If he was used to] silver utensils,
	Y.	he must sell them, and use brass ones.
III.	Z.	[If he was used to] brass utensils,
	AA.	he must sell them and use glass ones.

BB. They told [the following story]: A family from Bet Nebaltah[36] was [visiting] in Jerusalem. They were related to the family of Arnon, the Jebusite [i.e., their family was among the original inhabitants of Jerusalem].[37]

CC. The sages sent them three hundred gold sheqels, for they did not want them to [be forced to] leave Jerusalem [due to a lack of money].

T. 4:11

Several distinct units (A-F, G-U, V-AA and BB-CC) provide additional information on the proper treatment of poor people. The two parallel rules at A-C and D-F make the point that poor people are not obligated to support charitable institutions. Nevertheless, if a poor person wishes to donate money, food or clothing, he is accorded the proper respect. We next turn to the case of a householder who has become poor (G-Q+R-U). Such a person is entitled to be maintained at the standard of living to which he is accustomed. The prooftext for this rule, Q, draws in its wake quite secondary expansions at R and S, as well as precedents at T and U. The third unit (V-AA) claims that the appropriate action for a person who becomes poor is to adjust his lifestyle to a new economic situation. Such a person must sell his property and buy new belongings of a lesser quality. Finally, the story at BB-CC makes the point that harsh economic circumstances should not force any family to emigrate from Jerusalem (cf. M. Ket. 13:11).

T. 4:12-13

- A. "[As regards] one who says, 'I shall not be supported by others'--
- B. "they act considerately toward him, and support him by giving [money to this poor person] as a loan, and [when he cannot repay the amount] they convert it to a gift,"[38] the opinion of R. Meir.
- C. But sages say, "They give [the poor person money] as a gift, and [when he refuses to take the charity] they convert it to a loan."
- D. R. Simeon says, "They say to him, 'Bring us some collateral,' in order to allow him to take money."

T. 4:12

- E. [As regards] one who says, "I cannot support myself"--
- F. they act considerately toward him, and support him by giving [this poor person money] as a gift, [and only if he refuses to accept the charity] do they convert it to a loan.

T. 4:13

When giving charity, the poor must be treated with dignity and respect. Accordingly, Meir claims (A-B), charity initially should be given as a loan, so that the poor person may retain some of his pride when taking the money. Later, if the poor person is unable to repay, the loan is converted to a simple gift. Sages' lemma (C) and the anonymous rule at E-F present an alternative view. Only if the poor person, out of his personal pride, refuses to take the charity should the townspeople claim that the money is given as a loan. Simeon's gloss (D) requires a tiny bit of collateral against any gift of charity. In line with A-B, this has the effect of treating the gift as a loan, and allows the poor person to retain his dignity.

8:8-9

- A. Whoever possesses two hundred zuz [i.e., enough money to support himself for a full year, from one harvest season to the next],[39] may not collect gleanings, forgotten sheaves, peah, or poorman's tithe [that have been designated from this year's crops].
- B. If he possesses two hundred [zuz] less one dinar [i.e., one hundred and ninety-nine zuz],
- C. even if one thousand [householders each might] give him [one dinar], all at the same time, [so that the poor person potentially possesses far more than two hundred zuz]--

	D.	lo, this person may collect [produce designated for the poor]. [When he gathers this food, he has not yet received any money from the householders, and so in fact is poor.]
	E.	[If he possesses two hundred zuz that he cannot freely use, because the money serves as] collateral for a creditor or for his wife's marriage-contract--
	F.	lo, this person may collect [produce designated for the poor].
	G.	They may compel him to sell neither his house nor the tools [of his trade in order that he might acquire through this sale two hundred zuz in cash]. [That is to say, only people with less than two hundred zuz in liquid assets may gather poor-offerings. Since this person's money is used to provide shelter or equipment, he is permitted to gather the poor-offerings.]

M. 8:8

		H.	Whoever possesses [as little as] fifty zuz, yet conducts business with them--
		I.	lo, that person may not collect [produce designated for the poor, because he derives a steady income from his money].
I.	J.	And anyone who does not need to collect [poor-offerings], but [nonetheless] collects [them],
	K.	[as punishment for this action] will depart from this world[40] only after he [in fact] comes to depend on other people.
II.	L.	And any person who is neither lame, dumb, nor handicapped, but [acts] as if he had [such a condition],
	M.	[as punishment for this action] will die of old age only after he actually [suffers from this condition].[41]
III.	N.	But anyone who needs to collect [poor-offerings], but does not collect [them],
	O.	[as a reward for his action] will die of old age only after [he has become able] to support others from that which belongs to him.
	P.	And with regard to this person Scripture states, "Blessed is the man who trusts in the Lord, whose trust is the Lord" (Jer. 17:7).
	Q.	And so too, a judge who judges for justice's sake [is blessed, as at N].[42]
	R.	As it is stated [in Scripture], "Justice and only justice shall you follow" (Deut. 16:20).
	S.	But any judge who accepts a bribe, and on its account changes his judgment,
	T.	will die of old age only after his eyes have grown weak.
	U.	As it is stated [in Scripture], "And you shall take no bribe, for a bribe blinds the clear sighted" (Ex. 23:8).

M. 8:9 (Y. Soṭah 3:4[19a]; B. Soṭah 21b; B. Ket. 68a, 105a; ARN 3; Mekhilta Mishpatim 20 [Horowitz-Rabin, p. 328]; Sifre Deut. 144 [Finkelstein-Horowitz, p. 199]; Tanḥ. Shoftim 1, 8 [Buber, Shoftim 7])

The tractate concludes by defining who is eligible to receive poorofferings and poorman's tithe. The main point is that anyone who cannot support himself throughout the year falls into the category of a poor person. Accordingly, a person with less than two hundred zuz (one year's support) may gather produce designated from this year's crops (A). This simple definition is refined in several secondary rules at B-I. In each of these cases, the person does not have money in hand with which to buy food and other necessities. For example, a poor person might possess less than two hundred zuz, yet have the prospect of receiving a large sum of money (B-D). Or perhaps the money a person possesses is committed as collateral (E-F), shelter (G) or equipment (G). Since in each case the person has less than the minimum two hundred zuz in liquid assets, we deem him eligible to collect poor-offerings. At H-I, the framers take up the case of a person who possesses less than two hundred zuz, yet does not fall into the category of a poor person. We speak of a householder who invests as little as fifty zuz, and so generates a steady income. Since he can live off the income from his capital, he is not permitted to gather produce designated for the sustenance of the poor.

Standing back for a moment, we see that the foregoing definition of poverty contrasts sharply with the one presented in Scripture. In Scripture's rules, certain categories of persons, those who are legally or socially disadvantaged, are regarded as poor. For example, at Lev. 19:10, widows, orphans, and resident aliens are entitled to collect the various poor-offerings without regard to the sums of money they possess. Mishnah's framers, by contrast, define poverty only in terms of capital. In their view, anyone who possesses less than a specified amount of money falls into the category of poor person and may collect poor-offerings. Clearly, the simple monetary definition provided by this pericope would apply to all people whether or not they fell into one of Scripture's categories. Mishnah's framers thus have moved beyond Scripture to a purely economic definition of a poor person.

Three formally parallel rules, J-K, L-M and N-O+P, conclude the discussion by contrasting those people who have the right to collect poor-offerings but do not gather the food with those who take that to which they are not entitled. Those who falsely claim to be poor eventually will be forced to collect charity (J-K, L-M). By contrast, poor people who rely not on charity but on the support of God eventually will enjoy economic prosperity (N-O). The prooftext at P is followed by two tangentially related rules (Q-R, S-U) that contrast judges who take bribes with those who do not.

T. 4:14

    A.   One who acts as though (1) he was blind, (2) his stomach was distended, or (3) his joints were swollen, [in order to gain sympathy of charity] (cf. M. 8:9T),

    B.   will not depart from this world before this actually is the case (M. 8:9U).

Acting as if injured in order to collect undeserved charity will lead to eventual punishment (cf. M. 8:9T-U).

T. 4:15

A. Charity collectors are not permitted to separate [their own money] from [that which they collect for charity by placing their own money in a separate purse, lest it appear that they steal for themselves some of the money they gather as charity].[43]

B. Even if his friend paid him money that he owed him, even if he found money in the road, he may not take it [for himself].

C. As it is written [in Scripture], "You shall be free of obligation before the Lord and before Israel" (Num. 32:22).

D. But they may separate [their own money] from [that which they collect for charity] if they are collecting within a private courtyard, or within [their own] shop. [Since they are on their own private property, not in the public domain, it is clear that they are not stealing from charity but taking what legitimately is theirs.]

Charity collectors must avoid even the appearance of cheating the community. Thus a collector must not be seen publicly accepting money and putting it into his own purse (A-C). If the person is in his own shop, or in private property, by contrast (D), he may accept money owed to him because no one will imagine that he is stealing some of the money he collects for charity.

T. 4:16

A. [As regards produce in the status of] second tithe--

B. (1) they may not use it to repay loans or [other] debts,
(2) they may not use it to repay favors received,
(3) they may not use it to ransom prisoners,
(4) they may not use it to purchase (ʿwsyn) groom's men's-gifts,
(5) and they may not give any part (dbr) of it as charity, [lest the poor person eat it without observing the produce's special status].

C. But (1) they may send part of it [to another] as an act of loving-kindness (gmylwt ḥsdym),

D. but he must inform [the other person of the produce's status],

E. and (2) they may give it to a citizen who is known to scruple [regarding the proper dispensation of consecrated produce] (ḥbr ʿyr) as a favor.

Second tithe is included here because of the mention of charity at B5. Since second tithe is consecrated for a particular use,[44] it may not be used to carry out a second obligation (B1-5), including the giving of charity. One may give second tithe as an act of loving-kindness or as a favor, however, providing that it will be disposed of in accordance with the law.

T. 4:17

A. [If] one pledged ('mr) to give [money to charity],
B. and then gave [this money],
C. they accord him merit (śkr) both on account of pledging [to give] and on account of actually [giving] (śkr m^csh).
D. [If] he pledged to give [money to charity],
E. but then [when the time came to pay his pledge, he] no [longer] had enough [cash] in hand to give [the full amount that he had pledged],
F. they accord him merit on account of pledging [to give] just as [they would have accorded him] merit on account of actually [giving].
G. [If] he did not pledge [to give money to charity],
H. but said to other people, "Give!"
I. they accord him merit on account of this,
J. as it is stated [in Scripture], "...and for this word (dbr hzh) [i.e., the word "Give!"] the Lord will bless you" (Deut. 15:10).[45]
K. [If] he did not say to other people, "Give!"
L. but placed [a poor person's mind] at ease (mnyḥ lw) with kind words,
M. from what [verse may we derive] that he should be accorded merit for his act?
N. It is stated [in Scripture], "...and for this word [i.e., the kind words spoken to the poor man] the Lord will bless you" (Deut. 15:10).

The pericope presents four levels of charitable activity, in order of descending significance (A-C, D-F, G-J, K-N). Each of these deeds deserves merit, from the most complete act of charity, pledging and giving (A-C), to the simplest, merely comforting the poor (K-N). Deut. 15:10 serves as a prooftext for the final two cases and indicates that words as well as gifts of money may be deemed praiseworthy.

T. 4:18

A. Monobaṣes the King [of Adiabene] went and gave away [to the poor] (ᶜmd wbzbz) [all of] his treasures during years of famine (bṣrwt).[46]
B. His brothers sent [the following message] to him:
C. "Your ancestors stored up treasures and increased the wealth [left for them by] their ancestors. But you went and gave away all of these treasures, both your own and those of your ancestors!"

I.
D. He replied to them, "My ancestors stored up treasures for this lower [world], but I, [through giving charity (ṣdqh)], have stored up treasures for [the heavenly world] above, as it is stated [in Scripture], 'Faithfulness will spring up from the ground below, [and righteousness (ṣdq) will look down from the sky]' (Ps. 85:11).

II.
E. "My ancestors stored up treasures [for the material world], where the [human] hand can reach (šhyd šwltt bw), but I have stored up treasures [for the

Peah Chapter Eight 155

non-material world], where the [human] hand cannot reach, as it is stated [in Scripture], 'Righteousness (ṣdq) and justice are the foundation of your throne, [steadfast love and faithfulness go before you] (Ps. 89:14).

III. F. "My ancestors stored up treasures [of a type] that produce no [real] benefits (pyrwt), but I have stored up treasures [of the sort] that do produce benefits, as it is stated [in Scripture], 'Tell the righteous (ṣdyq) that is shall be well with them, for they shall reap the benefits (pyrwt) of their deeds' (Is. 3:10).

IV. G. "My ancestors stored up treasures of money, but I have stored up treasures of souls (šl npšwt), as it is stated [in Scripture], 'The fruit of the righteous (ṣdyq) is a tree of life, and a wise man saves the souls [of poor people] (npšwt)' (Prov. 11:30).

V. H. "My ancestors stored up treasures [that eventually, after their deaths, would benefit only] others, but I have stored up treasures [that will benefit] myself [both in life and in death], as it is stated [in Scripture], 'It shall be a righteousness (ṣdqh) to you before the Lord your God' (Deut. 24:13).

VI. I. "My ancestors stored up treasures in this world, but I have stored up treasures for myself in the world-to-come, as it is stated [in Scripture], 'Your righteousness (ṣdqyk) shall go before you, [and the glory of the Lord shall be your rear-guard]' (Is. 58:8)."

The story of King Monobaṣes' exceptional generosity provides a setting for the parallel exegesis of six verses. Each unit contrasts the King's righteous act of giving charity (ṣdq/ṣdqh) with the actions of his ancestors, who merely hoarded money for themselves. The pericope as a whole thus carries forward T. 4:17's notion that acts of charity are praiseworthy.

T. 4:19

    A. Charity (ṣdqh) and righteous deeds (gmyltwt ḥsdym) outweigh all other commandments in the Torah.

I. B. Nevertheless ('l'), charity [can be given only to the] living, but righteous deeds [can be performed for the] living and the dead.

II. C. Charity [is given only] to poor people, but righteous deeds [are done for both] poor and rich people.

III. D. Charity [is given as an aid for a poor person's] finances, but righteous deeds [aid both a poor person's] finances and his physical needs.

A general statement on the importance of both charity and other righteous deeds (A) prepares the way for the triplet that follows (B, C, D). These rules contrast charity and righteous deeds, placing a higher value and emphasis on the latter.

T. 4:20-21

A. Said R. Joshua b. Qoraḥ, "From which [verse may we derive the fact] that anyone who loses sight [of the importance of giving] charity (hm⁽ᶜ⁾lym ⁽ᶜ⁾ynyw mṣdqh) [is viewed] as if he worshipped idolatry?

B. "It is stated [in Scripture], 'Take heed lest there be a base (blyᶜl) thought in your heart, and you say, "[The seventh year, the year of release, is near," and your eye be hostile to your poor brother, and you give him nothing...]' [Deut. 15:9].

C. "And elsewehere (lhln) [Scripture] states, 'If you hear... that certain base men (blyᶜl) have gone out among you, ...saying, "Let us go and serve other gods," ...you shall surely put the inhabitants of that city to the sword, destroying it utterly...'" (Deut. 13:12-15).

D. "Just as in the latter case 'base' explicitly refers to idolatrous worship, so too in the former case 'base' refers to [something deemed equivalent to] idolatrous worship."

T. 4:20

E. Said R. Eleazar b. R. Yosé, "From which [verse may we derive the fact] that charity and righteous deeds are great peace-[makers] and intercessors between [the people of] Israel and their father in heaven?

F. "It is stated [in Scripture], 'For so says the Lord: Do not enter their house of mourning, or go to lament or bemoan them. For I have taken away my peace from this people, says the Lord, [namely], my steadfast love (ḥsd) and mercy (rḥmym)' [Jer. 16:5].

G. "Steadfast love (ḥsd)--this refers to righteous deeds (gmylwt ḥsdym).

H. "Mercy (rḥmym)--this refers to charity.

I. [The verse thus] teaches that charity and righteous deeds are great peace-[makers] between [the people of] Israel and their father in heaven.

T. 4:21

Two passages of Scriptural exegesis present further information regarding charity and righteous deeds. Deut. 13:12-15 and 15:19 are adduced in order to prove that refusing to give charity is tantamount to idol-worship (A-D). The second unit (E-I), focusing on Jer. 16:5, claims that charitable acts and righteous deeds serve as advocates for the people of Israel in the face of divine judgment.

APPENDIX
MISHNAH TRACTATE PEAH IN SIFRA AND SIFRE DEUTERONOMY

The following appendix contains those sections of Sifra and Sifre Deuteronomy[1] that quote passages of Tractate Peah. These two documents of Scriptural exegesis systematically work through Leviticus' and Deuteronomy's laws of poor-offerings, which as we know, provide the general information underlying Mishnah's system of poor-support. Sifra and Sifre, for their part, attempt to provide a base of Biblical authority for Tractate Peah's rules. Thus, throughout Sifra and Sifre, a short explanation of a given verse or phrase draws in its wake verbatim citations of Mishnah. In all, these documents claim to show precisely how the detailed laws of Tractate Peah emerge directly out of the relevant verses.

Together, Sifra and Sifre Deuteronomy treat virtually all the poor-offerings mentioned in Tractate Peah. Within their discussion of these gifts, moreover, they touch upon each issue dealt with by Mishnah. Where Tractate Peah contains rules governing the definition and distribution of a particular offering, Sifra and Sifre too treat both issues. In all, Sifra takes up those offerings mentioned at Lev. 19:9-10: peah, gleanings, separated grapes, and defective clusters. Similarly, Deut. 24:19-22, which mention forgotten sheaves and separated grapes, set the agenda for Sifre Deuteronomy. The following table shows in detail how Sifra and Sifre Deuteronomy carefully derive Mishnah's rules.

Why did the editors of Sifra and Sifre create these commentaries to Scripture's laws of poor-relief? Tractate Peah raises a question of authority, because it presents its rules as binding law, yet with scarcely a quotation of the Mosaic Codes. The underlying assertion is that Mishnah's rules have their own independent authority equal to that of the Sinaitic legislation. In answer to the implied claim, Sifra and Sifre Deuteronomy respond that Tractate Peah's rules are authoritative solely because they rest upon Scripture. For Sifra and Sifre, Mosaic revelation alone can bestow the authority claimed for Mishnah's laws.[2]

My translations include the relevant materials found in Sifra Qedoshim 1:6-3:7 and in Sifre Deuteronomy Chs. 110, 282-285 and 336. The translations are based on the texts presented by Weiss (Sifra) and Finkelstein-Horowitz (Sifre Deuteronomy).

I. Sifra

Lev. 19:9-10		Mishnah's Topic	Sifra	Mishnah Cited
Peah	1.	How much produce to designate (M. 1:2-3)	Qed. 1:9-10	M. 1:3
	2.	What types of produce (M. 1:4-5)	Qed. 1:7-8	M. 1:4-5
	3.	What constitutes a field (M. 2:1-3:7)	Qed. 1:6,11-2:4	M. 2:1-4,7
	4.	How is produce distributed (M. 4:1-5)	Qed. 3:4-7	M. 4:1-2
Gleanings	1.	Definition (M. 4:10-5:2)	Qed. 2:5	M. 4:10
	2.	Distribution of gleanings (M. 5:3)	Qed. 2:6	--
Separated Grapes	1.	Definition (M. 7:3a)	Qed. 3:2	M. 7:3
	2.	Free Access (M. 7:3b)	Qed. 3:2	M. 7:3
Defective Clusters	1.	Definition (M. 7:4)	Qed. 3:1,3	M. 7:4
	2.	When does the law take effect (M. 7:6,8)	--	--

II. Sifre Deuteronomy

Deut. 24:19-22		Mishnah's Topic	Sifre Deut.	Mishnah Cited
Forgotten Sheaves	1.	Definition (M. 5:7-6:3)	#110,282,283	M. 5:7, 6:3
	2.	Scriptural Basis of Law (M. 6:4)	#283	M. 6:4
	3.	Ambiguous Cases (M. 6:5-7:2)	#283	M. 6:5-6
Separated Grapes	1.	Definition (M. 7:3a)	#283	M. 7:3
	2.	Free Access (M. 7:3b)	#283	M. 7:3
Defective Clusters	1.	Definition (M. 7:4)	#285	M. 7:4
	2.	When does the law take effect (M. 7:6-8)	#284	M. 7:7

I. Sifra

Sifra Qed. 1:6

A. "When you harvest [the yield of your land, you shall not completely reap the corner of your field as you harvest]" (Lev. 19:9).

B. [The emphasis on "when you harvest] excludes [the following cases from the requirement of setting aside peah]:

C. [a field that] (a) robbers harvested, (2) ants devastated, or that (3) the wind or cattle trampled (M. 2:7A).

D. "When you harvest [the yield of your land, you shall not completely reap the corner of your field as you harvest]" (Lev. 19:9).

E. [The emphasis on "when you harvest"] excludes [a second sort of case, namely one in which] a gentile [owns and] harvests [the field].

F. On the basis [of the foregoing exegesis, E, the sages] said:

G. [As regards] a gentile who harvested his field and afterward converted [to Judaism]--
[the produce that he had harvested is exempt from the restrictions of
(1) gleanings, (2) forgotten sheaves, and (3) peah.
R. Judah obligates [the convert] to [obey the law of] the forgotten sheaf, because [the law of] the forgotten sheaf [takes effect] only after [the conclusion of] the binding [process, which takes place after the gentile had converted (M. 4:6. A-D)].

Sifra Qed. 1:7

A. [On the basis of Lev. 19:9's opening phrase, "When you reap your harvest of your field...,] I can derive only [that the obligation to set aside peah applies to produce] while one reaps [it].

B. From what [phrase, then, might I determine that the obligation likewise relates to produce] while one merely plucks [it for a random snack]?

C. Scripture states [at the end of Lev. 19:9, "...you shall not completely reap the corner of your field] as you harvest." [The repetition of the word "harvest" is taken to mean that the obligation of setting aside peah applies to all types of harvesting, both reaping and snacking.]

D. From what [phrase, then, might I determine that the obligation to set aside peah applies not only to grain as one reaps it, but also to grain] already harvested [and brought to the threshing floor, but from which peah was not set aside]?

E. Scripture states, "[When you reap] your harvest...," [thereby implying that peah must be set aside from all produce the Israelite harvests].

F. [On the basis of Lev. 19:9's phrase, "When you reap the harvest of your Land,"] I can discern only [that the obligation to set aside peah applies to] grain.

G. From what [phrase, then, might I determine that the obligation likewise applies to] legumes?
H. Scripture states, "[When you harvest] your Land...," [thereby implying that all produce of the Land of Israel is subject to the law of peah].
I. From what [phrase, then, might I determine that peah must also be set aside from groves of] trees?
J. Scripture states, "When you reap the harvest of your field...," [thereby implying that the produce of any field, even an orchard, is subject to the law].
K. [On the basis of Lev. 19:9's phrase, "the harvest of your field...,"] it is possible that vegetables, squash, gourds, melons, and cucumbers all are included in the [above stated] general rule [that all of the Land's yield is subject to the law of peah]. [From what phrase might I determine that this is not the case?]
L. Scripture states, "[When you harvest] the yield [of your land]..."
M. Now the term "yield" is reserved only for [produce that is] <u>(1) edible, (2) privately owned, (3) grown from the Land [of Israel], (4) harvested as a single crop, and (5) can be preserved in storage</u> (M. 1:4B-C).
N. <u>This [general rule likewise] excludes vegetables, for even though they are harvested as a crop, one cannot preserve them in storage</u> (T. 1:7A)
O. <u>This [general rule likewise] excludes dates, for even though one can preserve them in storage, they are not harvested as a crop</u> (T. 1:7B).
P. <u>Grain and legumes are included in this general principle</u> [M.1:4C].

<u>Sifra Qed. 1:8</u>

A. <u>And among types of trees, the fruit of (a) a sumac tree, (2) carob trees, (3) walnut trees, (4) almond trees, (5) grape vines, (6) pomegranate trees, (7) olive trees, (8) and date palms is subject to designation as peah</u> (M. 1:5A-C).

<u>Sifra Qed. 1:9</u>

A. "[When you reap your harvest of your land,] you shall not completely reap the corner of your field [as you harvest] (Lev. 19:9).
I. B. Now "corner" must refer to the completion [of the harvesting of that field]. [This point is implied by the phrase "you shall not completely reap the corner..."].
II. C. And "corner" must refer to [leaving unharvested the appropriate] specified [portion of the yield] (so Rabad). This point is implied by the phrase "you shall not completely reap the corner portion..."].
III. D. And "corner" must refer to the rear [of the field]. [This point is implied by the juxtaposition of the following two phrases: "you shall not completely reap... your field"].
E. On the basis [of the foregoing interpretations, at B, C, and D, the sages] said:

F. [If] he designated [some produce as peah], whether at the beginning or at the middle [of the field], lo, this [grain] is peah,
providing that he leaves at the rear [of the field] no less than one-sixtieth [of the crop] (M. 1:3A-B).

Sifra Qed. 1:10

A. R. Simeon said, "For [the following] four reasons, a person must designate [produce as] peah only [while harvesting] the rear of his field:
"On account of:
(1) robbery from the poor,
(2) the idleness of the poor,
(3) appearance's sake,
(4) and because [Scripture] states, "You may not completely harvest the rear corner of your field" (Lev. 19:9).
"Robbery from the poor--how so?
"This assures that the farmer will not find an opportune moment and say to a poor relative, 'Come and collect [all of] this peah for yourself.' [If the farmer was allowed to designate all of the peah for his own family, the other poor people in the town would not have fair access to the produce, thus robbing them of what rightfully is theirs (cf. M. 8:6).]
"The idleness of the poor--how so?
"This assures that poor people will not be sitting around and watching [the farmer] all day, saying, 'Now he is designating peah!' Rather, since [the farmer designates produce as peah while harvesting the rear of his field, the poor person] may go and gather poor-offerings from another [person's] field, and may return to collect [the peah] at the end [of the harvest].
"Appearance's sake--how so?
"This assures that passers-by will not say, 'Behold how so-and-so harvested his field and did not designate [any produce as] peah for the poor!'
"Because [Scripture] states, 'You may not completely harvest the rear corner of your field' (Lev. 19:9)--[how so?].
"Since the produce actually designated as peah will not have been collected before the farmer finishes harvesting his field, when he does finish it will appear that he never designated any produce] (T. 1:6A-H with variations).

Sifra Qed. 1:11

A. "[When you reap the harvest of] your field...(Lev. 19:9)."
B. [The phrase "your field"] excludes [from the law of peah] the field of other people. [That is, each householder is required to set aside peah only from his own property.]
C. R. Simeon b. Judah says in the name of R. Simeon, "[The phrase] 'your field' excludes [from the law of peah a field that is] jointly owned with a gentile."

D. [The phrase] "your field" [is stated] to impose the obligation [to set aside a separate portion of produce as peah from] each and every field [owned by a single farmer].

Sifra Qed. 2:1

A. On the basis [of the foregoing conclusion that the phrase "your field" implies that each field is to have a separate portion of peah (Sifra Qed. 1:11D), sages] said:

B. And these [landmarks] establish [the boundaries of a field] for [purposes of designating] peah:

(1) a river, (2) pond, (3) private road, (4) public road, (5) public path, (6) private path that is in regular use both in the dry season and in the rainy season, (7) uncultivated land, (8) newly-broken land, (9) and [an area sown with] a different [type of] seed.

"And [as regards] one who harvests unripe grain [for use as fodder]--[the area he harvests] establishes [the boundaries of a field, since it now may be deemed uncultivated land; see 7]," the opinion of R. Meir.

But sages say, "[The area he harvests] does not establish [the boundaries of a field], unless he also has ploughed [the stubble] under, [thereby creating newly-broken ground; see 8] (M.2:1A-D)."

C. [As regards] an irrigation ditch that [divides a tract of land so that the tract] cannot be harvested as one--

R. Judah says, "[It] established [the boundaries of a field]."

"And any hills that are hoed with a mattock [i.e., hills that divide a tract of land and that are hoed manually] (Is. 7:25)--

even though an ox cannot pass over them with its plough,

[the farmer] designates peah for the entire [tract of land, as one field] (M2:2A-E).

Sifra Qed. 2:3

A. All [of the landmarks listed at M. 2:1, cited at Sifra Qed. 2:1B,] establish [the boundaries of a field planted with] seeds,

but as for establishing [the boundaries of an orchard of] trees, only a fence [does so].

But if the branches [of several trees] are intertwined with each other, [even a fence] does not establish [a boundary between them].

Rather, [the farmer] designates [a single portion of produce as] peah on behalf of all [of the trees whose branches are intertwined] (M. 2:3A-D).

Sifra Qed. 2:4

A. And as regards carob trees, [which have extensive root systems that intertwine, as do the branches at D], all that are within sight of each other [constitute a single orchard, and a single portion of fruit is designated as peah on behalf of all of them together].

Said Rabban Gamaliel, "In my father's household they used to designate one [portion of produce as] peah on behalf of all the olive trees that they owned in every direction [i.e., all that they owned together].

"But as regards carob trees, all that are within sight of each other [constitute a single orchard, and a single portion of produce is designated as peah for all of them together]."

R. Eliezer bar Ṣadoq says in [Gamaliel's] name, "So too: [They designated one portion of produce as peah for all] of the carob trees that they owned in the locale, [whether or not they were in sight of each other]" (M. 2:4E-H).

Sifra Qed. 2:5

A. [You shall not gather] the gleanings after your harvest (Lev. 19:9).
B. [This prohibition does] not refer to gleanings [dropped during] random plucking, [but only to those dropped during the harvest itself].
C. "...the gleanings of your harvest." [The juxtaposition of "gleanings" and "harvest" implies that gleanings can refer] only to that which falls due to the process of harvesting.
D. On this basis they said:
E. What [produce is in the status of] gleanings?
That which falls [to the ground] during the harvest.
[If a householder] was harvesting [his field, and] harvested an armful, [or] plucked a handful,
[and] a thorn pricked him so that [the produce] fell from his hand to the ground--
lo, [this produce] belongs to the householder.

I. [Produce that falls from] within the [householder's] hand, or [from] within his sickle, [i.e., that which he already has taken into his possession], belongs to the poor.

II. [Produce that falls from] the back of the [householder's] hand, or [from] the back of his sickle, [i.e., the produce fell before the householder had taken possession of it], belongs to the householder.

III. [Produce that falls from] the tip of the [householder's] hand, or [from] the tip of his sickle--
R. Ishmael says, "[Such produce] belongs to the poor."
R. Aqiba says, "[It] belongs to the householder" (M. 4:10A-L).

Sifra Qed. 2:6

- A. "You shall not gather the gleanings [after your harvest]... [You shall leave them] for a poor person..." (Lev. 19:10).
- B. [The juxtaposition of "You shall not gather" and "for a poor person" implies that] you may not help one poor person [rather than another]. [The householder must remain uninvolved in the distribution of poor-offerings; cf. M. 4:1-4.]
- C. [The juxtaposition of] "You shall not gather" [and "for a poor person" likewise implies that] one must warn a poor person regarding his own [field, that the poor person may not gather the poor-offerings from that field].

Sifra Qed. 3:1

- A. "You shall not strip your vineyard bare of defective clusters" (Lev. 19:10).
- B. On the basis [of this verse sages] said:
- C. [As regards] a vineyard [the produce of which] entirely is defective clusters--
  R. Eliezer says, "[The fruit] belongs to the householder [i.e., the clusters do not fall into the category of defective clusters because the norm in that vineyard is clusters that are not well formed]."
  R. Aqiba says, "[The fruit] belongs to the poor, [i.e., the clusters are deemed defective, because they lack the definitive characteristics of well-formed clusters]."
  Said R. Eliezer, "[Scripture states], 'When you harvest the grapes of your vineyard, you shall not return to gather the defective clusters' (Deut. 24:21). "If there is no harvest [of normal clusters, because the entire yield is defective], how can there be defective clusters [left after the harvest]?"
  Said to him R. Aqiba, "[Scripture also states], "And you shall not strip your field bare of defective clusters' (Lev. 19:10). "[This verse indicates that the law applies] even if [the] entire [yield of the vineyard] is defective clusters, [such that there is no harvest of normal clusters]."
  Aqiba continues:] "If that is the intent of Lev. 19:10], why does [Scripture] state, 'When you harvest the grapes of your vineyard, you shall not return to gather the defective clusters' (Deut. 24:21) (M. 7:7A-H)?
- D. "[Scripture states this] because it is possible that since the verse permits the poor [to gather the] defective clusters, they might come and take them at any time they wish, [even though the farmer has not yet harvested his portion of the crop]. Therefore Scripture states, 'When you harvest, you shall not strip your vineyard bare of defective clusters.'
- E. "[This verse, i.e., Deut. 24:21, proves that] the poor may not claim the defective clusters before the harvest, [for the law of defective clusters takes effect only when the farmer claims the normal bunches for himself, by harvesting them]. [Before this time, none of the grapes can enter the status of defective clusters]" (M. 7:7I).

Sifra Qed. 3:2

A. "You shall not gather the separated grapes of your vineyard" (Lev. 19:10).

B. [Because of Lev. 19:9's opening phrase "When you harvest...," Lev. 19:10's phrase "separated" can refer only to [that which separates] because of the harvest, [but not to fruit that separates due to some external constraint].

C. On the basis [of this interpretation sages] said:

D. [If a householder] was harvesting, [and] cut an entire cluster, [and] it became entangled in the leaves [of the vine], [so that the cluster] fell from his hand to the ground, and separated [into individual grapes], lo, [the individual grapes, together with the remaining cluster], belong to the householder, [since the fruit fell due to some external constraint]. [Only produce that falls to the ground at random, for no apparent reason, enters the category of the separated grape.]

One who places a basket under the vine while he harvests, [in order to catch the grapes that separate and fall, so that they will not enter the status of separated grapes], lo that man steals from the poor.

Concerning him it is stated, "Remove not the landmark of the poor" (gbwl ^{c}wlym). [This is a play on words on Prov. 22:28, which reads, "Remove not the ancient landmark." (gbwl ^{c}wlm) (M. 7:3A-H).

Sifra Qed. 3:3

A. What [produce is subject to the law of] the defective cluster (^{c}wllt), [such that it belongs to the poor]?

Any [cluster of grapes] that has neither a shoulder [i.e., a wide upper-part] nor a pendant [i.e., as cone-shaped lower-part].

If [a cluster of grapes] has either a shoulder or a pendant, [or both], it belongs to the householder, [for it is deemed well formed].

If it is uncertain [whether a cluster has at least one of these two definitive features, a shoulder or a pendant], [it is deemed a defective cluster and belongs] to the poor.

[As regards] a cluster [that appears to be] defective, [for it grows] on the [portion of the vine that] lies [on the ground] ('rkbh), [such a cluster cannot hang down, and so appears to have neither a shoulder nor a pendant, even though in fact it may possess these features]--

if [the cluster] is harvested along with the [normal] clusters, lo, it belongs to the householder [i.e., it is deemed a well-formed cluster].

But if [the cluster] is not [harvested with the normal clusters], lo, it belongs to the poor [i.e., it is deemed a defective cluster].

[As regards] a single grape [i.e., one that does not grow within a cluster]--

R. Judah says, "[It is deemed] a [normal] cluster, [and belongs to the householder]."

But sages say, "[It is deemed] a defective cluster, [and belongs to the poor]" (M. 7:4A-N).

Sifra Qed. 3:4

A. "[You shall abandon them] for the poor" (Lev. 19:10).
B. Perhaps [one might infer from this phrase that poor-offerings must be given] to other poor people [i.e., non Israelites].
C. Therefore Scripture states, "[You shall abandon them for the poor] and the sojourner." [The sojourner here referred to is taken to be an Israelite.]
D. If [poor-offerings must be given to] sojourners, perhaps [this phrase is meant to include giving the offerings to] resident aliens.
E. [This cannot be the case because] Scripture states, "[You shall abandon them for the poor, the sojourner, and to the Levite..."
F. Just as [the term] Levite clearly refers to a member of the covenant [i.e., an Israelite], so too [the term] sojourner, [in this context], refers to a member of the covenant.

Sifra Qed. 3:5

A. Or: "[You shall abandon them] for the Levite and for the poor" (Lev. 19:10).
B. Perhaps [these two phrases indicate that one must give the poor-offerings to these people] whether or not they are in need.
C. [To prove this is not the case], Scripture states, "[You shall abandon them] for the poor."
D. Just as [the term] "poor" refers to someone who is in need and a member of the covenant, so too all [those listed as recipients in Lev. 19:10] must be in need and members of the covenant.
E. "[When you reap the harvest of your field, you shall not reap it to its very corner, neither shall you gather the gleanings after your harvest.] You shall abandon [them for the poor] (Lev. 19:9).
F. The householder places the produce before them, and they divide it.
G. Even if ninety-nine [poor people] say that [the householder should harvest and] distribute [the produce], and [only] one [poor person] says that [the poor should harvest and] take [the produce by themselves] (M. 4:1E),
H. even if the one who says the poor should divide the produce themselves is healthy and strong, [and will be able to take more than any other poor person],
I. they listen to the single individual, [who said that the poor should take the produce], for he has spoken according to the law (M. 4:1F-G).
J. Perhaps in the case of produce suspended from a trellis or the produce of a palm tree (M. 4:1H) the same rule, that the poor should divide the offerings for themselves, hold true?

K. [To indicate that this is not the case, Scripture states, "you shall abandon] them [i.e. the offerings]." [The indirect object is taken to mean that the householder must abandon only those items that will benefit the poor. He has no right, by contrast, to leave for them produce that they will have to collect in dangerous situations.]

L. [In this case, when collecting the produce is likely to endanger the poor], <u>even if ninety-nine [poor people] say that [the poor should harvest and] take [the produce by themselves], and [only] one [poor person] says that [the householder should harvest and] distribute [it to the poor]</u> (M. 4:11),

M. even if the one who says the householder should divide the produce is old and sickly, [and thus will gain more than he would be able to take for himself],

N. <u>they listen to the single individual, [who said that the householder should divide the produce], for he has spoken according to the law</u> (M. 4:11-K).

<u>Sifra Qed. 3:6</u>

A. On what basis do you claim that [the householder] should divide produce on a trellis or a date palm, but that [the poor] should divide [for themselves] all other types of produce [set aside as poor-offerings] (cf. M. 4:1-2)?

B. After Scripture made a general statement, ["When you harvest...", (Lev. 19:9)], it made a limiting statement, ["...the harvest of your Land", (Lev. 19:9)].

C. Scripture states, "...the harvest [of your Land]." Now what characterizes [the action of] "harvesting" is that a minor can reach up as easily as an adult. This excludes [the cases of produce on] a trellis or [the fruit of] a date palm, for [in these cases] a minor cannot reach up as easily as an adult.

D. <u>R. Simeon says, "[So too]: Smooth nut-trees</u> (M. 4:1D) are deemed like [produce on] a trellis or [the fruit of] a date palm, [because gathering the poor-offerings from these trees could endanger the poor].

<u>Sifra Qed 3:7</u>

A. On what basis [may we determine that] (1) <u>produce about which there is a doubt [as to its status as] gleanings [is deemed to have the status of] gleanings</u>, (M. 4:11F) (2) produce about which there is a doubt [as to its status as] forgotten sheaves [is deemed to have the status of] forgotten sheaves, [and] (3) produce about which there is a doubt [as to its status as] <u>peah</u> [is deemed to have the status of <u>peah</u>?

B. Scripture states, "You shall abandon them for the poor. I am the Lord your God." [The term "abandon" implies that the householder must leave behind even that produce which might belong to him.]

II. Sifre Deuteronomy

Sifre Deut. #110

A. "[At the end of every three years you shall bring forth all the tithe of your produce in the same year, and lay it up within your towns.] [And the Levite, because he has no portion or inheritance with you,] and the the sojourner, the fatherless, and the widow within your towns... [shall come and eat and be filled]" (Deut. 14:28-29).

B. Perhaps [these two phrases indicate that one must give the poor-offerings to these people] whether or not they are in need.

C. And do not wonder, because [Scripture also] states, "You shall not... take a widow's garment in pledge," [with the result that one might think that the verse applies] whether [the widow] is poor or rich--

D. [to prove this is not the case], Scripture states, "[You shall abandon them] for the poor"--just as the word "poor" refers solely to a poor person, so too all [these cases] refer to poor people.

E. Perhaps [this verse indicates that poorman's tithe must be given] to members of the covenant and to [those who are] not governed by the covenant [i.e., to both Israelites and gentiles alike].

F. [To prove that this is not the case], Scripture states, "...giving it to the Levite..."--just as [the term] "Levite" refers to a member of the covenant, so too all [those listed as recipients of poorman's title] must be members of the covenant.

G. "...and they shall come and eat and be filled" (Deut. 14:29).

H. [This implies that you must] give the poor enough poorman's tithe to satisfy them.

I. On the basis [of the preceding exegesis, sages] said:

J. [When dispensing poorman's tithe] they may give to [each of] the poor people at the threshing floor no less than:

(1) one-half qab of wheat,

(2) one qab of barley (M. 8:5A-B).

K. "[Those] within your towns [shall come and eat and be filled]" (Deut. 14:29).

L. [This verse] teaches that one may not take [poorman's tithe] from the Land [of Israel] abroad [to feed poor people there].

M. [On the basis of the foregoing exegesis, sages] said:

N. A family from Bet Nebultah was [visiting] in Jerusalem.... [The sages] sent them gold pieces, for they did not want them to [be forced to] leave Jerusalem [due to a lack of money].

Sifre Deut. #282

A. "When you harvest [the yield of your land, you shall not completely reap the corner of your field as you harvest]" (Lev. 19:9).

B. [The emphasis on "when you harvest] excludes [the following cases from the requirement of setting aside peah]:

C. [a field that] (a) robbers harvested, (2) ants devastated, or that (3) the wind or cattle trampled (M. 2:7A).

D. "When you harvest [the yield of your land, you shall not completely reap the corner of your field as you harvest]" (Lev. 19:9).

E. [The emphasis on "when you harvest"] excludes [a second sort of case, namely one in which] a gentile [owns and] harvests [the field].

F. On the basis [of the foregoing exegesis, E, the sages] said:

G. [As regards] a gentile who harvested his field and afterward converted [to Judaism]--
[the produce that he had harvested is exempt from the restrictions of (1) gleanings, (2) forgotten sheaves, and (3) peah.
R. Judah obligates [the convert] to [obey the law of] the forgotten sheaf, because [the law of] the forgotten sheaf [takes effect] only after [the conclusion of] the binding [process, which takes place after the gentile had converted (M. 4:6. A-D)].

H. "[When you reap your harvest in your field, and have forgotten a sheaf] in your field, [you shall not return to gather it] (Deut. 24:21).

I. "[This phrase, 'your field'] excludes [from the law of the forgotten sheaf a case in which] one was binding [sheaves] in another person's field," the opinion of R. Meir.

J. But sages declare [such sheaves, bound in another's field], subject [to the law of the forgotten sheaf].

K. On the basis [of Meir's exegesis at A], you say:

L. [As regards] a sheaf that (1) workers forgot, but the household did not forget, (2) that the householder forgot, but the worker did not forget, or (3) in front of which poor people stood, or (4) if they covered it with straw, [thereby hiding the sheaf from sight so that the householder and his workers would forget it] -- lo, the [sheaf] is not [subject to the restrictions of the] forgotten sheaf (M. 5:7A-C).

Sifre Deut. #283

A. "[When you reap your harvest in your field], and have forgotten a sheaf [in the field, you shall not go back to get it]" (Deut. 24:19).

B. [The phrase, "a sheaf," implies that the law does] not [govern a case in which one forgot a small] grain pile [consisting of three sheaves]. [Thus the householder need not abandon for the poor three sheaves that he left in the field.]

C. May one [reason that the verse's reference to a single sheaf implies that the law does not apply] even to two [sheaves that have been forgotten in the field]?

D. [No, because] Scripture states [at Lev. 19:9], "It shall be for the poor and the sojourner." [Since two groups are named, we may infer that the law does in fact apply when two sheaves are left in the field] (see Finkelstein-Horowitz, p. 299).

E. On the basis [of the foregoing exegesis, C-D, sages] said:

F. <u>Two sheaves [of grain that are left side-by-side in a field] are [subject to the restrictions of the] forgotten sheaf.</u>

<u>But three [sheaves left side-by-side in a field] are not [subject to the restrictrions of the] forgotten sheaf.</u>

<u>Two piles of olives or carob [that are left side-by-side in a field] are [subject to the restrictions of the] forgotten sheaf.</u>

<u>But three [such piles left side-by-side in a field] are not [subject to the restrictions of the] forgotten sheaf.</u>

<u>Two stalks of flax [that are left side-by-side in a field] are [subject to the restrictions of the] forgotten sheaf.</u>

<u>But three [stalks left side-by-side in a field] are not [subject to the restrictions of the] forgotten sheaf.</u>

<u>Two [individual] grapes [that separate from a vine, and lie on the ground side-by-side] are [subject to the law of] the separated [grape]</u> (Lev. 19:9-10).

<u>But three [grapes lying side-by-side] are not [subject to the restrictions of] the separated [grape]</u> (M. 6:5A-H).

G. "[When you harvest... and have forgotten a sheaf] in the field..." (Deut. 24:19).

H. "[This verse] excludes tubers [from being subject to the law of the forgotten sheaf, because they are not sheaves]," the opinion of R. Judah.

I. But sages say, "[The phrase] 'in the field' [is meant] to include tubers [under the law of the forgotten sheaf, just like any other produce forgotten and left behind in the field] (cf. M.6:10).

J. "[When you harvest... and have forgotten a sheaf] in the field..." (Deut. 24:19).

K. [The phrase, "in the field," is required] to include [under the law of the forgotten sheaf] standing grain [which we might otherwise think is exempt (as at M.6:7).

L. For [we might have argued] in accordance with strict logic [that standing crops are exempt from the law of the forgotten sheaf, as follows at D-G]:

M. If a sheaf, upon which the poor have a weak claim, is subject to the law of the forgotten sheaf -- [the poor have a weak claim on sheaves because at most they will receive some produce as forgotten sheaves; they receive nothing as gleanings or <u>peah</u>]. --

N. is it not logical that a crop of standing grain, upon which the poor have a stronger claim, should be subject to the law of the forgotten sheaf? [I.e., the poor receive from standing crops portions as <u>peah</u> and gleanings, and then later

Appendix

forgotten sheaves. Since to begin with they have a strong claim on standing crops, this produce should be subject to the law of the forgotten sheaf.]

O. No! [Strict logic demands that standing crops are exempt from the law of the forgotten sheaf.] For if you say [that the law applies to] a sheaf, [which can be easily forgotten, so that its presence in the field] can prevent neither another sheaf nor a standing crop [that has been forgotten nearby from entering the status of the forgotten sheaf],

P. would you say [that the law applies to] a standing crop, [which almost certainly will never be forgotten, with the result that its presence in a field] does prevent a nearby sheaf or other standing crop from becoming subject to the law? [No. Hence, on the basis of logic it appears that the law of the forgotten sheaf should apply to standing crops] (cf. T. 3:6).

Q. [Therefore it is necessary for] Scripture to state, "in the field", to include [under the law of the forgotten sheaf all of a field's produce, including] as standing crop.

R. "[When you... forget a sheaf]... you shall not return to gather it" (Deut. 24:9).

S. [The phrase "you shall not return"] excludes [a case in which sheaves have been arranged for later collection at] the ends of rows. [The farmer does not return to the field when gathering these, but merely passes along the edge of the field.]

T. On this basis, [sages] said:

U. [As regards sheaves that the householder has left at] ends of rows [on one side of his field]--

[the presence of] a sheaf on the opposite side [of the field] proves [that the sheaves referred to at A are not forgotten]. [While harvesting the field, zig-zagging up and down the rows, the householder has arranged the sheaves at the end of each row for later collection. We therefore know that he has not forgotten them.]

[As for] a sheaf that [the householder] had picked up, in order to take it to the city [for sale], and that he then forgot [in the field]--

the [Hillelites] concede [to the Shammaites] that [the sheaf] is not [subject to the restrictions of the] forgotten sheaf. [By his deed, the farmer already has indicated that he intends to take the sheaf with him later when he goes to the city] (M. 6:3A-D).

V. "[When you... forget a sheaf]... you shall not return to gather it" (Deut. 24:19).

W. [The singular form, "to gather it," implies that we must consider] all [of the grain left behind, even if it is bound into two separate sheaves], as a single [mass]. [The farmers assume that large amounts of grain left in the field are exempt from the law, because the householder is unlikely to forget so sizable a quantity of produce. [If enough grain remains in the field, even bound into two separate bundles, the law does not apply.]

X. And what is the measure [of the largest amount of grain that can be deemed forgotten]?

Y. Sages measure it at a yield of two seahs.
Z. On this basis [sages] say:
AA. A sheaf that contains two seahs [of grain], and [that the householder] forgot, is not [subject to the restrictions of the] forgotten sheaf.
[As regards] two sheaves that [together] contain two seahs [of grain, e.g., each sheaf contains one seah]--
Rabban Gamaliel says, "[They belong] to the householder."
But sages say, "[They belong] to the poor" (M. 6:6A-E).
BB. "You shall not return to gather it" (Deut. 24:19).
CC. On the basis [of this phrase, sages] said:
DD. [As regards] a single stalk [of unharvested grain that stands] in [an area of land that already has been] harvested,
the top of which [single stalk] is as tall as the standing [crop next to it, so that the stalk perhaps appears to be part of the standing crop],
if [that stalk] is harvested at the same time as the standing [crop],
lo, it belongs to the householder, [that is, it is not deemed a gleaning].
But if [the stalk is] not [harvested at all, but remains standing after the harvest of the entire field is completed],
lo, it belongs to the poor, [that is, it is deemed a gleaning].
[As regards] a single stalk [of grain that is in the status of] gleanings [such that it belongs to the poor and is exempt from the separation of tithes], that was mixed with a heap [of grain that is not in the status of gleanings, and so is subject to the separation of tithes]--
[with the goal of returning to the poor person that one lost stalk, the householder must follow this procedure: He takes two other stalks of grain from the pile, and sets aside one for the poor. From the second, he] designates the tithes [required for the first] stalk, and then gives [that first stalk, now exempt from the separation of tithes], to a poor person. [This assures that the poor receive in exchange for the original stalk in the status of gleanings the proper amount of grain, one full stalk from which tithes need not be separated].
Said R. Eliezer, "But how can this poor person [receive] anything in exhange for [something that] had not yet come into his possession, [namely, the original stalk in the status of gleanings]?
"Rather, one transfers to the poor person [partial ownership of] the entire heap [of grain, so that now the poor person owns the stalk that was mixed in]. [Since he has acquired ownership of the gleaning, he now may trade it for a stalk of common produce.
[To this end, the householder must follow the procedure outlined at G.] He designates the tithes [required for] one stalk [of grain], and then gives [another stalk to a poor person] (M. 5:2A-K).
[Note that Sifre Deut. takes M. 5:2 to refer to the law of forgotten produce as it applies to standing crops, not to gleanings. See my remarks above.]

Sifre Deut. #284

A. "When you beat your olive trees, [you shall not go over the boughs again]..." (Deut. 24:20).

B. The earliest [Israelites] used to beat [the boughs] of their olive trees [with a rod, rather than picking the individual olives by hand]. They then were generous with [the olives that remained on the trees, and gave them to the poor].

C. On the basis [of the foregoing exegesis, sages] said:

D. [The fruit of] an olive tree [that is completely surrounded by other olive trees, for] it stands in the middle of three rows [of trees, that mark off] two rectangular [plots of grain], and that [the householder] left [unharvested], is not [subject to the restrictions of the] forgotten sheaf (M. 7:2A-C).

E. "When you beat your olive trees..." (Deut. 24:20).

F. [The phrase "your olive trees"] excludes [from the law of forgotten produce, olives that one left behind on the tree of] another [farmer].

G. "When you beat your olive trees..." (Deut. 24:20).

H. [The phrase "your olive trees"] excludes [from the law of forgotten produce, olives that one left behind on trees belonging to] the Temple.

I. "[When you gather the grapes of your vineyard], you shall not glean it afterward" (Deut. 24:21).

J. [The phrase "you shall not glean" implies that] you may not cause one poor person [to glean].

K. On the basis [of the foregoing exegesis, sages] said:

L. (1) One who does not allow the poor [freely] to collect [gleanings], (2) or who allows one [poor person] but not another, (3) or who assists [only] one of them, lo, that person robs the poor.
With regard to that person it is stated, "Do not remove the landmark of the poor," (gbwl ^cwlym). [This is a play on words for Prov. 22:28, which states, "Do not remove the ancient landmark" (gbwl ^cwlm)] (M. 5:6E-G).

M. "You shall not glean it afterward" (Deut. 24:21).

N. [The phrase "afterward"] teaches that the law of forgotten produce [left behind after one harvests] applies [to the produce of a vineyard].

O. "You shall not glean it afterward" (Deut. 24:20).

P. [The phrase "afterward"] teaches that the law of peah (i.e., produce left standing in the corner of the field after the harvest) applies [to the produce of a vineyard].

Q. "[You shall leave them] for the sojourner, the orphan and the widow" (Deut. 24:20).

R. Here [Scripture] states "sojourner and orphan" and there [at Deut. 24:19, Scripture] states "sojourner and orphan."

S. Just as the phrase "sojourner and orphan" stated in the latter case (Deut. 24:19) refers to [the law of the forgotten sheaf applying only to] a crop that produces two seahs [or less; see Sifre Deut. #283V-AA], so too here the phrase "sojourner and orphan" refers to [a case in which a vine produces] two seahs [or less].

Sifre Deut #285

A. "When you reap your vineyard, you shall not glean it afterward of defective clusters" (Deut. 24:21).

B. On the basis [of the word "reap," which applies only to well-formed clusters],

C. [As regards] a vineyard [the produce of which] entirely is defective clusters--
R. Eliezer says, "[The fruit] belongs to the householder [i.e., the clusters do not fall into the category of defective clusters because the norm in that vineyard is clusters that are not well formed]."
R. Aqiba says, "[The fruit] belongs to the poor, [i.e., the clusters are deemed defective, because they lack the definitive characteristics of well-formed clusters]."
Said R. Eliezer, "[Scripture states], 'When you harvest the grapes of your vineyard, you shall not return to gather the defective clusters' (Deut. 24:21).
"If there is no harvest [of normal clusters, because the entire yield is defective], how can there be defective clusters [left after the harvest]?"
Said to him R. Aqiba, "[Scripture also states], 'And you shall not gather defective clusters' (Lev. 19:10).
"[This verse indicates that the law applies] even if [the] entire [produce of the vineyard] is defective clusters, [such that there is no harvest of normal clusters].
[Aqiba continues:] "[If that is the intent of Lev. 19:10], why does [Scripture] state, 'When you harvest the grapes of your vineyard, you shall not return to gather the defective clusters' (Deut. 24:21)?
"[This verse, i.e., Deut. 24:21, teaches that] the poor may not claim the defective clusters before the harvest, [for the law of defective clusters takes effect only when the farmer claims the normal bunches of grapes for himself, by harvesting them]. [Before this time, none of the grapes can enter the status of defective clusters]" (M. 7:7A-I).

D. "You shall not glean it of defective clusters" (Deut. 24:21).

E. What [produce is subject to the law of] the defective cluster (^{c}wllt), [such that it belongs to the poor]?
Any [cluster of grapes] that has neither a shoulder [i.e., a wide upper-part] nor a pendant [i.e., a cone-shaped lower-part].
If [a cluster of grapes] has either a shoulder or a pendant, [or both],
it belongs to the householder, [for it is deemed well-formed].
If it is uncertain [whether a cluster has at least one of these two definitive features, a shoulder or a pendant],
[it is deemed a defective cluster and belongs] to the poor.

[As regards] a cluster [that appears to be] defective, [for it grows] on the [portion of the vine that] lies [on the ground] ('rkbh), [such a cluster cannot hang down, and so appears to have neither a shoulder nor a pendant, even though in fact it may possess these features]--
if [the cluster] is harvested along with the [normal] clusters,
lo, it belongs to the householder [i.e., it is deemed a well-formed cluster].
But if [the cluster] is not [harvested with the normal clusters],
lo, it belongs to the poor [i.e., it is deemed a defective cluster].
[As regards] a single grape [i.e., one that does not grow within a cluster]--
R. Judah says, "[It is deemed] a [normal] cluster, [and belongs to the householder]."
But sages say, "[It is deemed] a defective cluster, [and belongs to the poor]!"
(M. 7:4A-N).

F. "You shall not glean it of defective clusters" (Deut. 24:21).
G. [The phrase "afterward"] teaches that the law of forgotten produce [left behind after one harvests] applies [to the produce of a vineyard].
H. "You shall not glean it afterward" (Deut. 24:20).
I. [The phrase "afterward"] teaches that the law of peah (i.e., produce left standing in the corner of the field after the harvest] applies [to the produce of a vineyard].
J. "[You shall leave them] for the sojourner, the orphan and the widow" (Deut. 24:20).
K. Here [Scripture] states "sojourner and orphan" and there [at Deut. 24:19, Scripture] states "sojourner and orphan."
L. Just as the phrase "sojourner and orphan" stated in the latter case (Deut. 24:19) refers to [the law of the forgotten sheaf applying only to] a crop that produces two seahs [or less; see Sifre Deut. #283V-AA], so too here the phrase "sojourner and orphan" refers to [a case in which a vine produces] two seahs [or less].

Sifre Deut. #336

A. "[For Torah is no trifle for you, but it is your life], and thereby you shall live long [in the Land which you are going over the Jordan to possess]" (Deut. 32:47).
B. [Study of Torah] is one of the matters that one who does them enjoys benefit therefrom in this world and long life in the world to come [M. 1:1C with variations].
C. [It is stated] explicitly here [in this verse] regarding study of Torah. [From what verse] might we derive that honoring father and mother (M. 1:1D1) [likewise earns rewards both in this world and in the world to come]?
D. Scripture states, "Honor your father and your mother, so that you may live long" (Ex. 20:12).

E. [From what verse might we derive that] letting the mother bird go [while keeping her chicks is in the same category]?

F. It is written, "You shall surely send out the mother. But the chicks you shall take for yourself, in order that it may go well with you and that you may live long" (Deut. 22:6).

G. [From what verse might we derive that] <u>bringing peace [between one person and his fellow</u> (M. 1:1D3) likewise is in the same category]?

H. Scripture states, "All your sons shall be taught by the Lord, and great shall be the peace of your sons" (Is. 54:13).

NOTES TO INTRODUCTION

1. At first consideration, the offering left in the rear corner of the field, peah, seems to break with this principle of random selection. As we shall see, peah must be designated by purposeful and carefully planned actions of the householder. Nonetheless, the produce designated as peah is separated from the rest of the crop merely by its accident of growing in the rear corner of the field. The farmer's act of designating the produce merely indicates to the poor that the grain he has left standing indeed has the status of a poor-offering. See below, note 6.

2. Seven of the Division's eleven tractates deal with the Temple or priestly rations: Demai, Terumot, Maasrot, Maaser Sheni, Hallah, Orlah, and Bikkurim. Of the remaining four, Berakhot is unrelated to the overall theme of agriculture, while Kilayim and Shebiit take up agricultural issues mentioned in Scripture.

3. The Holiness Code (Lev. Chs. 17-26) makes it clear that both the poor and the priests possess none of the Land. In the case of the priests, it is evident that, in compensation for this lack, ordinary householders must render to the priests a portion of their crops. See also Lev. 27:30; Num. 18:8-24.

4. For a discussion of the Biblical promise of prosperity to all Israelites living in the Land, see Brueggemann, The Land, pp. 48-50.

5. See for example, M. Maas. Chs. 2-3; Jaffee, Tithes, pp. 63-105.

6. In the case of peah, the householder himself, through quite deliberate action, must designate the produce for the poor (see T. 2:7-8). The crucial fact, however, is that he plays no role in determining which produce the poor will receive. How so? As T. 1:6K-L explicitly state, the farmer must designate whatever grows in the rear corner of the field, regardless of its quality or amount.

7. The notion that God's choice is reflected through random chance is expressed fully in the following passage of the Talmud of the Land of Israel:

Y. San. 6:3

> You find that: when Achan committed sacrilege, Joshua began to attempt to appease the Holy One, blessed be he, saying to him, "Lord of the world, Tell me who this man is [who committed sacrilege]."
>
> God said to Joshua, "I am not going to inform on any creature, and not only so, but if I did so, I should turn out to commit an act of slander. But go and arrange the Israelites in their tribes, and cast lots on them. Forthwith, I shall produce him."
>
> This is in line with that which is written, "So Joshua rose early in the morning and brought Israel near, tribe by tribe, and the tribe of Judah was taken; and he brought near the families of Judah, and the family of the Zerahites was taken; and he brought near the family of the Zerahites man by man, and Zabdi was taken; and he brought near his household man by man, and Achan the son of Carmi, son of Zabi, son of Zerah of the tribe of Judah, was taken" (Josh. 7:16-18).
>
> Achan said to Joshua, "Are you going to seize me by a mere lot? In this entire generation, there are only two who are truly faithful, you and Phineas. Cast lots between yourselves, and one of you will be trapped by the lot! Not only so, but your teacher, Moses, died only thirty or forty days ago. Now did Moses, our rabbi, teach us, 'By the testimony of two witnesses [will the accused by put to death]' (Deut. 17:6)? Now have you already begun to err?"

At that moment Joshua foresaw through the Holy Spirit that he would eventually divide up the Land of Israel by lots.

That is in line with the following verse of Scripture: "Joshua cast lots for them in Shiloh before the Lord; and there Joshua apportioned the land to the people of Israel, to each his portion" (Josh. 18:10).

[So Joshua reasoned:] "Will you then say on this basis that we are giving a bad name by casting lots? And not only so, but if the lots now are confirmed, then all Israelites will say, 'The lots were confirmed in a capital case, all the more so in property cases [e.g., such as in the division of the Land].' But if the lots now are nullified, then all the Israelites will say, 'In a capital case the lots were nullified, all the more so in property cases!'" [Hence, the lots must validly reveal God's will] (Neusner, Talmud, Vol. 31).

8. See M. Ter. 1:7, 3:5; Peck, Terumot, pp. 62-63, 113-116.

9. The tractate makes a second point in connection with each of the poor-offerings, namely, that this food must be of an anomalous nature. How does this anomaly arise? When the farmer either reaps his field, cuts a few stalks, or binds a sheaf of grain, he claims ownership of the produce. Food that previously had belonged to God alone is not partially acquired by the householder for himself and for his household. The anomaly arises when the farmer drops or leaves behind some of the food he reaps. This produce, which escapes from the farmer's possession at just that moment when he attempts to effect full acquisition, must be given to the poor. The poor-offerings thus are anomalous because the householder first acquires ownership of them but then does not retain them in his possession.

10. See M. 4:6-8 for an example of this explicit comparison between poor-offerings and priestly rations.

11. See Sarason, Demai, pp. 3-6; Jaffee, Tithes, pp. 5-6.

12. T. 1:5 makes it clear that the farmer is supposed to leave grain standing as peah when he reaps his field. He then must designate this food as peah. Nonetheless, if he does not set aside the produce while reaping, he must separate and designate the appropriate portion as peah during binding or threshing.

13. M. Maas. 1:5-8; Jaffee, Tithes, pp. 5, 43-61.

14. As a free-standing unit, the discussion of Scripture could have been placed either before the definitions at A or, as the framers have chosen, after them. Their choice seems to me to bear no meaning.

15. See Noth, Leviticus, pp. 139-141; IB Leviticus, pp. 197-198.

16. See Noth, Leviticus, p. 141. On the prohibition against the priests' ownership of a portion of the Land of Israel, see Num. 18:20, 24; IB Numbers, pp. 229-233.

17. See Elliger, Leviticus, pp. 247, 309, on the relationship between Lev. 19:9 and 23:22.

18. On the nature of the rules in Deuteronomy's "Egyptian Series," see Carmichael, Deuteronomy, p. 203.

19. Of course, not every tractate of Mishnah stands so close to Scripture's rules. For examples, see Neusner's discussions in "Scripture in Appointed Times," p. 112, and in Judaism, pp. 167-229.

20. The Roman numerals correspond directly to the parts of the outline above.

21. We may assume that such Israelite groups as the Essenes at Qumran and the early Christians certainly were aware of Leviticus' and Deuteronomy's injunctions regarding poor-support. The fact that they knew the same Scriptural rules as Mishnah's framers, yet did entirely different things when dealing with poor-relief, again shows the wide range of options available in treating this topic.

22. See Nickelsburg, pp. 55-56.

23. See Nickelsburg, p. 122; Vermes, Perspective, pp. 29-44.

24. See Vermes, pp. 163, 169-175.

25. See Vermes, DSSE, pp. 29, 116.

26. See Driver, p. 250; Vermes, DSSE, p. 96.

27. See the Community Rule, 6:11-18; Vermes, DSSE, p. 82.

28. The only exception to this notion is represented by M. 8:7, which discusses the soup-kitchen and communal fund. But the main thrust of the tractate is to focus on the individual's gifts to the poor.

29. Supporting the poor with whatever gift one could afford would signal the compassion needed to live a life suitable for the new order. See Batey, p. 24; Johnson, p. 76.

30. See also Hengel, Property, p. 11.

31. See Batey, p. 21.

32. See Hengel, Property, p. 40; Batey, pp. 56-59.

33. See Batey, pp. 56-59.

34. Now this restatement of the Biblical rules in fact represents a remarkable choice on the framers' part, for this was by no means their only option concerning poor-support. In some tractates, the framers work out issues not at all suggested by Scripture, or merely relevant to Scripture in the most general way (consider, for example, Tractate Parah). Similarly, some tractates begin with Scripture's facts, but move in essentially unprecedented directions (Tractate Shabbat, for example). See Neusner, Judaism, pp. 221-222; Neusner, Scripture and Appointed Times, pp. 110-111, 115, for a comprehensive treatment of Mishnah's various relationships to Scripture.

35. See E.D. Hirsch, Validity, who persuasively argues that the proper reading of prose texts consists of a search for the author's intended meaning. Hirsch effectively counters the view of "new criticism" that we must banish all considerations of the author's meaning. For a full statement of the opposing view, see Fish, Is There a Text in This Class?, pp. 22-67.

36. Other exegetical traditions have claimed that meaning is carried not through syntax and literary form, but through other means. As we shall see below, this claim, typical of rabbinic commentaries, produces entirely different results from analysis of Tractate Peah.

37. Neusner, Purities, Vol. XXI, pp. 164-234, amply describes the five syntactic patterns that characterize all of Mishnah's rules. This limited repertoire of rhetorical forms indicates the care with which the framers formulated their material.

38. Again, see Neusner, ibid., on the various literary patterns characteristic of Mishnaic discourse.

39. Examples of the list are found at M. 1:1, 1:4, 1:5, 2:1, 3:6, 4:5. Further discussion of the list can be found in Jaffee, Tithes, pp. 15-19; Peck, Terumot, pp. 23-25; and Sarason, Demai, pp. 11-23.

40. See Porton, "Dispute." Further examples of the dispute form are found at M. 2:1, 2:4, 3:2, 3:4, 3:6, 4:5, 4:9, 4:10, 4:11, 5:3, 5:4, 6:1-2, 6:5, 6:6, 7:5, 7:6, 7:7, and 8:5.

41. Other examples of simple repetition are found at M. 3:7-8 and 6:5-6.

42. Another example of a triplet is found at M. 4:8.

43. Many of Tractate Peah's thematic units correspond directly to the chapter markings in standard editions of Mishnah. Some, however, comprise only a part of a chapter or cross the divisions of chapters. Nonetheless, I follow the standard chapter markings because these are uniform in all editions and allow me regular breaks to discuss the tractate's unfolding.

44. My translation is literal insofar as I attempt to reproduce Hebrew word order. But my overall approach is to provide a "free" rendition, one that adds explanatory language as needed, seeks to translate the sense of a phrase (even if this means translating two occurrences of a single word differently), and attempts to reproduce metaphor and idiom where possible. On this approach to translation as it applies to ancient translations, see Barr, "Typology of Literalism."

45. Of course, this translation also allows the reader to identify phrases that do not fit within an established pattern. By recognizing such glosses or appendices we can more easily see the central theme of the unit itself.

46. It should be noted that textual variants in Tractate Peah rarely are of importance for the interpretation of a passage as a whole. For the most part, the variants concern only the spelling of a word or the presence or absence of particles, conjunctions, and articles.

47. See M.D. Herr, EJ, Vol. 15, p. 1284, for the consensus view of Tosefta's age and location of redaction.

48. See Neusner, Purities, Vol. 21, passim, on the relationship between the syntax of Mishnah and Tosefta. My translation and commentary follow the critical text prepared in Lieberman, TZ, and the analysis in Lieberman, TK.

49. Herr, E.J., Vol. 14, p. 1518, states, "Since it appears that the Sifra [and Sifre, see p. 1520] in the present form... were not known to the two Talmuds, it would seem to have been compiled and arranged in... (the Land of) Israel not earlier than the end of the fourth century C.E...."

50. I hasten to add that neither view is inherently better. Rather, the concerns of the academic community differ from those of the primarily theological community I have just described. In the framework provided by the univerity, how any rule fits within its larger literary and conceptual context is paramount; the message of the framers' essay, likewise, is my first priority.

NOTES TO CHAPTER ONE

1. Two contradictory positions are expressed at M. 1:3A-B: First, peah may be any portion of a field's produce, and second, peah must be left standing in the rear corner of the field. According to both opinions, however, each field must have a distinct portion of its produce designated as peah. This common proposition forms the basis of all of Chapter Two, which is devoted to defining a field for the purposes of designating peah.

2. See Maimonides, Commentary.

3. Bert, GRA, TYY, Danby, p. 10, and Lieberman, TZ, p. 41, all state that r'ywn may mean the number of times an Israelite must appear in the Temple-court during each of the three pilgrimage festivals (so Y. Peah 1:1 [15a]). Maimonides, Commentary, points out, however, that in Mishnah r'ywn refers to the offering that the pilgrim brings, but not to the pilgrim himself (see also Kasovsky, Conc. Mish., IV, p. 1630ff; M. Hag. 1:1-2). Additionally, since the term follows two other offerings in our list (M. 1:1B1-2), it seems clear that it refers to the appearance-offering. Bert, who cites both possibilities, claims that the confusion stems from M. Hag. 1:2, which in fact lists a specific measure for the appearance-offering. Bert believes the commentators attribute a different meaning to the word in its present context in order to prevent the two rules from contradicting each other.

4. Maimonides, Commentary, and Bert distinguish between righteous deeds that are accomplished by rendering physical assistance, and those accomplished through giving money. According to these commentators, only physical actions have no limit; monetary gifts are limited to one-fifth of a person's wealth. This distinction is not at all indicated in the text. TYT, GRA, and MR, by contrast, state that whether a righteous deed is accomplished through physical action or through giving money, no limits govern its performance (see B. Ket. 50b, the basis of this view).

5. See Maimonides, Commentary.

6. Proper analysis of a Mishnaic list must pay attention not only to the superscription, but also to the interplay of the elements themselves. This view is fully articulated in Jaffee, "Lists," pp. 19-20; see also Jaffee, Tithes, p. 16.

7. Maimonides, Commentary, asserts that all five elements of the first list in fact do form a unity. In his view, the list contains those acts that are deemed more meritorious the more generously they are performed. For the case of offerings, that is, the greater the value of the item designated, the better. Similarly, with regard to righteous deeds and study of Torah, one receives greater rewards the more one accomplishes. This view may be rejected, however, on two grounds. First, no mention is made in the list itself about the rewards or merits one receives for performing these actions or offerings. This notion seems to be introduced here on the basis of the second list, which explicitly deals with the rewards for one's actions. Second, this principle does not account for the exclusion from the list of other possible elements. Certainly charity is more praiseworthy when given in greater amounts, yet it is not included on the list.

8. Perhaps B4-5 were added to the core of this first list on the basis of materials present in the second. This would account for the repetition between the two lists, as well as for the fact that the first list is not uniform. See Bauer, Die Mischnah, p. 10.

9. I follow Lieberman, TK, p. 126, who identifies qrn as punishment received in the world-to-come, and pyrwt as the consequences of one's actions in this world. See M. 1:1C.

10. See Jastrow, II, P. 1303-4, s.v. ṣrp, Hithpa.

11. Reading lm^{c}sh with E, ed. princ.

12. Again reading with E, ed. princ.

13. Lieberman, TK, p. 127, claims that pyrwt here refers to an action produced by a good or an evil intention. See the parallel passage at B. Qid. 40a.

14. TYY claims that B should be read as a stich separate from C:

> B. "And even though they said, '[They may designate as peah no less than one-sixtieth of a field's produce,' cf. M. 1:2A], still peah has no fixed measure [as an upper limit]."

This interpretation harmonizes M. 1:1's rule that peah has no measure with M. 1:2A, which states that the proper amount of peah is at least one-sixtieth of a field's yield. Since this explanation ignores the continuation at C, however, it may be rejected.

15. I translate ᶜnwh in accordance with M. 6:7 (see also Sens, MS, TYT). In that context, the word clearly means "crop." Along these lines, Kohut, Aruch, IV, p. 224, s.v. ᶜnwh, and Jastrow, II, p. 1092, s.v. ᶜnwh, link the word with Biblical Hebrew ᶜnbh, "yield of a vineyard." I reject the alternative suggestion of translating ᶜnwh = "poverty" as in TYY and Danby, p. 11, since Mishnah never uses the word with that meaning (see Kasovsky, CM, III, p. 1389, s.v. ᶜnwh).

16. Bert, MS, and GRA all harmonize M. 1:1 and M. 1:2. They claim the rule that no measure pertains to peah (M. 1:1) refers only to a measure specified in the Torah, the written law. The contrary rule that one must designate one-sixtieth of the field's produce (M. 1:2) they characterize as a rabbinic injunction. Thus the two rules are not contradictory; rather they refer separately to the written Torah and to the oral one. This notion, of course, is not indicated by the text at all, and is merely an attempt to eliminate contradictions within Mishnah.

17. Lieberman, TK, p. 126, attempts to account for the measure provided at A, one-sixtieth of a field's produce, on the basis of the amounts required for other agricultural offerings. He claims that all offerings must comprise at least this amount of the yield (cf. M. Ter. 4:3). His explanation is not satisfactory, however, for he never explains why one-sixtieth is an appropriate minimum for any offering.

18. TYT correctly points out that A and B-C must be independent of each other, for they repeat precisely the same point. That is to say, the notion that one must designate one-sixtieth (or more) of his field's yield is repeated at Cl, which states that the farmer must designate an amount of peah befitting the size of his field.

19. Maimonides, Gifts 1:15, claims that A and B-C are fully continuous and harmonious. He views A as providing the minimum amount of produce that may be designated as peah. B-C then require the farmer to designate more than this amount under certain conditions. This harmonization is not contained within the text, which quite clearly contains two distinct rules.

20. Swp (rear), tḥlh (front), and 'mṣᶜh (middle) are used in this context to refer to parts of the field that correspond to the farmer's actions during the harvest (Albeck, p. 42). The farmer begins harvesting his crop at the front of the field and continues up and down the rows (the middle). He works his way toward the rear of the field, ending his harvest in the rear corner. Thus the location of these parts of the field are determined by the where the farmer begins reaping the produce.

21. So Maimonides, Commentary, and MR. But Sens and Bert claim that one need not leave any produce as peah at the rear of the field unless he has left less than the appropriate measure (one-sixtieth of the crop) in the middle or front of the field. Only in such a case, they argue, must the householder designate additional produce at the rear of the field, in order to bring the total amount of peah up to one-sixtieth of the crop. This interpretation seems to be based on an attempt to harmonize A and B, which appear to me to be contradictory rules.

22. Maimonides, Commentary, Bert, MS, and GRA all suggest that šyyr should be read as hš'yr, "allow to remain." M. 1:3C then would read:

> C. R. Judah says, "If [the farmer] leaves one stalk [at the rear of the field], he relies upon it [to fulfill his obligation] regarding peah."

These commentators all interpret Mishnah in light of T. 1:5F-G, which harmonizes M. 1:3A-B and C-E. Read in this way, Judah (C-E) takes a position midway between the anonymous rule at A and Simeon's lemma at B. That is, Judah rules that while peah validly may be designated in any part of the field (as at A), a symbolic amount of produce, one stalk, must be left in the field's rear corner (as at B). I have chosen to follow Sens, MR, and Albeck, p. 42, and to translate šyyr as "retain," based on Mishnah's usage of this word in other contexts (see M. 3:7-8A; M. B.B. 9:6; T. 1:5E-G).

23. I follow Sens and MR, who suggest that the pericope is composed of two completely independent rulings, A-B and C-E. Most commentators, by contrast, view the pericope as three continuous rules (A, B, C-E). See above, note 22.

24. See for example T. 1:1C-D; M. Ter. 4:5, Peck, Terumot, pp. 148-149; M. Bik. 2:4, Wenig-Rubenstein, in Green, Approaches, Vol. 3, p. 74.

25. So Lieberman, TK, p. 131.

26. So Maimonides, Commentary. See also Kohut, Aruch, VIII, p. 106, s.v. šmr, and Bauer, Die Mischna, p. 13, who translate gehütet and aufbewahrt wird respectively.

27. The proper names of the trees listed at E:
'wg (sumac) = Rhus Coriaria; EJ, XV, p. 311; Löw, Flora, I, pp. 200-202;
ḥrwbyn (carob) = Ceratonia Siliqua; EJ, V, p. 201; Löw, Flora, II, pp. 393ff;
'gwz (walnut) = Juglans Regia; EJ, XIII, pp. 625-626; Löw, Flora, II, pp. 41-42;
šqdym (almond) = Amygdalaus Communis var. Dulcis or Amara; EJ, I; p. 666, Löw, Flora, III, pp. 242ff.;
gpnym (grapevines) = Vitis Vinifera; EJ, XIII, pp. 619-620; Löw, Flora, I pp. 48-51;
rmwnym (pomegranate) = Punica Granatum; EJ, XIII, p. 841; Löw, Flora, III, pp. 80ff.;
zytym (olive) = Olea Eurpaea; EJ, XIII, pp. 623-624; Löw, Flora, II, pp. 287-293;
tmrym (date palms) = Phoenix Dactylitera; EJ, XIII, pp. 623-624; Löw, Flora, II, pp. 306 ff.

28. See M. Maas. 1:1 and Jaffee, Tithes, pp. 28-30.

29. See M. 3:2, which presents a dispute concerning whether the farmer must designate peah from each patch he harvests or from only one patch on behalf of the entire field.

30. I follow Albeck, p. 42, who claims that all of the fruit of each tree listed at D-E ripens at one time, as a single crop. Unlike other trees, then, this fruit is harvested as a single crop (cf. M. 1:4B4), and so is subject to the law.

31. tmr (fig tree) = Ficus Carica, EJ, VI, p. 1273; Löw, Flora, I, pp. 224 ff. Lieberman, TK, p. 132, supplies the language needed to understand this stich.

32. šyzpyn (Jujubes) = Zizyphus Vulgaris; EJ, IX, p. 788; Löw, Flora, III, pp. 138-141.

33. I follow Lieberman, TK, pp. 132-133, who explains that bnwt swh refers not to the bleached color of the fruit, but to the tree-bark's color.

34. ḥlḥlḥyn (peas) = Lathyrus Sativus; EJ, XIII, pp. 619-620; Löw, Flora, II, p. 437.

35. On the meaning of myrwḥ, see Maimonides, Commentary, and Bert.

36. So Bert.

37. Produce that is edible, privately owned, and grown from the ground is subject to the separation of tithes (M. Maas. 1:1; Jaffee, Tithes, pp. 28-30). Such produce does not become subject to the law, however, until the farmer processes it, thus indicating his claim of ownership (cf. Maimonides, Commentary; Sens; M. Maas. 1:6; Jaffee, Tithes, pp. 43-51).

NOTES TO CHAPTER TWO

1. See Chapter One, n. 1.

2. Peah is designated from produce standing in the field, but agricultural offerings given to the priests are designated at the threshing floor. This hints at a fundamental distinction between poor-offerings and priestly dues. As we shall see (M. 4:1, 8:1), poor-offerings have no consecrated status. Priestly rations, by contrast, are deemed holy. For further discussion of this matter, see above, pp. 72-74 and 138-139.

3. For an example of another case in which natural categories are decisive, see M. Ter. 2:4. One may not separate heave-offering from one kind of produce on behalf of another kind. Moreover, such a separation is not valid even post facto. That is to say, in cases where taxonomic categories determine the validity of the offering, human actions are completely disregarded. See Peck, Terumot, pp. 92-93.

4. M. Men. 10:8 explicitly refers to the use of young grain as fodder. Maimonides, Commentary, however, claims that šḥt should be interpreted as grain that is not fit for any purpose, "waste." Following his view would not affect the substance of the law or of my comment.

5. As my interpolations at C-D indicate, the central issue here is whether or not an area that already has been harvested becomes analogous to uncultivated land. For this interpretation, see TYT.

6. At M. 1:3, sages and Simeon dispute whether or not peah is specific to the rear corner of each field. Both sides agree, however, that a separate portion of produce must be designated on behalf of each field. The motivation for this view is probably Scripture, which states, "You should not harvest the corner of your field" (Lev. 19:9). See Maimonides, Commentary.

7. MR suggests that the ambiguity arises here because cutting young grain does not constitute "harvesting," but is veiwed as thinning out the crop. This action cannot establish a field's boundaries, he claims, unless the farmer indicates his intention by ploughing the area. I follow TYT.

8. Tosefta here reverses "private path" and "public path" in its quotation of M. 2:1A-B. See Lieberman, TK, p. 134.

9. Maimonides, Commentary and Gifts 3:19, interprets A-B in light of T. 1:8b. According to that pericope, an irrigation ditch establishes a boundary only if it is sufficiently large that the farmer connot reach across it.

10. I follow Lieberman, TK, p. 137, for problems of interpretation and translation.

11. So Maimonides, Commentary.

12. On the translation of this phrase, see Danby, p. 11.

13. Löw, Flora, II, pp. 402-404, discusses the extensive root systems of carob trees. He claims that their roots can extend as far as fifty meters. See also EJ, V, pp. 201-202.

14. The mention here of Gamaliel and his father shows that the Patriarch's actions, by virtue of his office alone, provide a sufficient precedent for legal rulings. On the common use of Gamaliel's actions as precedents for anonymous legal rules see Kanter, Gamaliel, pp. 238-242; 247-248.

15. See Kanter, Gamaliel, pp. 25-26. He correctly notes that Gamaliel's lemma (M. 2:4F-G) must have been formulated independently of its present context.

16. Several commentators, notably Bert and TYT, attempt to harmonize the two contrasting opinions present in Gamaliel's ruling. See below, n. 18.

17. While E+G and F+H provide contrasting definitions of an orchard, they are not in standard dispute form. That is to say, the two opinions do not respond to a common superscription nor to each other. For further information of the dispute as a standard form, see Porton, "Dispute," pp. 18-19.

18. I have interpreted "in every direction" in accordance with the meaning given by Jastrow, II, p. 1458, s.v. rwḥ ii, and Kasowsky, CM, IV, p. 1660, s.v. rwḥ. Compare Maimonides (Commentary), Bert, and GRA. These commentators harmonize the two parts of Gamaliel's lemma, claiming that bkl rwḥ means "in each individual direction." Following this explanation, a separation portion of produce was designated for olive trees

on each side of the farm. This is in line with Gamaliel's ruling for carob trees: all trees planted in close proximity to one another comprise a single orchard. Nevertheless, the two parts of Gamaliel's ruling must be in opposition to one another, or we cannot account for Eliezer's finding it necessary to correct them (cf. H).

19. At A-B TYY adds the underlined phrases:

   A. One who sows his field with [only] one type of seed], even if he brings the crop to the threshing floor in two lots [that he harvested at separate times],
   B. designates one [portion of produce as] peah [from the entire crop, while at the threshing floor].

Contrary to the bulk of the tractate, this commentator believes the peah is designated at the threshing floor, not from unharvested produce in the field (see Chapter Two, n. 2; and below, M. 4:1). In his view the condition of the produce prior to the designation at the threshing floor is inconsequential. Even if the produce derives from two separate fields, it has been brought together at the threshing floor as a single crop from which only one portion need be designated as peah. This interpretation, however, is not hinted at by the text. Furthermore, it cannot account for the second rule, C-D, that a farmer must designate two portions of produce as peah from two separate species that have been brought to a single threshing floor.

20. Jastrow, I, p. 689, s.v. lblr, connects lblr with the Latin librarius, a legal copyist. See Lewis and Short, p. 1061.

21. The "Pairs" usually are thought to be the men listed by twos in M. Abot 1:4, 6,8,10,12, as well as M. Hag. 2:2. See Bert, Danby, p. 446, n. 7, and Neusner, Pharisees, I, pp. 61-158, for further information.

22. Sens correctly claims that human action determines the boundaries of a field only if the chapter's earlier definitions (see M. 2:1) are ambiguous.

23. Maimonides, Commentary, Sens, and Bert provide the interpolation at M. 2:7A1. In contrast they note that an Israelite householder who hires gentiles to harvest his field indeed does become liable to designate peah.

24. Maimonides, Commentary and Jastrow, II, p. 1423, s.v. qrsm, link qrsmwh with BH krsmwh, to bite or nibble.

25. So MR. But MS and Bert read "...for the obligation to designate peah on behalf of the grain that has been harvested devolves upon the standing crop." In their view the farmer must designate peah for the entire field, not because he completes the harvest, but because the thieves obviously will not give to the poor any portion of what they have stolen. As I have shown, however, the judgement depends on who harvests the rear corner of the field.

26. At M. 1:3 Simeon and sages dispute whether or not peah is specific to the rear corner of the field. The entire discussion in this pericope assumes Simeon's theory is valid. He rules that none but the grain growing in the field's rear corner can satisfy Scripture's requirements.

NOTES TO CHAPTER THREE

1. So Sens. Maimonides, Commentary, claims that this refers to a householder who plants some patches of his field and leaves other portions unsown. This interpretation may be rejected, however, on the basis of the context supplied at E.

2. So Bert. I reject Maimonide's interpretation of m'ḥt yd (see Commentary) as "from a single place" because the rule then would not parallel the other parts of the discussion (cf. M. 3:3 I, which also speaks of the purposes for which part of the field is harvested).

3. Bert points out that these rules (I-M), while entirely consonant with the surrounding material's meaning, depart from its form. This formal balance, at B-C, F-G, and Q-R, is established by the phrases "from each and every one [of the plots]" and "from one [plot] on behalf of all [of the plots together]." At J, L, and M, however, the formula shifts to "from the former by themselves and from the latter by themselves." Accompanying this stylistic shift is a change in the formal structure of the rules. Note that I-M alone is not framed as a dispute. It therefore appears that these rules, while carrying forward the present investigation, are not original in this context.

4. This section on parent-onions seems to have been included here simply because of the mention of onions at M. 3:3. The rules thus support a theory of redaction based only on topic. Mishnah's usual theory, we recall, takes into account both topic and underlying principle.

5. I follow the interpretation of this crux in Sens.

6. Reading hyw lw with E, ed. princ.

7. Lieberman, TK, pp. 138-139, claims that this assumption is necessary because the farmer thins out only the poorest quality plants which could not be preserved in storage (see M. 1:4-5). Nothing in the text supports this assertion and it would not affect the validity of the assumption that these onions are exempt from designation as peah because they could not be stored. Only on the basis of such an assumption does Judah's qualification make sense following M. 3:3D.

8. So Sens. Jastrow, II, p. 1374, s.v. qlḥ, claims that qlḥy 'yln does not refer to trees at all, but rather to "the stems of plants in his field [without the soil]." In this context, however, the term must refer to the live, growing part of the trees, the subject of the pericope.

9. The situation is analogous to M. 2:7-8, where the farmer sells part of the produce of his field but does not sell the field itself. In both cases, the sale has no effect on the status of the field (although at M. 2:7-8 the sale does affect who must designate peah). See MR.

10. So Maimonides, Commentary, and Danby, p. 13.

11. A prozbul transfers title of a loan to a court. To prevent this loan from being cancelled by the Sabbatical year, the borrower must own at least a tiny piece of land. Because he owns this land, the loan is deemed secure and is not actually outstanding during the Sabbatical year (M. Sheb. 10:2). See Newman, Sabbatical Year.

12. In addition to presenting two theories of real estate, the pericope also offers two readings of M. 1:4-5's definition of what produce is subject to the laws of peah. Specifically, M. 1:4B3 claims that all food grown from the Land is subject to the law. Of the two positions advocated here, only Aqiba reads this criterion literally. The other authorities interpret "land" to mean a sizable portion of real estate.

13. Maimonides, Commentary, links all of the measurements at A-D to the amounts of food that must be given to each poor person as part of poorman's tithe (M. 8:5). His explanation is not sufficient, however, for M. 8:5 never mentions "an area that measures six-by-six handbreadths" (C) or "an area that produces enough to require two sickle strokes" (D). Instead, I follow Sens and TYT who explain these rulings principally in light of M. Kil. 2:10.

14. At E., Maimonides, Commentary, and Bert ignore the phrase "any land at all," and translate instead:

> E. "[If] he had consigned to his wife some land [constituting an equal share in the state with his sons], she forfeits...."

According to this interpretation, as I have explained above, the woman's marriage settlement must be forfeited because her share of the estate almost certainly will be greater than two-hundred zuz, her total claim on the estate. I have chosen not to follow this interpretation, however, for it ignores the central principle of the triplet; even a minuscule area of land has unlimited value.

15. Maimonides, Commentary, points out correctly that the issue of the pericope as a whole is whether or not a small piece of land can indicate the householder's intention for his entire estate. Nevertheless, both Maimonides and Bert wish to harmonize the three cases. These two exegetes claim that the rules regarding one's wife (D-F) or one's slave (G-K) apply only when the householder is deathly ill (as at A-C). This harmonization is not indicated by the text, which provides a fresh superscription for each case (D, G) and does not repeat the key phrase, "while upon his death bed." In addition, see MS and MR, who explicitly state that the householder at D-E is not ill.

16. So Bert. MR claims that the householder's statement that he retains one ten-thousandth of his property refers explicitly to the slave. I reject this suggestion, for the text does not make this claim and is fully comprehensible without the interpolation.

NOTES TO CHAPTER FOUR

1. The notion that the poor must have free access to their produce applies to gifts other than peah. M. 5:6, for example, claims that poor people must be allowed to collect freely all that which God gives them.

2. Human action also initiates the system of tithes. Jaffee, Tithes, pp. 1-6, makes the point that produce becomes subject to the separation of tithes only after a farmer claims it for purposes other than a random snack. God's representatives, the priests and Levites, have no claim on the tithes until an Israelite first takes the produce. Similarly, the restrictions of the law of gleanings do not apply until the householder has acquired ownership of the produce.

3. In order to acquire possession of something, Mishnah requires one physically to take the object into his possession. Without this action, no claim of ownership is established (see M. B.M. 1:3-4; Sheb. 10:9).

4. For a discussion of the Biblical depiction of the Land of Israel as a source of affluence and success, see Brueggemann, The Land, pp. 48ff.

5. M. Maas. 1:1 states that only privately owned food is subject to the separation of tithes. See Jaffee, Tithes, pp. 28-30.

6. So Maimonides, Commentary, and Bert.

7. Bert, TYT, and Albeck, p. 49, propose that this passage reflects an important secondary concern for the welfare of the poor. While the poor attempt to climb the trees, they might push and shove each other so that some of them fall. In particular, these exegetes claim, this reasoning stands behind Simeon's insistence that the householder distribute peah designated from nut-trees with smooth trunks (D). This notion, which is not indicated by this pericope at all, seems to have been imported here from M. 4:4. That rule explicitly claims that the safety and welfare of the poor are of central concern in determining how peah should be allocated.

8. See M. Arak. 7:5, which states, "A person may not consecrate something that he does not own."

9. On the proper acquisition of movables see M. Sheb. 10:9; M. Qid. 1:4; M. B.M. 4:2; and M. B.B. 5:7, 9:7.

10. My interpretation of A-B follows GRA. But Maimonides, Commentary, and Bert interpret at B:

> B. he is entitled to no part [of the peah, neither that which he properly acquired, nor that which he unfairly tried to gain].

These two commentators then ask why the poor person should not be allowed to keep the produce that he originally picked and threw over the remaining grain. With regard to this food, at least, he seems to have accomplished a proper act of acquisition. Both exegetes follow T. 2:1, and claim that the produce is taken from the poor person as a penalty for his impertinent actions. While this interpretation is a plausible extension of Mishnah, we must note that the text itself gives no indication of this explanation.

11. M. 4:1, we recall, states that the householder must himself harvest and distribute peah from produce growing on trees and trellises. In light of Mishnah's explanation at C, MR asserts that protecting the poor from dangerous situations is the underlying concern at M. 4:1 and in this entire chapter. See above, pp. 73, n. 7.

12. So Y. Suk. 4:2 [54b]. See Lieberman, TK, pp. 148-149.

13. M. 1:4 states that only produce used for human consumption is subject to the laws of peah.

14. Simeon's view that a jointly owned field is an integral whole accurately reflects M. 3:5. If individuals jointly own a single field, together they are responsible for designating one portion of peah.

15. The triplet at A-G explicitly mentions sheaves only at C-D and E-F+G. On this basis, I follow Maimonides, Commentary, in interpolating the issue of the law of the forgotten sheaf at A-B. But see MR, who claims that A-B refers not only to forgotten sheaves, but to all other poor-offerings as well. The formal balance of this triplet, however, indicates that the particular interest here is the law of the forgotten sheaf.

16. See M. Maas. 1:5-8; Jaffee, Tithes, pp. 43-51.

17. Albeck, p. 50, claims that the law of the forgotten sheaf applies immediately after the produce is harvested, without regard to when it is bound into sheaves. This view seems to ignore the operative language at B and C, "after it was bound," which implies that the moment of binding is crucial. See also Albeck's comments to M. 5:7-8, pp. 54-55.

18. As Maimonides, Commentary, and Bert point out, the person at A-C must be an ordinary householder. If he were poor, he would have the right to collect the poor-offerings for himself and to give them to whomever he wished.

19. Eliezer (B) apparently carries forward the common Mishnaic principle that a person's agent may perform any action on his behalf. See, for example, M. Ber. 5:5.

20. All privately owned produce of the Land of Israel must be tithed, in accordance with M. Maas. 1:1. See Jaffee, Tithes, pp. 28-30.

21. Contrary to the remainder of the pericope, B claims that all produce that falls to the ground during the harvest has the status of gleanings. Nevertheless, this does not seem to be evidence of a theory separate from the one I have explained, for this general statement is followed closely by the qualifications in the units at C-E and F-L. See Maimonides, Commentary.

22. Albeck explains C-E's ruling on the basis of a theory entirely different from that which I have expressed. In his view, only produce that falls while the householder actually is reaping it enters the status of gleanings (p. 51). The produce at C-E, he claims, fell after the householder had harvested it and so did not become subject to the law. His view is unacceptable in light of F-G and H-I, which holds that only what the farmer first claims (by harvesting), and then drops, is governed by the law of gleanings. I follow Bert. and MR, who state that the focus of C-E is the constraint that the thorn places upon the householder. This seems to be the only element at C-E that might account for a ruling different from that of F-G.

23. T. 2:13 makes this point in a general way about all poor-offerings. Householders may not give the produce to chosen individuals, for they thereby would determine what produce was destined for the poor (see M. 4:1-2).

24. Primus, Aqiba, pp. 18-19, phrases the discussion at F-L solely in terms of the completion of the harvest. In his view any produce that falls after the completion of the harvest has the status of gleanings. This accurately reflects the facts, but misses a crucial point. The completion of the harvest is important only because it means that the householder has acquired ownership of the produce. As I have explained, this initiates the system whereby God claims some produce for the poor.

25. See M. 7:3, Lieberman, TK, p. 148.

26. Reading with E, ed. princ. See Lieberman, TZ, p. 47.

27. See B. Hul 132b. The gifts listed as examples at T. 2:13J (the shoulder, the two cheeks, and the stomach) are given to the priests from and unconsecrated animal that an Israelite slaughters.

28. See M. Maas. 5:7, which explicitly states that ants stole any grains of produce found in their holes.

29. So Bert.

30. For the notion that we must prevent householders from taking produce that might be reserved exclusively for the poor, see MR.

31. Lieberman, TK, p. 154, reads nqdryn, as in E. This changes the meaning of neither the text nor the commentary.

NOTES TO CHAPTER FIVE

1. For rules governing the consecrated status of heave offering, see M. Ter. 4:7-10:12.

2. Haas, Second Tithe, pp. 1-3, explains that second tithe may be exchanged for other produce because it has a lesser degree of sanctity than other priestly rations. This lower amount of holiness means that the produce is attached less strongly to a single individual who designates the produce from his crops.

3. For the use of sheaves in transporting produce to the threshing floor, see White, Roman Farming, p. 184. He first states that baskets were used for this purpose, but immediately thereafter refers to the sheaves that contain the produce.

4. For this meaning of kdy npylh, see M. B.M. 9:5, Y. B.M. 9:5 [12a], Jastrow, II, p. 924, s.v. npylh, and Maimonides, Commentary. Bert and TYT hold that this phrase means "the amount [of produce] that normally falls [as gleanings]." This interpretation is problematic, because it contradicts Mishnah's use of the phrase in other contexts. Furthermore, it harmonizes Simeon's opinion with the anonymous rule at E. According to this latter view, Simeon merely holds that the farmer gives to the poor the amount of gleanings that the field probably would produce, precisely the amount specified at E. On formal grounds, however, we expect Simeon to dispute E (see Porton, "Dispute," pp. 22ff). I therefore have chosen the present translation on both formal and substantive grounds.

5. So Danby, p. 363, n. 1.

6. The prodedure interpolated at H is required to solve a problem arising from Mishnah's phrasing. Without this addition, H reads:

H. [in order to return to the poor person that one lost stalk, the householder takes another stalk of grain, that he will give to the poor. But first [he] designates the tithes [required for that] one stalk and [then] gives it to [a poor person].

The problem now is clear. A full stalk of grain in the status of gleanings fell into the heap, yet in exchange the poor person will receive less than a full stalk. In order to prevent the poor person from being cheated, Y. 5:2 [18d], followed by all commentators, suggests the procedure I have indicated. Tithes are separated from one stalk on behalf of another that the poor person will receive.

7. Maimonides, Commentary, says that the determining factor is the stalk's appearance. If it looks like the remaining standing crop (i.e., if it is approximately the same height as the standing crop, B), it is exempt from the law of gleanings. This interpretation, however, ignores C-F, which explicitly state that the decisive factor is the farmer's act of harvesting.

8. At M. 3:1-4, the Shammaites hold that a field consists of whatever area of land the farmer harvests as a single unit. His action, not the physical characteristics of the land, is decisive. This basic principle also is operative here. What the farmer does during the harvest determines how the law is to be applied.

9. Bert, TYT, and Albeck, p. 52, hold that M. 5:2A-F actually refer to the law of the forgotten sheaf. The produce belongs to the householder, they say, because of the standing crop nearby (cf. M. 6:8, which states that sheaves forgotten near a standing crop are not subject to the restrictions of the law). The ruling is included here, says Albeck, because it deals with cases of doubt, the subject of M. 4:11-5:2. This interpretation seems to me unlikely. The rule is placed between two other laws that clearly do treat the law of gleanings (M. 5:1, 5:2G-K), and should be read in that context.

10. See M. Mid. 5:4, Jastrow, I, p. 525, s.v. ṭwpḥ. Maimonides Commentary, presents another possibility. He claims that ṭpyḥ means "inferior barley," and so interprets at A:

A. "They may not [irrigate by] turning [a water wheel] in [a field planted with] inferior barley," the opinion of R. Meir. [This is because irrigation will cause excessive damage to the barley, so that the poor will not receive useful produce.]

According to this reading, however, sages' view no longer responds to A. For a possible explanation, see below, n. 12.

11. So Albeck, p. 53.

12. Lieberman, TK, p. 155, reads at B:

B. But sages permit [the irrigation], for it is impossible [for householders properly to tend their fields without it].

That is, following K and P, he reads 'ypšr [='y 'pšr]. I have translated the text before me, without correction. The substance of the law is unaffected by the variant reading.

13. So E, ed. princ. See Lieberman, TZ, p. 49.

14. M. Hal. 1:3 states that all poor-offerings are exempt from the separation of tithes. See also M. 1:6.

15. Two secondary interpretations of this principle are possible. First, we have the notion that a landowner by definition is not a poor person, and so may not gather poor-offerings. This interpretation is made less likely by the rule at D-E. Here sharecroppers own a portion of the field, yet explicitly are deemed poor. Second, our concern may be to assure that these agricultural offerings are differentiated from that which the field's owner retains, as required for all offerings (cf. M. Ter. 4:5, M. Bik. 2:4). That is to say, a person may not keep offerings required of produce he owns, even if he otherwise

is entitled to them. For example, a priest or Levite must give to another the tithes separated from a field that he owns, even though he otherwise has a right to gather this produce for himself (cf. M. 1:6I-J). Similarly, a poor person must allow other poor people to collect poor-offerings designated from a field he owns. While this explanation is plausible, it seems secondary to the concern that all poor people have free access to poor-offerings. M. 5:6, which follows our pericope, takes up precisely this issue of free access. The continuity in underlying principles makes it clear that the pericope's primary point is that the poor must be allowed to gather the food without external interference.

16. See Albeck (p. 53), and Jastrow (I, p. 120, s.v., 'rys, ii).

17. So Albeck, p. 54, and Danby, p. 16, n. 1, who interpret <u>cwlym</u> as "poor people." This, they say, is an antithetical use of "those who ascend" for "those who have descended" in fortune. Maimonides, <u>Commentary</u>, interprets the phrase to refer to the returnees from the Egyptian exile, who received gifts from God upon their return to the Land of Israel. In the context of this pericope, however, only the former interpretation is appropriate.

18. Read 'rysyn for crysyn (E, <u>ed. princ.</u>, Lieberman, TZ, p. 50). Note that M. 5:5D-E states that a sharecropper may not collect poor man's tithe from a field he sharecrops. Gleanings, however, are allowed to him because they are not part of the produce which the sharecropper owns. Cf. M. 5:5, below.

19. Delete wh<u>c</u>kwrwt, a variant spelling of the word that follows, whḥkwrwt (see Lieberman, TK, p. 157).

20. In order to allow Tosefta to correspond fully to Mishnah, I have separated T. 3:1 into four parts. Tosefta itself makes no such distinction.

21. So V. E, <u>ed. princ.</u>, and Y. 5:7 read "is subject." However, that reading contradicts the general theory developed in M. 5:7, and in the pericope itself (cf. F-H; the use of the particle 'p at F implies that the preceeding is a negative construction). Y. explains its reading on the basis of Deut. 24:19, which states, "and you have forgotten a sheaf <u>in the field</u>,...." According to the Talmud, the law of the forgotten sheaf does not apply to sheaves once they are transported to the city, and so the farmer's actions while in the city have no effect on sheaves in the field. Thus even if the householder in the city remembers the sheaf which his workers have forgotten, the sheaf is deemed subject to the law. I have translated the text before me, since it is consistent with M.'s theory and since it shows no hint of the distinction between city and field. See Lieberman, TK, p. 158ff.

22. So Jastrow, I, p. 616, s.v. kwtb<u>c</u>h.

23. So Jastrow, I, p. 620, s.v. kwmsh.

24. So Jastrow, I, p. 506, s.v. ḥrrh.

25. The interpolation is supplied by Maimonides, <u>Commentary</u>, TYT, and Bert. Since the householder intends to keep these bundles of produce in the field, we know that they are not forgotten.

26. White, <u>Roman Farming</u>, p. 426, states that a roofed structure was used to prevent damage caused by rain to produce stored until threshing. Following Albeck, p. 55, I assume that a grain-heap was used for similar storage. If the farmer leaves some sheaves in this heap, the law does not apply. The sheaves are not forgotten, but merely remain in storage.

27. I follow Maimonides, <u>Commentary</u>, who says that the end of processing (gmr ml'kh) refers to storage immediately before threshing the produce. Compare Jastrow, I, p. 255, s.v. gmr.

28. For problems of text and meaning, see Lieberman, TZ, p. 50; TK, pp. 161f, whom I follow.

NOTES TO CHAPTER SIX

1. In many places I translate šḵḥ (usually rendered "forgot") as "left behind," because the law clearly assumes that the sheaf was not forgotten and does not fall into the category of the forgotten sheaf.

2. Distinguishing characteristics, important as mnemonic devices at E-G and H-J, also play a central role in the rules of lost objects (see for example M. B.M. 2:5). If a lost object has a distinctive feature, we assume that its owner does not give up hope of regaining his property. Whoever finds the object will be able to trace the owner through the special marks. In the present case, the Shammaites hold that a sheaf with distinctive features will be remembered, and so cannot enter the category of forgotten sheaves. See also Lieberman, TZ, p. 51.

3. Ownerless property is exempt from the separation of tithes (see M. Maas. 1:1; Jaffee, pp. 28-30). In light of this fact, one formulation of the issue at A-C is as follows: Are the poor required to separate tithes from produce given to them as a gift? The Shammaites hold that they need not. Food given to them alone may be deemed ownerless, and so exempt from tithing. The Hillelites hold that such property is not truly ownerless, and so the poor must separate tithes. Although this issue may account for the importance of the question posed at A-C, its point in context is different. As I have explained, the pericope's main interest lies in the effect of human intention upon the law.

4. The three disputes before us take up a common theme but do not comprise a triplet. A triplet, we recall, is a set of three rules that express precisely the same point in precisely the same formal pattern. In the present case, however, no stich repeats the language of the corresponding stich in the other disputes. Since the similarity is merely topical but not formal, we have no triplet.

5. Hḥzyq here means "pick up" (see Jastrow, I, pp. 444-445, s.v. ḥzq). In this context the phrase cannot have its usual meaning in Mishnah, "to acquire possession," because the householder already acquired full possession of the grain when he bound it into a sheaf (as at M. 5:8).

6. The phrase "they agree..." (D) has no possible antecedent other than the Houses (see M. 6:1-2). Furthermore, the protasis at C formally matches the superscriptions of the two Houses-disputes at M. 6:1-2D-F, G-I [i.e., substantive + š + ... + wšḵḥw + ...šḵḥ/'ynw šḵḥ]. On this basis, I claim that C-D conclude the series of Houses-disputes.

7. Bert, TYT, and Albeck, p. 56, read M. 6:3 and 6:4 as a single harmonious pericope. In their view M. 6:3A-B set up rules regarding the "ends of rows" in a field, which follow at M. 6:4. I reject this interpretation because of the intervening rule at M. 6:3C-D. Instead, I follow Maimonides, Commentary, and MR, who claim that A-B and C-D address the same issue, how a farmer's intentions may be indicated by his actions. See also Lieberman, TK, p. 166.

8. On B as a citation of M. 6:2H-J, see Lieberman, TZ, p. 51.

9. So E, ed. princ. V repeats "R. Eliezer" twice through dittography. See Lieberman, TZ, p. 51.

10. So Y. 6:2[29a]; E, V, and ed. princ. read "are not." See Lieberman, TK, p. 163.

11. V mistakenly reads at D "the bottom sheaf." In line with E, ed. princ., and Lieberman, TZ, p. 51, this phrase must be shifted to F.

12. So E, ed. princ.; see preceding note.

13. The notion that one must act directly upon an object in order to indicate his intentions for it also is expressed at M. 4:3. As we recall, the pericope states that a poor person may acquire ownership of peah only by physically taking it. Merely covering it with his cloak does not sufficiently indicate his intention to acquire it. See above, pp. 74-75. See also M. Sheb. 10:9, which requires an explicit act in order to indicate acquisition.

14. Although the pericope presents two divergent opinions on the same problem, it does not comprise a true dispute. As I have explained, the two rulings do not respond to each other, but merely treat a single situation. Porton ("Artificial Dispute," p. 18) says that "in a true dispute both comments should deal with the problem set forth in the superscription, and the two comments should respond to each other." The present pericope meets the first of these requirements, but not the second. In form, then, I classify it as an artificial dispute.

15. See Jastrow, II, p. 1109, s.v. <u>c</u>rb (i).

16. So E, <u>ed. princ.</u>, and Lieberman, TZ, p. 51. V reads: ten fields.

17. Maimonides, <u>Commentary</u>, Bert, TYT, and MR all interpret the pericope in light of T. 3:4b, which claims that the focus of the rule is the direction that the workers move when gathering the sheaves (cf. B). This interpretation is not supported by the text. Instead, I follow Albeck, pp. 56-57, who explains the pericope in terms of the worker's position within each row of the field.

18. Albeck, p. 57, explains that three measures of produce are not subject to the law of the forgotten sheaf because they comprise a small grain-heap. As we recall (M. 5:8), produce placed within a grain-heap is not subject to the law, for the householder has not forgotten it but purposely left it in storage. The text, however, does not mention a storage-heap, and so I have explained the rules only in view of Mishnah's own earlier laws.

19. Maimonides, <u>Commentary</u>, Bert, and MR account for the different views of the Shammaites and the Hillelites by reference to two verses in Scripture. These commentators claim that the Hillelites base their ruling on Lev. 19:9, which states that gleanings must be given to (1) poor people and (2) sojourners. Since two groups are mentioned, two measures of produce are deemed subject to the law. The Shammaites, on the other hand, base their lemma on Deut. 24:19, which states that forgotten sheaves must be given to (1) sojourners, (2) orphans, and (3) widows. Since this verse refers to three groups, three measures are deemed subject to the law. This interpretation in no way is reflected by Mishnah itself.

20. See Kanter, <u>Gamaliel</u>, pp. 48-49, who states that the issue here "appears to be an offshoot of a problem extensively discussed at Yavneh: whether individual items of acts are to be considered separately or together in the application of a law." In the present case, we wish to know whether distinct sheaves each must contain the requisite two <u>seahs</u>, or whether several sheaves might combine so that they are excluded from the category of forgotten produce. Here we may carry the reasoning a step further. The dispute focuses on whether or not we take account of the farmer's actions in binding grain into separate sheaves. The alternative, presented by Gamaliel, is that all produce left behind in the field forms a single mass, even if contained in separate sheaves. His notion, it seems, is that the farmer has left behind a large amount of a single species of produce; hence we may assume that the food has not been forgotten. The dispute before us, therefore, presents options familiar from other contexts in the tractate (see M. 3:1-4, 6:1-2). In this case, as in others, we wish to know whether the farmer's actions are decisive or whether natural categories--defined, for example, by the limits of one particular species--determine the application of a law.

21. In the debate at F-I Gamaliel agrees with the general principle of M. 6:5, but endorses the opinion of neither House. The Hillelites claim that three sheaves left together in a field are deemed outside the law. The Shammaites exclude any group of four sheaves left behind in a field. Gamaliel, however, rules that two sheaves are exempt from the law, merely by virtue of the fact that they appear to be stored. Thus, he agrees with M. 6:5 in principle, but not in detail.

22. On this meaning of <u>tph</u> see Maimonides, <u>Commentary</u>, and Jastrow, I, p. 547, s.v. <u>tpyḥ</u>, ii. But compare M. 5:3 and M. Shab. 17:6, where the same word refers to the pitchers on a water wheel (so Maimonides, <u>Commentary</u> to M. 5:3).

23. Jastrow, II, p. 1092, s.v. ʿnwh, I, claims that the word means God's response to prayers for fertility (see Maimonides, Commentary; Hos. 2:33). More likely perhaps is the second possibility he mentions, that the phrase is linked to BHʿnbh, "a full crop." On this meaning, see Bauer, Die Mishnah, p. 47, who translates "[qutes] Gerstenkorn," and M. 1:3.

24. Maimonides, Commentary, and Bert link this rule to M. 5:2, a pericope that refers to a single stalk of unharvested grain that stands near an unharvested crop. In their view, M. 5:2 provides an example of the present issue, namely, how an unharvested crop might prevent produce left nearby from becoming subject to the law of the forgotten sheaf. See my argument against this view, above, p. 89-92.

25. MS claims that the sheaf and the standing crop must be of the same species. This supposition, however, is not reflected in the text at all. Furthermore, when the householder returns to harvest the standing crop, he will have the opportunity to collect any sheaves left nearby, whether or not they belong to the same species. Accordingly, such sheaves cannot fall into the category of the forgotten sheaf.

26. Maimonides, Commentary, and Bert both claim that Scripture's own formulation implies that the law of the forgotten sheaf applies to standing crops. These commentators cite Deut. 24:19, which states that the law applies to produce "...forgotten in the field." But it is unlikely that the verse is meant to include all produce remaining in the field, whether or not bound into sheaves. The beginning of the verse explicitly states, "when you forget a sheaf in the field...," thus implying what the bulk of the tractate takes for granted: Only sheaves are subject to the laws of forgotten produce.

27. The householder's action of harvesting produce initiates the system of agricultural offerings. This notion, presented here for the case of forgotten sheaves, is common throughout this tractate. See for example, M. 4:10, which treats the laws of gleanings. See also M. Maas. 1:1; Jaffee, Tithes, pp. 28-30.

28. So Lieberman, TK, p. 167.

29. On problems of text throughout this pericope, see Lieberman, TZ, p. 52, and TK, p. 168.

30. So E, Lieberman, TZ, p. 53.

31. In order to make the rule at C-E balance B, Lieberman, TK, p. 168, suggests the long interpolation at E. Although not indicated by the text, it is necessary in order to understand these rules.

32. Maimonides, Commentary, claims that each of the three pairs of produce listed at A-C presents precisely the same case of ambiguity. In each case, he says, we speak of produce of a single species, some harvested and some unharvested. In his view, therefore, garlic and onions (C) actually refer to two different types of tubers, some of which are uprooted and some of which remain in the ground. While this interpretation results in a harmonious list of four elements, all harvested and unharvested, I reject it because it does not take account of the fact that garlic and onions, as a pair, are one of Mishnah's stereotypic ambiguities. Maimonides would separate this pair in order to produce a smooth and even list. The interpretation that I follow is presented by most commentators, notably Bert and MS. See also Albeck, p. 58.

33. K lacks the rest of D and all of E.

34. Garlic and onions comprise the genus Allium. Onions belong to the species Cepa, while garlic belongs to the species Sativum. See Löw, Flora, II, pp. 125-131.

35. Maimonides, Commentary, Bert, MS, and MR all read Yosé's lemma as a dispute of the anonymous rule at A-D. According to them, Yosé holds that the pairs of produce listed at A-B do join together unless separated by produce belonging to the poor. On both substantive and formal grounds, however, I read E-H as an independent rule. The issue of ownership, central at E-G, is not in play at A-D, which take up the effects of physical differences. Furthermore, since the two rules respond neither to a common

superscription nor to each other, they do not comprise a single formal unit. We must note that the redactor apparently has placed the two rules side-by-side because they utilize a common apodosis, "...these pairs do/do not join together."

36. Albeck, p. 58, states that the produce listed at A1-2 and B3 is not subject to the law because it never is used as food. According to this interpretation, B4 alone presents a case in which the binding process has not yet been completed. This argument is problematic, for in some cases the laws of poor-offerings govern produce that never is used as food. Parent-onions, for example, are not used as food, yet are deemed subject to the designation of peah (see M. 3:4). Furthermore, it seems likely that all of the elements in the list at A-B are brought together to make a single point: Unbound grain cannot become subject to the law of the forgotten sheaf. See also Maimonides, Commentary, and MS.

37. My interpolation at A2 is not indicated by the text at all. Nonetheless, as TYY correctly points out, it is required by context. In light of this explanation, A1-3 all refer to a single situation: a person harvests and binds, yet cannot clearly see the sheaves in order to gather them.

38. Maimonides, Commentary, reads the three rules at A-B, C-D, and E-F as a unitary essay. He thus claims that the worker mentioned at C-D and E-F is one of the people listed at A. The rules regarding intention at C-F, however, would apply equally well to any harvester, whether blind or not. The unit as a whole thus does not form a clearly defined formal entity. Nevertheless, Maimonides is correct in noting that the rules take up a single topic, the role of intention in the laws of the forgotten sheaf.

39. So Bert and Sens. But Albeck, p. 59, claims that the rule at D should read:

D. [the large sheaves that he leaves behind] are not [subject to the restrictions of the] forgotten sheaf.

He claims that these large sheaves are mixed among the small sheaves, and so hidden from the harvester's sight, but not forgotten. I reject this possibility, since the large sheaves could not easily be covered by small ones. Since these big sheaves are in plain sight, the law applies to them. The small sheaves that are left behind, however, are not subject to the law. The householder never intended to gather them.

40. This case attracts the interest of Mishnah's framers because, as we recall from M. 5:7, sheaves that are hidden from sight should be exempt from the restrictions of the law. In fact, TYY and Albeck, p. 59, claim that the produce a blind harvester leaves behind should not be subject to the law because it was hidden from sight, not forgotten (cf. M. 5:7). However, neither commentator explains why these sheaves are in fact deemed subject to the law, as B rules. As I have explained, this is because the harvester began to harvest even though he knew that he almost certainly would leave some sheaves behind.

41. So Y. 6:11[19d], followed by all commentaries.

42. Lieberman, TK, p. 169, states that the sacrifices offered on behalf of the father are thank-offerings. On the basis of a parallel passage in Ruth Zuta (2:16) he suggests that A should read:

"A certain righteous man forgot a sheaf in the middle of his field. On that very day he prepared a great feast. His son said to him..."

Lieberman says that this alternative better fits the context provided by B. His reading, of course, does not affect the story's main point, which is at C.

43. So E, ed. princ.; V reads: does not transgress.

196 Support for the Poor

NOTES TO CHAPTER SEVEN

1. I follow K and most other MSS, which delete "even." This word apparently appears here in the printed versions through dittography from M. 7:2J.

2. I follow Y. 7:1[20a] and Bert in interpreting zyt hnṭwph bš⁽c⁾ tw as a participial construction: "An olive tree that exudes [oil] when ripe." Maimonides, Commentary, however, explains that this phrase refers to a tree growing in the city of Netofa, in Galilee. The former explanation seems to me preferable, for it better suits the present context, which demands that the phrase refer to a tree with distinctive features. Furthermore, as Yerushalmi explains, the city probably was named after its trees, not vice-versa.

3. Maimonides, Commentary, followed by Albeck, p. 59, interprets byšny as referring to a tree transplanted from Beth Shean. I reject this interpretation because of the context provided by the remainder of the stich at G. We expect byšny to complement and balance špkwny, which clearly refers to a tree that produces large quantities of oil. Byšny therefore must follow its simplest meaning, "a dry producer," i.e., one that produces very little oil.

4. The situation at M. 7:2 parallels that of M. 3:1. In both cases two rectangular plots of grain are marked off by olive trees:

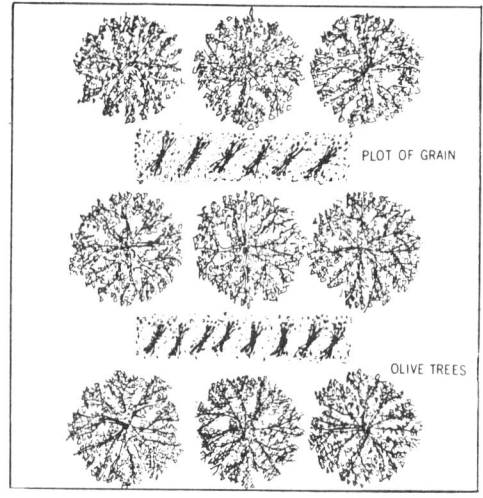

At issue in this pericope is the status of the center tree. Maimonides, Commentary, provides a similar illustration. Albeck, p. 60, however, claims that the olive tree in question is not one of the nine trees shown above, but a tenth planted among them. I discern no evidence for his supposition.

5. So MR and Albeck, p. 60, who claim that the tree is exempt from the law because of its special location. Maimonides, Commentary, and Bert hold that the law does not apply, because the tree is hidden from sight (cf. M. 5:7). On the basis of the context provided at M. 7:1, however, I reject their explanation. It seems preferable to explain the present rule in terms of the immediately preceding one than to harmonize it with a pericope from an entirely different chapter.

6. This rule reflects the notion that the householder can render an entire crop subject to the restrictions of forgotten produce merely by beginning to harvest one portion (see M. 6:7-8). Accordingly, olives that remain unharvested on trees that the farmer has already begun to reap can fall into the category of forgotten produce.

7. K lacks both C and D.

8. See Jastrow, I, p. 121, s.v. 'rkwbh

9. I follow MR in interpreting 'rkbh as a ground-trained vine. Maimonides, Commentary, and Albeck, p. 61, explain that this term refers to a small side-branch of the main vine. Nonetheless, they explain the ambiguity precisely as I have stated it.

10. See White, Roman Farming, who explains how thinning a vineyard of the poorest quality clusters is essential to the growth of that which remains.

11. This issue of when the law of the defective cluster begins to apply also gives rise to the rules at M. 7:7-8. In those pericopae, the law is deemed to apply either when the clusters first appear on the vine (M. 7:8), or when the vineyard is harvested (M. 7:7). Only MR draws our attention to this parallel. The remainder of the commentators attempt to harmonize the present pericope with the rules of peah. They claim that the law of the defective cluster appplies as soon as peah has been designated. I can find no support for their view. See in particular TYT.

12. Lieberman (TZ, p. 54) claims that the vineyard at A is sold before the defective clusters within it have appeared. This has the effect of harmonizing Tosefta with M. 7:7-8's notion that the law of the defective cluster applies as soon as such clusters appear. His assumption, however, is not indicated by the text. I follow the simple sense of "A gentile who sold his field to an Israelite for harvesting...," which implies that the beginning of the harvest is the moment when the law takes effect.

13. As we recall, M. 7:5 presents a dispute over when the law of the defective cluster takes effect. Tosefta assumes Judah's view (M. 7:5B), that the law applies only after the harvest has begun. Meir (M. 7:5C), by contrast, holds that the law takes effect as soon as the defective clusters appear.

14. TYT claims that krm, "a vine," refers to all trees that produce edible fruit. Within the context supplied by this chapter, however, it seems clear that we deal only with grape vines (cf. M. 7:3, 7:5-7).

15. The penalty that the householder must pay when redeeming second tithe for his own cash equals twenty-five percent of the purchase price. This is referred to as "the added-fifth" for it equals one-fifth of the final total (i.e., twenty percent of the purchase price + penalty).

16. So Albeck, p. 61.

17. We note that the Hillelites' view (F) is expressed in an unexpected manner. On grounds of formal balance between the two disputes, F should parallel C, "[The laws of separated grapes and defective clusters] do not apply." Despite the present formulation of their view, it is clear that the Hillelite opinion is meant to serve as the opposite of the Shammaite position. See T. M.S. 5:19.

18. See Haas, Second Tithe, pp. 171-2, 216, n. 11.

19. MR points out that Eliezer's view (M. 7:7B) also guarantees the act of designation and differentiation required of all agricultural offerings. Farmers must retain at least a small amount of their produce, or they do not meet the obligation to set aside produce for the poor (see M. 1:3D-E for the application of this principle to the laws of peah).

20. Reading with K. All other MSS. lack: "If so."

21. So Maimonides, Commentary, Bert and TYT.

22. MR says Yosé's lemma implies that the law of the defective cluster does not take effect until the harvest begins. This, says MR, explains why the Temple has a claim on a portion of the defective clusters. The farmer's dedication is valid, for he still

controls the defective clusters at the moment when he dedicates the vineyard. Thus the produce that grew before the dedication, i.e., produce fully within the householder's control, must be given to the poor. But that part of the defective clusters that grew after the farmer had dedicated his vineyard to the Temple does not belong to the poor. Our understanding of Yosé's lemma does not depend upon this view, yet MR's interpretation is a logical extension of Yosé's position. For further discussion of this view, see TYT.

23. Even though grapes cannot be bound into sheaves, they are deemed subject to the laws governing forgotten sheaves. This serves to prevent waste of valuable produce that the farmer leaves behind. See Maimonides, Commentary.

24. So Lieberman, TK, p. 175.

25. Lieberman, TZ, p. 55, reads D-F as secondary to M. 7:8E. He claims that gdwly (at T. 3:15F) refers to a case in which the householder dedicated his vineyard to the Temple after the defective clusters had appeared (cf. gydwlym at M. 7:8E). D-F do not fit this context, however, and Lieberman's interpretation is unlikely. My translation attempts to make sense of the stich in light of M.-T.'s other rules, which state that the law applies as soon as the defective clusters begin to grow. See M. 7:8A-D.

NOTES TO CHAPTER EIGHT

1. TYT notes that B. Taan. 6b presents the full list, "gleanings, forgotten sheaves, peah, and poorman's tithe," in place of "gleanings" (as at M. 8:1A). According to this version, he claims, M. 8:1 systematically deals with all poor-offerings mentioned in the tractate.

2. So Y. Peah 8:1, which claims that nmwšwt refers to old people who feel their way with canes. See also Jastrow, I, p. 751, s.v. mwš.

3. The second rainfall refers to rain of sufficient quantity for new crops to begin to grow at the end of summer. M. Taan. 1:4, 3:1, and M. Ned. 8:5 fix the time when these rains usually fall, the month of Marḥeshvan, as the beginning of the new agricultural season. See also Jastrow, II, p. 1442, s.v. rby^{ch}.

4. M. 1:3 presents this same principle, that the poor must be given an adequate amount of food, with respect to the designation of peah. See also GRA and MR.

5. It seems odd, at first glance, that the poor are deemed credible with regard to olive oil, for this produce already has been processed. We recall, however, that the distribution of poorman's tithe is part of the normal process of separating tithes (see Sarason, Demai, pp. 1-11). This tithing procedure, in its entirety, is carried out at the threshing floor. In the case of olives, this means that the poorman's tithe is given out in the form of oil (as at M. 8:3K). On the other hand, olives that are subject to the laws of forgotten produce, that is, those left on the crown of a tree (see M. 8:3L), are taken by the poor before any processing has occurred. We therefore assume that the poor cannot possess oil that derives from this source.

6. So Maimonides, Commentary, and Bert. But compare Jastrow, I, p. 715, s.v. lps, who claims that the phrase means householders give to the poor "a bit of stew."

7. So Maimonides, Commentary, Bert. and MR.

8. So Lieberman, TK, p. 178. On the basis of this contradiction, he states that E-F do not comprise part of Judah's lemma.

9. Lieberman, TK, p. 178, claims that C-D probably are tacked on to Judah's lemma, since they deal with the contrast between Israelites and gentiles. This is only tangentially related to the issue at A-B, that poor people are believed only with regard to food of the types that householders usually give them. Nevertheless, says Lieberman, the formal parallelism at B and C indicates that the two rules must be read as a single unit.

10. So Lieberman, TK. p. 178.

11. The commentators offer two distinct interpretations of M. 8:6A. I follow Sens, TYT and Albeck, p. 64, who assume that the priests, Levites and Israelites mentioned are poor people receiving poorman's tithe. The alternative view, taken by Maimonides, Commentary, and by MR, is that priests, Levites and Israelites who are householders all must give the same amount of produce to the poor as poorman's tithe. Following this interpretation, A would read:

> E. This measure [for each type of produce, specified at M. 8:5], applies to priests, Levites, or Israelites, [when these householders] distribute poorman's tithe].

I choose the former interpretation, however, since it alone speaks of the equitable distribution of poorman's tithe, the context provided by the pericope's two other rules.

12. So Maimonides, Commentary, Bert., TYT and MR.

13. For the relative values of these measures, see EJ, XVI, pp. 387-388.

14. See also Y. Pes. 10:1[37c], which specifies the amount of food needed for two meals. Cf. MR and TYT, who claim that Yerushalmi's explanation merely carries forward Abba Shaul's lemma (C-D).

15. I cannot account for the fact that the farmer here is allowed to keep for his own relatives 50 percent of the poorman's tithe. MR provides one possible explanation. He notes that so long as the farmer gives away at least as much grain as he keeps, he does not distribute the food in an unfair manner. See also T. 4:2b, which claims that the farmer may retain for his relatives as much as two-thirds of the poorman's tithe.

16. Maimonides, Commentary, and Bert claim that the farmer at D-E does not have enough produce to distribute as poorman's tithe because he saved some of this food for his own relatives (as at B-C). The connection between these two rules is not indicated in the text, however, and appears to be a simple harmonization of the units.

17. So Jastrow, II, p. 1290-91, s.v. ṣnw^c. Lieberman (TK, p. 154), on the basis of M. Dem. 6:6, suggests equating "decent people" with "ḥaberim." In his view, we speak of people who wish to avoid giving food to the poor because the poor will not eat the produce in a state of cleanness. Lieberman thus interprets C to mean that these people should give the poor something to eat forthwith, while the food remains ritually clean. I follow Jastrow, however, since the context provided at D fits only his interpretation.

18. So Lieberman, TK, p. 154. On a farmer's right to snack on untithed produce, see also Jaffee, Tithes, pp. 2-3; TK, p. 154, n. 32.

19. So E, ed. princ., Lieberman, p. 178. V reads: "When dispensing poorman's tithe...." The substance of the law is unaffected by either reading.

20. So Lieberman, TK, p. 180.

21. So Lieberman, TZ, p. 56.

22. See B. Ket. 26a; Lieberman, TK, p. 181.

23. Lieberman, TK, p. 181, states that the New Moon messenger traveled as far as Namarin (Tel Namarin). See also Klein, p. 108.

24. I follow E in deleting this stich, for Tosefta never presents a case in which a stricter rule applies to the holy things of the country than applies to the holy things of the Temple.

25. So Jastrow, I, p. 563, s.v. yd.

26. I follow TYT in explaining that C refers to food. Read in this way, C provides balance for the stichs at A and E, both of which explicitly refer to edibles. Maimonides, Commentary, and Bert., however, state that C refers to giving to the poor person a bed and mattress on which to sleep. I can discern no support for their position.

27. So Jastrow, II, p. 1676, s.v. tmḥwy.

28. See Bert and TYT, who claim that a loaf worth a dupondius is sufficient for at least two meals.

29. B. B.B. 8b, cited by Maimonides, Commentary, and Sens, explicitly explains the ruling at H in terms of M. Sheq 5:2 and M. San. 1:1.

30. Lieberman, TK, p. 184, offers a quite different explanation of why strangers are not supplied with clothing. He claims that the verb mkyr, "to know," here means "to know whether or not a person actually is poor." In his view, people that the townsfolk know to be poor are given full support. Strangers, by contrast, might actually be freeloaders who do not require the community's support. To prevent this misuse of public funds, strangers are given only food.

31. So V, ed. princ.; E reads: "on a day to day basis, bkl ywm."

32. So E., V, ed. princ. read: "ᶜny hᶜyr, the town's poor." On the meaning of psy hᶜyr, see Lieberman, TZ, p. 57.

33. E reads: "peruṭah." Lieberman, TK, p. 184, rejects this reading because it obscures the basic difference between the soup-kitchen and the communal fund. He claims that money alone is contributed to the communal fund, while the soup-kitchen is supported by gifts of food.

34. So Lieberman, TK, p. 185.

35. Lieberman, TK, p. 185, notes that the phrase lyṭr' bŝr bṣpwry is taken by B. Ket. 66b as referring to a pound of poultry. On the basis of Epstein, Tarbiẓ 1945, p. 270, however, he provides the interpretation that I follow.

36. So E; ed. princ. reads: "Gebaltah;" V reads: "Nebaṭlah."

37. On the Jebusites as the original inhabitants of Jerusalem, see IDB 2:807-808, EJ 9:1307-1308. See also Lieberman, TK, p. 187.

38. So Lieberman, TK, p. 187, who bases his explanations on the interpretation offered at B. Ket. 67b.

39. M. Ket. 5:1 makes the point that two hundred zuz is approximately one year's supply of money. Hence, when a man divorces his wife, he must give her two hundred zuz, so that she may support herself for a full year.

40. At M. 8:9K, ms K reads: "will die of old age...." This brings M. 8:9K in line with the parallel stichs at M. 8:9M, O and T.

41. L-M follow Q in the standard printed versions, but belong here. See Albeck, p. 66.

42. So Albeck, p. 66.

43. Lieberman, TK, p. 188, offers an alternative explanation of A. He claims that, reading with ed. princ., A should be rendered:

> A. Charity collectors are not permitted to make change, [so that they do not appear to distribute that which they collect].

This interpretation, however, ignores the explicit explanation at B, and so may be rejected.

44. Second tithe, we recall, must be taken to Jerusalem and consumed within the city. See Haas, Second Tithe, pp. 1-3.

45. Lieberman, TK, p. 190, claims that the descending order of the pericope is broken by G-J. On the basis of B. B.B. 9a, Lieberman says that making others give charity is more meritorious than giving charity oneself. I reject this harmonization, however, for it is not indicated by the text, and breaks the symmetry of the passage.

46. So Jastrow, I, p. 184, s.v. bṣwrt.

NOTES TO APPENDIX

1. These documents of Scriptural exegesis are generally thought to have been redacted in Palestine, no earlier than the fourth century A.D. See M.D. Herr, EJ, Vol. XIV, pp. 1518-1520.

2. A larger polemic underlies Sifra Negaim -- namely, that reason unaided by revelation is insufficient as a basis for Mishnah's authority. This notion scarcely occurs in the materials considered here (see Sifre Deut. 283's treatment of M. 6:7). Nonetheless, as we have seen, the materials as a whole are consistent with that claim. See Neusner, Purities, Vol. VII, Negaim. Sifra.

INDEX TO BIBLICAL TEXTS

I. Hebrew Bible

Genesis
- 2:18 — 149

Exodus
- 23:8 — 151
- 20:12 — 175

Leviticus
- 19:9 — 17, 31, 32, 33, 44, 47, 71, 82, 84, 109, 157, 159, 160, 161, 163, 165, 166, 167, 169, 170, 178, 184
- 19:10 — 17, 31, 32, 33, 109, 131, 132, 152, 157, 164, 165, 166, 170
- 19:11 — 35
- 19:12 — 35
- 19:13 — 35
- 19:14 — 35
- 19:15 — 35
- 19:16 — 35
- 19:17 — 35
- 19:18 — 35
- 19:22 — 134
- 19:24 — 122, 129, 130
- 22:6 — 176
- 23:22 — 17, 31, 178
- 27:30 — 17, 31, 177
- 27:31 — 17, 131
- 27:32 — 17
- 27:33 — 17

Numbers
- 18:3-24 — 31, 177, 178
- 32:22 — 153

Deuteronomy
- 8:7 — 18
- 8:8 — 18
- 8:9 — 18
- 8:10 — 18
- 13:12 — 156
- 13:13 — 156
- 13:14 — 156
- 13:15 — 156
- 14:22 — 130
- 14:23 — 130
- 14:24 — 130
- 14:25 — 97, 130
- 14:26 — 97, 130
- 14:27 — 97, 130
- 14:28 — 97, 137, 168
- 14:29 — 97, 137, 168
- 15:8 — 149
- 15:9 — 156
- 15:10 — 154
- 15:19 — 156
- 16:16 — 42
- 16:17 — 42
- 16:20 — 151
- 17:6 — 177
- 18:1 — 17
- 18:2 — 17
- 18:3 — 17, 83
- 18:4 — 17
- 18:5 — 17
- 24:9 — 171
- 24:13 — 155
- 24:19 — 25, 26, 31, 32, 33, 34, 101, 106, 107, 108, 119, 122, 125, 157, 169, 170, 171, 172, 173, 175, 191, 194
- 24:20 — 27, 31, 32, 33, 173, 175
- 24:21 — 17, 31, 32, 33, 132, 157, 164, 169, 173, 174, 175
- 24:22 — 31, 32, 157
- 32:47 — 175
- 26:1 — 42, 67
- 26:2-11 — 42
- 26:12 — 17, 31, 32, 33, 131
- 26:13 — 32, 33, 131
- 26:19 — 42

Joshua
- 7:16-18 — 177
- 18:10 — 178

Psalms
- 66:18 — 43
- 85:11 — 154
- 89:14 — 155

Proverbs
- 1:29 — 43
- 1:30 — 43
- 1:31 — 43
- 11:30 — 155
- 22:28 — 96, 126, 165
- 24:26 — 70

Isaiah
- 3:10 — 43, 155
- 3:11 — 43
- 7:25 — 55
- 54:13 — 176
- 58:8 — 155

Jeremiah
- 6:19 — 43
- 16:5 — 156
- 17:7 — 151

II. Intertestamental Literature

Wisdom of Ben Sira
- Chs. 1-2 — 33
- 4:4 — 33
- Chs. 11-14 — 33
- Ch. 51 — 33

III. New Testament

Mark
- 10:25 — 34

Luke
- Ch. 16 — 34

Galatians
- 2:10 — 34

INDEX TO CLASSICAL RABBINIC TEXTS

I. Mishnah

Berakhot
5:5 188

Peah
1:1 21, 41, 42, 44, 45, 175, 176, 179, 181, 182, 188
1:2 21, 41, 44, 45, 181, 182
1:3 21, 41, 45, 47, 48, 53, 59, 161, 180, 182, 184, 185, 194, 197, 198
1:4 21, 41, 45, 50, 64, 65, 77, 160, 179, 183, 186
1:5 21, 41, 48, 65, 77, 160, 179, 186
1:6 21, 17, 37, 41, 49, 50, 51, 72, 81, 190, 191
2:1 21, 36, 53, 54, 55, 57, 60, 63, 66, 162, 179, 180, 184, 185
2:2 21, 53, 55, 56, 63, 66, 162
2:3 21, 53, 56, 65, 162
2:4 21, 53, 56, 163, 180, 184
2:5 21, 38, 53, 57
2:6 21, 53, 57
2:7 21, 53, 57, 60, 195, 169, 185, 186
2:8 21, 53, 57, 58, 60, 186
3:1 22, 37, 61, 62, 103, 190, 193, 196
3:2 22, 61, 62, 103, 180, 183, 190, 193
3:3 22, 61, 62, 64, 103, 185, 186, 190, 193
3:4 22, 61, 62, 63, 104, 180, 190, 193, 195
3:5 22, 61, 65,66, 103, 188
3:6 22, 61, 66, 68, 179, 180
3:7 22, 61, 68, 69, 180, 182
3:8 22, 61, 68, 180, 182
4:1 22, 49, 71, 72, 74, 75, 77, 81, 93, 94, 143, 166, 167, 183, 184
4:2 22, 71, 782, 73, 74, 75, 77, 81, 93, 94
4:3 22, 71, 73, 74, 75, 77, 94, 192
4:4 22, 71, 73, 75, 77, 94, 187
4:5 22, 71, 73, 75, 76, 77, 179, 180
4:6 17, 71, 77, 78, 79, 80, 81, 159, 169, 178
4:7 17, 71, 79, 80, 178
4:8 17, 71, 79, 80, 178, 180
4:9 22, 71, 81, 82, 114, 180
4:10 23, 71, 72, 82, 84, 85, 90, 95, 97, 109, 121, 126, 163, 180, 194
4:11 23, 71, 72, 85, 86, 95, 109, 127, 167, 180
5:1 23, 87, 88, 90, 91, 95, 109, 190
5:2 23, 87, 89, 90, 92, 95, 109, 172, 190, 194
5:3 23, 87, 92, 95, 180, 193
5:4 23, 87, 93, 95, 180
5:5 24, 87, 93, 94, 95, 96, 194
5:6 24, 87, 95, 96, 173, 187, 191
5:7 24, 87, 97, 98, 102, 106, 112, 126, 169, 188, 191, 195, 196
5:8 25, 78, 87, 88, 98, 99, 100, 102, 112, 117, 118, 188, 192, 193
6:1 25, 101, 102, 103, 104, 109, 121, 180, 192, 193
6:2 2, 101, 102, 104, 105, 122, 123, 180, 192, 193
6:3 25, 101, 104, 105, 106, 107, 171, 192
6:4 25, 101, 107, 108, 122, 134, 192
6:5 25, 101, 108, 109, 110, 111, 112, 123, 124, 170, 180, 193
6:6 25, 101, 110, 112, 124, 172, 180
6:7 25, 67, 101, 102, 111, 116, 124, 182, 196, 201
6:8 26, 101, 102, 111, 113, 114, 115, 116, 196
6:9 26, 101, 116, 117
6:10 26, 101, 117, 118
6:11 26, 101, 118, 119
7:1 26, 121, 122, 123, 124, 125, 196
7:2 26, 121, 123, 124, 125, 136, 173, 196
7:3 27, 109, 121, 125, 126, 131, 135, 165, 189, 197
7:4 27, 121, 126, 127, 128, 131, 132, 135, 165, 166, 174, 175
7:5 27, 121, 128, 129, 135, 180, 197
7:6 23, 121, 122, 129, 130, 135, 180, 197
7:7 28, 121, 131, 132, 135, 164, 174, 180, 197
7:8 28, 121, 122, 132, 133, 134, 135, 197, 198
8:1 28, 137, 138, 139, 140, 183, 198
8:2 29, 137, 139, 140, 142
8:3 29, 137, 139, 140, 142, 198
8:4 29, 137, 140, 142
8:5 29, 137, 142, 143, 145, 168, 180, 186
8:6 29, 137, 142, 146, 199
8:7 29, 137, 138, 146, 147, 148
8:8 30, 137, 146, 150, 151
8:9 30, 137, 138, 150, 152, 200

Demai		II. Tosefta	
6:6	199		
Kilayim		Peah	
2:10	67, 186	1:1	45, 183
Shebiit		1:2	43, 45
10:2	186	1:3	43, 45
10:9	187, 192	1:4	43, 44, 45
Terumot		1:5	46, 51, 178, 182
1:7	178	1:6	47, 161, 177
2:4	184	1:7	49, 160
3:5	178	1:8	54, 55, 56, 59, 184
4:3	182	1:9	55, 59, 60, 64
4:5	183, 190	1:10	64
4:7	146	1:11	64, 65
Maaserot		1:12	69
1:1	51, 65, 76, 81, 183, 187, 188, 192, 194	1:13	69
		2:1	74, 75, 188
1:5-8	178, 183, 188	2:2	75
5:7	189	2:3	83
Maaser Sheni		2:4	95
5:3	122	2:5	76
Hallah		2:6	48
1:3	190	2:7	73, 177
4:1	114	2:8	73, 177
Bikkurim		2:9	78, 79
2:4	183, 190	2:10	79
Shabbat		2:11	81
17:6	193	2:12	77
Sheqalim		2:13	83, 126, 189
5:2	146, 200	2:14	84
Taanit		2:15	84, 85
1:4	198	2:16	86
3:1	198	2:17	77
Hagigah		2:18	139, 143
1:1-2	181	2:19	91
2:2	185	2:20	92
Katubbot		2:21	91, 92
1:2	69	3:1	95, 96, 97, 98, 100, 103, 191
5:1	200	3:2	104, 105
13:11	150	3:3	96, 105, 106
Nedarim		3:4	106, 107, 113, 193
8:5	198	3:5	109, 110, 117
Qiddushin		3:6	114, 116
1:4	187	3:7	115
Baba Mesia		3:8	118, 119, 120
1:3-4	187	3:9	124, 136
2:5	192	3:10	124, 125
4:2	187	3:11	127, 128
9:5	189	3:12	129
Baba Batra		3:13	134
5:7	187	3:14	134
9:6	182	3:15	134, 198
9:7	187	3:16	135
Sanhedrin		4:1	141
1:1	147, 200	4:2	144, 146, 199
Abot		4:3	144
1:4-12	185	4:4	144
Menahot		4:5	144, 145
10:8	184	4:6	144, 145
Arakhin		4:7	144, 145
7:5	187	4:8	147
Middot		4:9	148
5:4	190	4:10	148, 149
		4:11	148, 149

4:12	150	Qiddushin	
4:13	150	40a	181
4:14	152	Baba Batra	
4:15	153	8b	198
4:16	153	9a	201
4:17	154, 155	Hullin	
4:18	154, 155	132b	189
4:19	155		
4:20	156	V. Sifra	
4:21	156		

Maaser Sheni
   5:19   131, 197

III. Talmud Yerushalmi

Peah		1:6	159
1:1	181	1:7	159, 160
5:1	89	1:8	160
5:2	190	1:9	160, 161
5:7	191	1:10	161
6:2	192	1:11	161, 162
6:11	195	2:1	162
7:1	125, 196	2:2	162
8:1	198	2:3	162
Pesahim		2:4	163
10:1	199	2:5	163
Sukkah		2:6	164
4:2	188	3:1	164
Baba Mesia		3:2	165
9:5	189	3:3	165, 166
Sanhedrin		3:4	166
6:3	177, 178	3:5	166, 167
		3:6	167
		3:7	167

IV. Talmud Babli

VI. Sifre Deuteronomy

Erubin		110	168
29a	143	282	169
Taanit		283	169, 170, 171, 172, 201
66	198	284	173, 174
Ketubbot		285	174, 175
50b	181	336	175, 176
26a	199		
66b	200		
67b	200		

GENERAL INDEX

Accident, separation of poor-offerings by
  17, 18, 23, 24, 27, 82, 88, 177
Actions of Israelite farmer
  19, 26, 31, 35, 42-44, 45, 53, 54, 58,
  61, 63, 64, 75, 76, 90, 99, 103, 104,
  108, 127, 151-152, 155, 156, 177, 181,
  182, 184, 188, 191-93
Agriculture, Division of
  11, 17, 35, 41, 177
Albeck, Hanoch
  7, 39, 40, 182, 183, 187, 188, 190-97,
  199, 1100
Ambiguity as focus of Mishnaic rule
  21, 23-28, 38, 49-50, 53, 54, 58, 64,
  72, 78, 88-89, 90, 102, 114, 116, 118,
  121, 126, 127, 129, 138, 158, 184-5,
  194, 197
Anomaly of poor-offerings
  72, 178
Apodosis
  37, 51, 195
Appearance's sake
  47
Appearance-offering
  42, 181
Appointed Times, Division of
  12, 178, 179
Aqiba
  13, 22, 28, 50, 51, 61-64, 67, 68, 71,
  72, 76, 82, 83, 85, 92, 131, 132, 142,
  163, 164, 174, 186, 189
Avery-Peck
  3, 7, 178, 179, 183, 184
Bar Kochba
  35
Barr, James
  7, 180
Batey, Richard
  7, 179
Bauer, Walter
  7, 39, 40, 181, 183, 194
Ben Sira
  33
Berakhot
  7, 177
Bertinoro
  7, 181-200
Bet Namer
  76
Bikkurim
  7, 11, 177
Blackman, Philip
  7, 39, 40
Brueggemann, Walter
  7, 177, 187
Buber, Solomon
  15, 58, 151

Carmichael, Calum
  8, 178
Carob trees
  56, 108, 160, 163, 170, 183-85
Chamber of Hewn Stone
  58
Chance, separation of poor-offerings by
  18, 25, 83, 84, 87, 97, 134, 138, 177
Christianity
  9, 33
Communal fund
  146-48, 179, 1100
Community Rule
  34, 179
Constantelos, Demitrios
  8
Corinth
  34
Damascus Rule
  34
Danby, Herbert
  8, 39, 40, 181, 182, 184-86, 189, 191
Davies, W.D.
  8
Dead Sea Scrolls
  15, 33, 34
Deceivers
  47, 48, 76
Definition of a field
  22, 53, 54, 61, 180
Demai
  8, 14, 177-79, 198
Deuteronomic Code
  31
Deuteronomy
  1, 2, 8, 15, 32, 33, 35, 107, 157, 158,
  168, 178, 179
Dispute
  13, 28, 37, 46, 47, 64, 67, 71, 76, 81,
  83, 85, 90-93, 103-105, 109, 110, 114,
  118, 127, 131, 180, 183-86, 189, 193,
  194, 197
Distribution of poor-offerings
  20, 23, 29, 30, 71, 73, 76, 81, 84, 93,
  104, 137, 143, 147, 148, 157, 158,
  164, 198, 199
Dosa
  76, 77
Egypt
  32
Egyptian Series in Deuteronomy
  178, 191
Eleazar
  16, 49, 50, 86, 105, 144, 145, 156
Eleazar b. Azariah
  16, 105

- 207 -

Eliezer
  5, 12, 21-23, 28, 53, 56, 57, 61, 66, 67, 81, 90, 91, 93, 105, 131, 132, 146, 163, 164, 174, 185, 188, 192, 197
Elliger, Karl
  8, 178
English
  3, 7, 15, 38, 40
Epstein, Jacob Nahum Haleri
  8, 200
Equal access to poor-offerings
  30, 73, 74, 87, 104
Eschaton
  34, 35
Essenes
  34, 179
Field
  17, 18, 20-28, 31, 36, 38, 41, 44-50, 53-67, 70, 71, 73, 76-82, 85-102, 104-110, 111-20, 122, 124, 128, 129, 132, 138-40, 158-62, 164, 166, 169-73, 175, 177, 178, 180-86, 188-95, 197
First Fruits
  17, 42, 45, 67
Fish, Stanley
  8, 147, 179
Forms used in pericopae
  5, 36, 38, 39, 63, 101, 110, 119, 179, 180, 193
Free access to poor-offerings
  27, 71, 74, 76, 96, 158, 187, 191
Frisch, Ephraim
  9
GRA (Elijah b. Solomon Zalman)
  9, 181, 182, 184, 187, 198
Galatia
  34
Gamaliel
  7, 10, 21-23, 25, 56-58, 71, 75, 76, 88, 110, 111, 114, 115, 144, 172, 184, 185, 193
Gentiles
  22, 23, 34, 58, 71, 77-79, 81, 82, 96, 97, 103, 104, 113, 114, 129, 141, 142, 159, 161, 168, 169, 185, 197, 198
Gereboff, Joel
  9
Grain heap
  88, 91, 98-100, 102, 110, 191, 193
Green, William S.
  9, 183
Haas, Peter
  9, 189, 197, 1101
Halakhah
  40
Ḥallah
  9, 177
Hands, A.R.
  9, 32, 43, 83, 144, 145
Haran, Menahem
  8
Heave offering
  17, 18, 87, 143-46, 184, 189

Hebrew Bible
  2, 31, 32
Hengel, Martin
  9, 179
Herr, M.D.
  180, 201
Hillel
  22, 25, 28, 37, 61-63, 101, 102-105, 109, 110, 130, 131, 149, 192, 193, 197
Hirsch, E.D.
  9, 179
Holiness of the Land of Israel
  31, 34, 35, 177, 189
Holiness Code
  31, 177
Horowitz, H.S.
  11, 42, 59, 78, 80, 85, 90, 96, 97, 104, 109, 110, 111, 117, 123, 127, 132, 133, 142, 151, 157, 170
Intending
  62
Intention
  20, 26, 36, 43, 44, 53, 61, 74, 100, 101, 103-106, 118-20, 134, 135, 181, 184, 187, 192, 195
Irrigation
  55, 56, 91-93, 118, 162, 184, 190
Ishmael
  11, 13, 72, 82, 83, 85, 163
Jaffee, Martin S.
  10, 177-79, 181, 183, 187, 188, 192, 194, 199
Jastrow, Marcus
  10, 91, 181, 182, 184-86, 189-94, 197-101
Jerusalem
  1, 7-11, 13-16, 34, 35, 42, 129-31, 146, 149, 150, 168, 1100, 1101
Jesus
  7, 34
Johnson, Luke T.
  10, 179
Joint ownership
  66, 78, 129
Joshua
  9, 12, 22, 61, 66, 67, 104, 105, 117, 156, 177, 178
Judah
  21, 22, 26, 27, 45-47, 49, 55, 56, 61, 64-66, 76-78, 80, 91-95, 98, 100, 117, 118, 121, 127, 128, 138, 139, 141, 142, 159, 161, 162, 165, 169, 170, 175, 177, 182, 186, 197, 198
Judah b. Beterah
  22, 61, 66, 67
Judaism
  1, 8-10, 12, 36, 178, 179
Judea
  35
Kafaḥ, Joseph D.
  11
Kahana, Abraham
  10

General Index

Kanter, Shammai
  10, 184, 193
Kasovsky, C.Y.
  10, 181, 182
Kilayim
  10, 11, 177
Kingdom of God
  34
Klein, Samuel
  10, 11, 199
Kohut, Alexander
  10, 182, 183
Land of Israel
  1, 10, 12, 17-22, 24, 30-32, 34-37, 39, 41, 48, 49, 53-56, 58, 61, 63, 66-70, 72, 79, 89, 91, 135, 137, 139, 143, 145, 146, 159, 160, 162, 167-69, 172, 175, 177, 178, 180, 184, 186-88, 190, 191
Landmarks as boundaries of fields
  36, 53, 54, 56, 57, 63, 162
Lauterbach, Jacob
  11
Levites
  29, 32, 50, 51, 84, 134, 140, 141, 142-44, 146, 166, 168, 187, 191, 199
Leviticus
  2, 8-10, 13, 31, 33, 35, 157, 178, 179
Levy, Jacob
  11
Lieberman, Saul
  8, 11, 15, 16, 47, 65, 79, 95, 98, 118, 125, 135, 136, 180-84, 186, 188-95, 197-101
List
  36, 37, 39, 42, 44, 49, 55, 96, 97, 122, 143, 146, 179, 181, 194, 195, 198
Löw, Immanuel
  11, 35, 48, 111, 112, 131, 183, 184, 194
MR (Ephraim Isaac of Premysla)
  3, 12, 40, 81, 112, 141, 181, 182, 184-89, 192-94, 196-99
Maaser Sheni
  9, 12, 177
Maaserot
  10, 11
MacMullen, Ramsay
  11
Maimonides
  10, 11, 13, 40, 42, 44, 55, 139, 180-100
Mandelbaum, Irving
  11
Marketplace
  62, 64, 65, 94
Measure
  18, 29, 42, 44-46, 67, 142, 145, 171, 172, 181, 182, 199
Meir
  23, 27, 54, 72, 75, 85, 92, 113, 114, 121, 123, 124, 128, 129, 142, 150, 162, 169, 190, 197

Metzger, Bruce
  14
Miasha
  58
Micklem, Nathaniel
  9
Minuscule portion of real estate
  22, 46, 61, 67-69, 186
Misappropriating poor-offerings
  72, 85
Mishnaic Hebrew
  1, 14, 36, 38
Mosaic Codes
  2, 17, 35, 39, 157
Moses
  11, 16, 58, 177
Naḥum the Scribe
  58
Neusner, Jacob
  3, 12, 13, 40, 178-80, 185, 1101
New Year
  91
Newman, Louis
  3, 13, 186
Nickelsburg, George
  13, 179
Noth, Martin
  13, 178
Numbers
  13, 35, 178
Olive trees
  26, 27, 32, 37, 56, 57, 62, 121-24, 138, 139, 163, 173, 184, 196
Omnipresent
  43, 44, 119
Orchard
  21, 53, 56, 57, 66, 91, 122, 138, 160, 162, 184, 185
Original meaning
  36-40
Orlah
  13, 134, 135, 177
Ownerless property
  21, 25, 45, 46, 50, 76, 77, 81, 82, 86, 102-104, 127, 135, 137-39, 192
Palestine
  9, 12, 35, 1101
Passover
  91, 130, 131
Patterns of pericopae
  1, 36, 38-40, 179
Paul
  3, 34
Pentecost
  42, 91
Phineas
  177
Physical characteristics as determinative of a field
  53, 63, 190
Pilgrimage
  42, 181

Porter, J.R.
  13
Porton, Gary G.
  13, 180, 184, 189, 193
Possession
  35, 51, 71, 72, 74, 75, 79, 82, 88, 90, 105, 139, 142, 163, 178, 187, 192
Priestly Writer
  31, 32
Priestly rations
  17-19, 29, 177, 178, 183, 189
Priests
  1, 17-19, 29, 31, 32, 35, 51, 84, 87, 89, 133, 137, 142-46, 177, 178, 183, 187, 189, 199
Primus, Charles
  13, 189
Private property
  48, 72, 93, 153
Processing, the moment of
  3, 18, 20, 24, 28, 29, 31, 51, 99, 100, 191, 198
Prozbul
  67, 186
Qumran
  34, 179
Rabad
  13, 160
Random separation of poor-offerings
  18, 19, 23, 27, 65, 71, 83, 84, 88, 97, 121, 125, 126, 143, 159, 163, 177, 187
Random snack
  65, 143, 159, 187
Rashi
  13
Real estate
  22, 61, 67, 69, 186
Robbers
  58, 59, 159, 169
Roman Empire
  1, 9, 11, 14, 16, 35, 38, 178, 189, 191, 197
Romm
  7, 9, 11, 12, 14, 15
Rosh
  3, 14
Sabbatical cycle
  29, 67, 102, 130, 131, 134, 135, 137, 140, 141, 186
Sacks, Nissan
  7-16, 39, 40
Ṣadoq
  49, 56, 163
Sarason, Richard S.
  14, 178, 179, 198
Scripture
  2, 17, 27, 30-33, 35, 36, 39, 43, 84, 119-21, 126, 130-32, 149, 151-57, 159, 160, 164, 166-68, 170, 171, 173, 175-79, 184, 185, 193, 194
Segal, M.H.
  14
Sens
  14, 16, 44, 55, 182, 183, 185, 186, 195, 199, 1100

Shammai
  22, 25, 28, 37, 61-64, 101, 102-105, 109, 130, 131, 190, 192, 193, 197
Sharecroppers
  24, 94, 96, 191
Shebiit
  13, 14, 177
Shiloh
  178
Sifra
  1, 2, 14, 39, 42, 45, 48, 54-56, 59, 73, 78, 82, 85, 110, 117, 126, 127, 130, 132, 157-67, 180, 1101
Sifre Deuteronomy
  1, 2, 14, 39, 42, 80, 85, 90, 96, 97, 109, 111, 117, 123, 127, 132, 133, 142, 151, 157, 158, 168, 169, 172-75, 180, 1101
Simeon b. Eleazar
  86, 144, 145
Simeon b. Gamaliel
  23, 88, 114, 144
Simeon of Miṣpah
  58
Sinai
  58, 105
Sirillo
  14
Smallwood, Mary
  14, 35
Smith, Jonathon Z.
  12, 15, 141
Soup kitchen
  29, 30, 137, 146-48, 179, 1100
Strack, Hermann
  11, 15
Structure of Tractate Peah
  1, 5, 19, 36-38, 40, 88, 186, 191
Study of Torah
  42, 45, 175, 181
Talmud
  7, 8, 10-16, 177, 178, 191
Ṭarfon
  9, 22, 61, 66, 67
Taxation
  18, 41, 148
Tcherikover, Avigdor
  15
Temple
  1, 10, 18, 19, 28, 35, 42, 50, 51, 59, 60, 71, 79, 80, 121, 122, 132-35, 145, 146, 173, 177, 181, 197-99
Temple-Treasurer
  50, 59, 80
Tenant-farmer
  18, 41
Terumot
  7, 15, 177-79, 183, 184
Thematic units
  36, 71, 180
Theophrastus
  15

Threshing floor
  18-20, 22, 24, 25, 28, 29, 50, 57, 58,
  62, 88, 94, 95, 98-100, 142-46, 159,
  168, 183, 185, 189, 198
Tithes
  10, 17, 18, 20-22, 29, 32, 41, 50, 51,
  65, 72, 76, 77, 79-82, 87, 90, 91,
  93-97, 103, 134, 137, 139-41, 143,
  145, 146, 172, 177-79, 181, 183, 187,
  188, 190-92, 194, 198, 199
Topographical features of a field
  61, 63
Torah
  10, 13, 41, 42, 45, 47, 105, 119, 155,
  175, 181, 182
Tractate Peah
  1, 2, 17, 19, 30, 31, 33, 35-42, 44, 45,
  53, 157, 179, 180
Triplet
  37, 38, 58, 78, 80, 83, 85, 129, 155,
  180, 186, 188, 192
Vermes, Geza
  15, 179
Von Rad, Gerhard
  15
Weinfeld, Moshe
  15

Welch, Adam C.
  16
White, K.D.
  16, 49, 50, 189, 191, 197
Wisdom
  33
World view
  2, 36, 39, 40
Yalon, Ḥanoch
  16
Yosé
  26, 28, 49, 50, 61-64, 68-70, 84, 96,
  116, 117, 121-23, 133, 146, 156, 194,
  197, 198
Zabdi
  177
Zabi
  177
Zahavy, Tzvee
  16
Zerahites
  177
Zuckermandel, Moses Samuel
  16